TWO OVER ONE GAME FORCE

REVISED — EXPANDED
UPDATED FOR THE 1990'S

by Max Hardy

Published by
Devyn Press, Inc.
Louisville, Kentucky

OTHER BOOKS BY MAX HARDY
Five Card Majors — Western Style (out of print)
Play My Card (with Bill Roney) (out of print)
New Minor Forcing
Fourth Suit Forcing
Forcing Notrump Responses
(above three as one book and separately)
Two Over One Game Force (original — out of print)
Splinters and Other Shortness Bids
Two Over One Game Force Quiz Book
Two Over One Game Force: An Introduction (with Steve Bruno)
Competitive Bidding With Two Suited Hands
The Problems With Major Suit Raises

Copyright © 1989 by Max Hardy

First Printing — June 1989
Second Printing — February 1991
Third Printing — March 1992
Fourth Printing — February 1994
Fifth Printing — September 1995
Sixth Printing — March 1997
Seventh Printing — March 1999

Printed in the United States of America.

Devyn Press, Inc.
3600 Chamberlain Lane, Suite 230
Louisville, KY 40241
1-800-274-2221

ISBN No. 0-910791-35-X

INTRODUCTION

It is said that the third time is "the charm". I hope that that saying has some roots in reality. This is the third book I have written about the bidding system that I prefer to play.

Five Card Majors Western Style was my first effort. I wrote and published it in 1974. At that time I had a standing date to play at Los Angeles Sectionals on Friday afternoons with Richard Walsh, the man who is to be credited with creating the "Two Over One" approach to bidding. He had worked out his system with his regular partners, John Swanson and Paul Soloway, and played it with great success with them and his wife of that time, Rhoda. This first book gave public access to what was then known as the "Walsh System". I was urged to write it by two of my students at that time, Anne Calderone and Corinne Kale. Corinne designed the cover for that first effort, and from her design I created the logo that now identifies Hardy Bridge Enterprises, Inc. and the Hardy Publishing Company.

The fact that I published **Five Card Majors** rather than pay to have another company publish it for me opened another door in my life. First Mike Lawrence, then Bobby Goldman, and then others brought me manuscripts to publish, and I became the first major publisher of bridge books in North America. But that is another story.

In 1981 another marvelous thing happened to me. Mary agreed to be my wife. Shortly before our marriage in December of that year I began writing the sequel to **Five Card Majors,** and in June of 1982 I published **Two Over One Game Force.** This second presentation of "the System" was considerably expanded over the first attempt, and there were major philosophical changes in the system to introduce. Dick Walsh had retired from bridge and moved to Switzerland, and many of the prevailing new ideas came from several sources. The most important change was the introduction of **Drury** in its modern context of showing a limit raise for opener's third or fourth seat major suit opening bid. Earlier, major suit opening bids were always very sound and promised five card or longer suits, but **Drury** allowed for light major suit opening bids in third and fourth seats and even paved the way to opening with four card suits in those positions.

Now another seven years have passed, and the need for a system update seemed apparent both to Mary and to me. Further, the mechanical problems of the existing text needed to be corrected. In this book you will find that the layout has been carefully structured so that it is never necessary to turn a page while you read the explanation of any example. That particular problem drove many readers of the previous book to distraction.

In this presentation you will find that I have gone to much greater lengths to explain than in previous efforts. Also, where I have strong personal preferences I have attempted to give reasons for my choices. In all, I feel satisfied that what you read here is the best attempt I have made to share with those who wish to play our preferred system, the knowledge of how it works.

Through all of the hours that I have spent working on the preparation of this book, Mary has been my right hand, helping, commenting, proofreading, and doing innumerable things to make my own task easier. It is to her that I dedicate this effort.

Max Hardy
3/29/89
Las Vegas, Nevada

TABLE OF CONTENTS

CHAPTER EIGHT - SLAM BIDDING 271

CHAPTER NINE - DUPLICATE PROCEDURES 291

CHAPTER I
OPENING BIDS

Opening Bids in Notrump

Opening bids and rebids of one or two notrump are used to show balanced hands that fall within specified point ranges. The choice of range for an opening bid of one notrump should compliment the bidding style in use. When opening bids tend to be sound, the rebid of one notrump will show at least 12 high card points, but when a light opening bid style is in use, the rebid of one notrump can show less.

The range of the one notrump rebid should not be so wide as to cause partner of the one notrump rebidder to have an evaluation problem. If that range exceeds four high card points, it becomes difficult for responder to know how to proceed.

Since ideally the rebid of one notrump should have a range of three or four high card points, when the rebid of one notrump shows at least 12 high card points, then that rebid can show as much as 15 high card points. It follows that the opening bid of one notrump with this agreement will show a minimum of 16 high card points.

If opening bids tend to be light, and one is permitted to open a balanced hand of 11 high card points, then the rebid of one notrump should be limited to no more than 14 high card points. With this agreement the range for an opening bid of one notrump should start at 15 high card points.

From this we see that style will determine our opening one notrump range. Sound bidding styles can play that an opening bid of one notrump shows 16 or a very good 15 high card points. Styles that permit light opening bids with balanced hands should arrange to have their rebids of one notrump restricted to a range of no more than four high card points, and should correspondingly start their opening notrump range somewhat lower.

Advocates of an extremely light opening bid style might even need to play that their opening bid of one notrump shows a range of 14 to 17 or 14 to 16 high card points in order to leave a reasonably defined range for their rebid of one notrump after an opening suit bid.

This presentation will assume that minimum opening bids with balanced hands promise at least a good 12 high card points whenever a rebid of one notrump is intended. The top of the one notrump rebid range will be a bad 15 high card points.

We define "bad" as a hand with no five card suit, poor intermediates (lacking in nines and tens), and bad shape (4-3-3-3 or a lackluster 4-4-3-2). When evaluating you should always add a point for a good five card suit.

The determination of the range of our one notrump rebid leads us to the determination of our opening notrump range. Since hands that are evaluated as having a "bad" 15 high card points have been placed in the category for a rebid of one notrump after a suit opening bid, our one notrump opening bids will start at a "good" 15 high card points.

To reiterate, a "good" 15 point hand will usually not have 4-3-3-3 distribution, it will have good spot cards, and it might also contain a five card (or six card) suit for which a point must be added.

The top of the range for an opening bid of one notrump should be such that the range, as suggested earlier, is not too wide. If a "good" 15 is the bottom of the range, the top of the range would best be a "good" 17 or a "bad" 18. An 18 high card point hand with reasonable distribution and good intermediates should be considered too strong for an opening bid of one notrump.

The gap between an opening bid of one notrump and an opening bid of two notrump is accommodated by the practice of having the opening bidder open with one of a suit (usually a minor suit) and make a jump rebid of two notrump. Exceptions to this auction become necessary when responder does not make the expected one-over-one response.

If responder makes a two-over-one response in a new suit, or if responder makes a (systemic) **Inverted Minor Raise**, when opener has a balanced hand that was too good for an opening bid of one notrump, but not good enough for an opening bid of two notrump, opener must then show his range by jumping to three notrump. Two notrump in each of those auctions would show minimum values.

The range of the "gap" notrump hands will be from a "good" 18 to a very poor 20 high card points. Any good 20 point balanced hand will be opened with two notrump.

The top of the range for an opening two notrump bid will be subject to partnership considerations. The recommendation is that any "good" 22 high card point hand should not be opened with two notrump, but merits an opening bid of two clubs, followed by a rebid of two notrump.

Opening bids of three notrump may be used to describe balanced hands that are very good, but today's tendency is to reserve that opening bid for some systemic purpose, and describe larger balanced hands by opening with two clubs and rebidding notrump at an appropriate level. Perhaps the easiest structure after opening with two clubs is to have the rebid of two notrump show a good 22 to 24, three notrump to show 25 to 27, and four notrump to show 28 to 30.

In addition to size considerations, opening bids or rebids in notrump should give consideration to shape. When the opening bidder voluntarily bids or rebids in notrump his message is that his hand is not unbalanced. Notice that the stipulation was not that the hand is "balanced", because there are some hand patterns that are not particularly balanced that should be described by bids in notrump.

By definition, an "unbalanced" hand is one which contains a singleton or a void. There are exactly six hand patterns which are not subject to that definition.

The most balanced hand that is possible is one with 4-3-3-3 distribution. If a card is moved from one three card suit and added to another, the pattern becomes 4-4-3-2. This is the most common of all hand patterns, and is still quite balanced.

By moving a card from one four card suit to the other, we arrive at a pattern of 5-3-3-2. This pattern is still reasonably balanced.

Further shifting, one card at a time, gives us three more patterns. These are not exactly balanced, but by definition, since they do not contain a singleton or a void, they are also not unbalanced.

The move of a card from one three card suit to the other gives us a pattern of 5-4-2-2. Not exactly balanced, but not unbalanced either.

The next card shift that does not produce a singleton or void is the move of a card from the four card suit to the five card suit, which produces a pattern of 6-3-2-2.

The final shift of a card from the three card suit to the six card suit gives us a pattern of 7-2-2-2. Again, not balanced, but still, by definition, not unbalanced.

These three hand patterns have been given the designation "semi-balanced", since they are neither fish nor fowl. They are not unbalanced, since they do not contain a singleton or void, but they are too lopsided to earn the designation "balanced".

In determining how to describe a hand with a semi-balanced pattern, the rule of thumb is this. If the honor strength falls primarily in the long suits, treat the hand as though it were unbalanced, and bid suits to describe the nature of the hand. If the honor strength falls in the doubletons, the hand should be described as though it were balanced by a bid in notrump at the point in the auction that also describes its size.

This means that an opening bid, or a rebid in notrump will show a hand in the high card point range specified by partnership agreement, and will also show a hand that is either balanced, or semi-balanced with honor cards in its short suit holdings.

The inevitable question asks whether it is permissible to open one notrump with a hand which contains a five card major. The answer is a provisional yes. When considering the possibility of opening a hand which contains a five card major with a bid of one notrump, take these matters into account.

First, there should be three cards in the other major. If partner transfers and then passes, were we to hold only two cards in his major suit, we would be in an inferior contract whenever he also happened to hold three cards in the five card major we have concealed with our opening bid of one notrump. Playing the 2-5 fit when a 5-3 fit exists in the other major will lead to poor results. A very bad five card major (Jxxxx or worse) should be treated as though it were a four card suit.

A second consideration should be whether the hand looks suit oriented or whether it looks notrump-ish. If the hand is all aces and kings, it will probably play better in a suit, and instead of opening with one notrump you will usually be better off if you open the bidding in the five card major suit.

If the honor holdings are mostly secondary cards (no aces and lots of queens and jacks) notrump should be given greater consideration. Also, when the hand with its 5-3-3-2 shape (most likely for this auction) contains a bad doubleton, an opening bid in the major suit will be more descriptive than an opening bid of one notrump. All of the following hands should be opened with a bid of one notrump.

Example 1:

a) Opener	b) Opener	c) Opener
♠ 95	♠ AQ	♠ AQ
♡ AQ86	♡ AQ	♡ KJ7
◇ KJ4	◇ KJ73	◇ AQ
♣ AQ98	♣ 97642	♣ 976432

d) Opener
- ♠ AQ
- ♡ AQ
- ◇ 9765432
- ♣ KJ

e) Opener
- ♠ Q97
- ♡ KJ975
- ◇ AQ
- ♣ KJ10

Example 1a) is a typical one notrump opening bid. Do not be dissuaded by the bad doubleton in spades. If you do not open with one notrump you will never be able to adequately describe the size and strength of this hand.

Example 1b) shows a semi-balanced hand with honors in the short suit holdings. It is best described by an opening bid of one notrump.

Examples 1c) and 1d) carry this thought to its ultimate conclusion. In each case, an opening bid of one notrump is more descriptive of the general nature of the hand than would be a bid in the poor long minor suit.

Example 1e) shows a hand with a five card major suit that can well be described with an opening bid of one notrump. If partner transfers to spades and then passes, we are as well placed (maybe better) than if we had opened with one heart. The short suit holdings are well protected if the ultimate contract happens to be in notrump.

Example 2:

a) Opener
- ♠ J5
- ♡ AQJ6
- ◇ K9
- ♣ KQJ94

b) Opener
- ♠ KJ4
- ♡ AJ
- ◇ KQ6
- ♣ KJ986

The hands in Example 2 should not be opened with a bid of one notrump.

Example 2a) is semi-balanced and has a weak doubleton. With two good suits it would be more descriptive to open with one club and reverse in hearts as your rebid (if that is systemically permitted).

Example 2b) has the right shape but is too strong for an opening one notrump bid. With eighteen points and a five card suit, your plan should be to open with one club and make a jump rebid of two notrump.

c) Opener	d) Opener
♠ Q108	♠ Q9
♡ K	♡ KJ975
◇ KQJ8	◇ AQ7
♣ AJ965	♣ KJ10

Example 2c) has the right high card strength, but the wrong shape. The singleton king makes the hand too weak for a reverse. Open with one diamond and rebid two clubs, but plan to take another bid if partner signs off by returning to two diamonds. Bid two spades if his original response was in that suit, or two notrump if his original response was in hearts. This auction denies a balanced hand, shows extra values, and tries for what appears to be the only possible game.

Example 2d) fails to qualify for an opening bid of one notrump because of the five card heart suit and only a doubleton spade. Open with one heart and rebid two clubs if partner responds one spade or one notrump (forcing). If partner then signs off by bidding two hearts, show your extra values by bidding two notrump.

Opening Suit Bids in First and Second Position

Opening suit bids in first and second position will show reasonable hands. All hands with 13 high card points should be opened. Hands with 12 high card points are opening bids when they have two plus defensive tricks and no rebid problem. Hands with 11 high card points are opening bids if the high cards are primary and placed in the long suits (it would be criminal to pass with AKxxx-Axxx).

Even some hands that have only 10 high card points are opening bids when those points are well placed and the hand has good shape (AQxxxx-KJxx).

The guide to whether or not to open with marginal high card holdings is the shape of the hand and placement of high cards. Do not open with a bad balanced 12 count in first or second seat, but a distributional 10 count with combinations of primary high cards in long suits should be opened.

Systemically, an opening bid in a major suit in first or second position promises a five card or longer suit. Dick Walsh, the patriarch of the system, would not open with a five card major suit when the quality was Jxxxx or worse. He treated those suits as though they were four, rather than five card suits. Your partnership should determine what quality is necessary for the opening of a five card major suit in first or second seat.

Minor suit opening bids show at least three cards in the suit bid. When the opening bid is in diamonds, opener will nearly always have a four card or longer suit. The only time an opening bid of one diamond is made with a three card suit is when opener holds four cards in each major and only two clubs. Rather than make a totally artificial opening bid of one club on a doubleton, opener makes the single exception and opens one diamond with a three card holding.

When opener holds a balanced hand with 3-3 in the minors, there is no problem. One club is the automatic opening bid.

When opener is balanced with 4-4 in the minors, there are two different thoughts as to which minor to open.

One thought is to open with one club, since the rebid being prepared is one notrump. One diamond would be correct if the planned rebid was in clubs, but to plan that auction is to plan to describe an unbalanced, rather than a balanced hand.

Partner has a full gamut of responses, including a chance to raise clubs. If the opening bid were one diamond, any time responder had a shapely minimum with long clubs he would not be able to describe his hand.

Another thought takes into account the possibility of interference by the opponents after the opening minor suit bid. If the opening bid has been one club, when the opponents interfere and responder makes a negative double, opener must rebid in diamonds, which gets the auction to a level that might be uncomfortable. If the opening bid, instead, has been one diamond on a balanced hand with 4-4 in the minor suits, after interference and a negative double, opener will have a more comfortable rebid in clubs.

Regardless of the choice of opening minor suit bids, when opener rebids one notrump he shows a balanced hand in the range of 12 to a bad 15 high card points. It stipulates that if weak notrumps were being used, he would have opened with a bid of one notrump. His rebid does not promise stoppers in any unbid suit. It is simply a description of size and shape.

The choice of opening bids with a balanced hand and 4-4 in the minor suits must be left to each individual partnership. If it is more important in your partnership to be able to raise clubs, you should agree to open with one club on these hands. If it is more important to be prepared to show both minor suits after interference and a negative double, you should open with one diamond on these hands.

A compromise is to agree to open with the better minor suit whenever you hold a balanced hand with 4-4 in the minor suits. This will work well most of the time.

Opening Suit Bids in Third and Fourth Position

In third and fourth position opening bid requirements change quite drastically from what they were in first and second seats. Opening bids in major suits may be made with four card holdings, but only when the strength of the hand is such that it would not normally be opened in first or second seat. Opener might have a hand with 10 to a bad 12 high points, and should simply take his best shot.

If he has a good four card major suit, that should be the shot that he takes. If his partner responds by bidding one notrump, that response is no longer necessarily a forcing call, and opener can pass. He will be able to do so comfortably with the knowledge that responder does not have a good fit for the major suit of the opening bid.

If responder held a fit for the major suit which opener bid in third or fourth seat, he could make a single raise, or with values for a limit raise he would bid two clubs. The two club response facing an opening major suit bid in third or fourth seat is the **Drury** convention in its modern form. It promises that responder has a limit raise for the major suit bid by the opener. With this convention available, it is possible to get to game when opener has a good hand, but to stay at the two level whenever opener has opened with less than full values or with a hand that would not accept a game invitation knowing of the limit raise in responder's hand.

When opener in third or fourth position has full opening bid values, he will not open with a four card major suit, but will bid as he would have in first or second seat. If he opens with a five card major suit and hears a response of one notrump, he will treat that call as a **Forcing Notrump** response, just as he would have if he had opened in first or second seat.

A minor suit opening bid in third or fourth position will most often have the full values expected for an opening bid. On those occasions when opener has less than full values, he will have opened in a minor suit holding reasonable support for each of the major suits. His plan is to pass if responder bids in either major suit. Occasionally, responder will take some other course of action, but opener will be able to cope with the auction if his preparedness includes support for both major suits whenever his values are less than expected.

Weak two bids in third position become quite undisciplined. Whenever your holding indicates that you should try to disrupt the situation for the opponents since the hand probably belongs to them, a weak two bid can be made on any reasonably good suit. Five card suits are common, and some brave souls even try to stir up action with weak two bids on good four card suits.

Example 3:

a) Opener
♠KJ875
♡Q93
◇K54
♣Q2

b) Opener
♠KJ105
♡Q84
◇Q62
♣K98

c) Opener
♠J65
♡KQJ97
◇K74
♣83

d) Opener
♠Q93
♡K62
◇K98
♣K1095

All Example 3 hands should be passed in first or second seat.

With Example 3a) open one spade in third or fourth seat, but pass any response except two clubs (Drury).

Example 3b) should be bid in the same way.

Example 3c) qualifies for a third or fourth seat weak two bid in hearts. The weak two bid in third seat is automatic, but in fourth seat is an absolute minimum and could open the door to a bad result. In fourth seat a weak two bid should be opened only if you are trying to create action.

With Example 3d) do not open in fourth seat, but in third seat open with one club and pass any response from partner.

Opening Suit Bids in Fourth Position

Although we have discussed opening bids in third and fourth position together, there are some different thoughts about opening the bidding after three passes. The first thought is that the reason to open is to achieve a plus score. After all, you do have the option to pass and have a score of zero rather than either a plus or a minus. Some special considerations do apply.

In situations where you are aiming to get a par result, the wisest course of action when you have marginal values is to pass. Settle for your average or better result (likely). Conversely, when you know that the state of your game requires action, you should open even with marginal values since you need to create a swing. You will rely on your playing skills to produce a plus score rather than the score that would be generated by passing out the hand.

When you are in doubt and need a guideline, count your "Pierson Points". This scale was suggested by Don Pierson, a former regular partner of John Swanson. With marginal hands, add the total of your high card points to the number of spades you hold. If the total is 15 or more, open the bidding, but if the total is less, pass.

The basis of this concept is that if the auction becomes competitive, when you hold sufficient length in spades to either bid them or defend against them, you are on reasonably firm ground to open the bidding with marginal values in fourth position. Weak two bids in fourth position are never of the minimum variety. Again, you do not open the bidding to the possibility of a minus score when you could pass the hand out. Weak two bids in fourth seat are not only maximum, but will often be hands that would be opened with a one bid in first or second seat.

The rationale for opening with a two bid instead of a one bid is twofold: to offer a good description to partner, and to deny the one and two levels to opponents who might otherwise compete.

Example 4:

a) Opener	b) Opener	c) Opener
♠ Q1085	♠ Q105	♠ KJ10963
♡ A93	♡ A93	♡ A93
◇ 54	◇ 854	◇ 54
♣ AJ92	♣ AJ92	♣ A2

Using the concept of "Pierson Points" Example 4a) would be an opening bid in fourth position, but Example 4b) should be passed. After opening one club with 4a) your plan is to pass any response, hopefully in a major suit.

Example 4c) would be opened with one spade in any other seat, but in fourth position you might consider opening with two spades instead. An opening weak two bid in fourth position is never of minimum variety, and often has sound opening bid values. Partner should expect a hand in the value range of about 10 to 14 high card points for a fourth seat weak two bid.

CHAPTER II
REBIDDING AFTER
OPENING BIDS
OF ONE OF A SUIT

Opener Rebids His Suit

In his first book after moving from England to become Bridge Editor of the New York Times, Alan Truscott commented about American bidding that the greatest weakness he had observed was that Americans "rush to rebid their five card suits". In the Two Over One System, there are some instances in which opener will be required to rebid a five card suit, but they are few and in specified auctions. Generally, when opener voluntarily rebids his first suit, it is six cards or longer.

When opener has started with one club and responder has bid one diamond, if opener rebids clubs he will always have a six card or longer suit. There is no hand that can have been dealt to him that will cause him to need to rebid clubs when holding only five.

If the response to one club has been either one heart or one spade, when opener rebids two clubs he will nearly always hold six or more. On rare occasions he might have opened with a good five card suit when also holding four poor diamonds and three-one in the major suits.

In such situations, when responder has bid opener's three card major, opener has the option of raising the major suit response even though he does not have the four card support that responder will expect. However, it is more likely that responder will have bid opener's short major suit, and the only option opener will have is the rebid of his good five card club suit. A rebid in notrump is out of the question since that would show a balanced hand.

If the response to one club is one notrump, when opener has the hand under discussion he will know that play in notrump is dangerous since responder must have no more than six major suit cards. Again, opener should remove to two clubs even though he has only five of them. Responder will nearly always have a three or four card fit for clubs, and since the opponents have at least nine cards in one of the major suits, a notrump contract would be in great jeopardy.

When the opening bid has been one diamond and responder has bid a major suit, a rebid in diamonds will usually show a suit at least six cards long. When responder has only five diamonds and is unbalanced, another rebid will be available. The exception occurs when opener has an unbalanced hand with five diamonds and four hearts, and responder has bid one spade. Here, opener may have to rebid a five card diamond suit, although some other options do exist.

Opener with a 3-4-5-1 pattern might raise responder's spades if his diamonds were poor and his spade holding included a high honor. With a 1-4-5-3 pattern which included a good three card club holding, responder could again avoid rebidding a mediocre five card diamond suit by electing to rebid in the good three card club suit.

The rebid of a three card club suit rather than the poor five card diamond suit cannot lead the auction astray, since responder will automatically take a "false preference" when holding two diamonds and three clubs with minimum values to cater to the possibility that opener has a 6-4 pattern.

When the opening bid has been one diamond and responder has bid two clubs, the auction is forcing to game. Opener has many options at his rebid. If opener rebids his suit, he promises five or more diamonds. Failure by opener to rebid his suit at this turn denies that he has as many as five diamonds. A rebid in either major suit denies five diamonds and promises four cards in the major suit of opener's rebid.

Such a rebid is not a reverse. It promises neither the shape nor the extra strength that are shown when a true reverse is made. If opener rebids two notrump after the two club response he denies holding as many as five diamonds, but could have a four card major.

His rebid indicates that notrump appears to be quite playable from his side as his hand is balanced with stoppers in both major suits. If responder holds a four card major in addition to a longer club suit, he should continue to describe his hand by bidding the four card major. In this fashion the four-four major suit fit can still be found whenever it does exist.

When opener has bid one heart and responder has bid either one spade or one notrump (forcing), or when opener has bid one spade and responder has bid one notrump (forcing), a rebid of opener's major guarantees that his suit is six cards or longer.

When opener has a 5-3-3-2 hand and apparently there is no other suit to bid, he can rebid one notrump after a one heart opening bid has received a one spade response.

After the opening bid of either major and a **Forcing Notrump** response, rebids in three card minor suits are systemic and occur with regularity. No hand exists in the system which either requires or permits the rebid of a five card major suit in any of these circumstances.

When opener has bid in a major suit and responder has made a game-forcing response in a new suit at the two level, circumstances change. Opener may be able to bid a second suit at the two level when he holds four cards in a suit ranking higher than responder's suit.

Systemically, a rebid of two spades after a one heart opening bid and a two over one response is not a true reverse, showing extra values, but since the auction is game forcing, opener merely shows his four card spade holding in addition to five or more hearts.

Opener might also be able to raise responder's suit or go to the three level to show his own second suit. Both of these actions promise extra values either in high cards or distribution. (This extra value requirement is subject to partnership preference. Since the two over one response has promised that the partnership has game going values, it is possible to agree that opener makes his most expressive rebid even though that might entail going to the three level with a bare minimum for his opening bid.)

Another option opener has available is a rebid of two notrump. When opener avails himself of this option, it must be truly descriptive. His hand should include stoppers in the unbid suits, and should also be otherwise balanced.

When opener is unable to make any of these descriptive rebids after a two over one response, he may have no option but to repeat the five card suit in which he opened the bidding. Responder must understand that opener's rebid of his original suit does not promise a suit of more than five card length. The rebid may simply have been one of necessity since any other call would have been a distortion. The repeat of opener's first suit is often simply a "catchall" which is used when no truly descriptive option is available.

Jump rebids of his original suit by the opening bidder will always show suits of six card or greater length. For the most part, they tend to show suits of good quality as well. Opener makes the jump rebid to emphasize his suit since that is the most important thing in his hand that needs description.

Example 5:

a) Opener
♠ K93
♡ 4
◇ J743
♣ AKJ98

b) Opener
♠ 9
♡ K852
◇ AQJ75
♣ K63

c) Opener
♠ 9
♡ KQ52
◇ Q7653
♣ AQ8

d) Opener
♠ K63
♡ KQ52
◇ AJ875
♣ 9

e) Opener
♠ K108
♡ K982
◇ AJ75
♣ Q9

f) Opener
♠ 1032
♡ KJ98
◇ AQJ5
♣ Q9

With Example hand 5a) opener will have bid one club with his good five card suit. If responder bids one diamond, opener can raise. If responder bids one spade, again responder can raise. Although responder usually expects four card support for the raise, no other action seems better. If responder bids one heart, opener has no choice other than to rebid his five card club suit.

With Example hand 5b) opener will have bid one diamond. If responder bids one heart opener has a happy raise. If responder instead bids one spade or one notrump, opener's only descriptive rebid is to repeat his five card diamond suit. If responder bids two clubs, opener is required to rebid diamonds, since any other rebid would deny a five card diamond suit.

Example 5c) is similar except that opener has bad diamonds and a good three card club suit. If responder bids either one spade or one notrump, responder makes a better description with a rebid in his three card club suit than with a rebid of his bad five card diamond suit.

Example 5d) is a situation in which opener's rebid after a response in either major suit should be a raise. If the response is one notrump, opener should rebid his diamond suit even though he is not proud of it. A pass would rely too strongly on black suit values in responder's hand, and responder is a favorite to have some sort of a fit for diamonds.

With Example 5e) opener would bid one diamond and raise a response of one heart. After a response of one spade opener would rebid one notrump. If responder instead has bid one notrump, opener will pass. If responder bids two clubs, opener can best describe by bidding two notrump. If there is a four-four heart fit, it will disclose itself when responder next bids three hearts.

14

Example 5f) is similar except that with bad spades, if the response to one diamond is two clubs, opener will rebid his four card heart suit rather than suggest notrump.

Example 6:

a) Opener	b) Opener	c) Opener
♠ AQ10854	♠ AJ107	♠ AQJ92
♡ K3	♡ KQJ63	♡ 83
◇ KJ4	◇ Q42	◇ A72
♣ 105	♣ 7	♣ Q54

Example 6a) shows a hand with which opener will bid one spade, and then rebid two spades after any response with his six card suit. If the response has been one notrump, the fact that his suit is six cards long will be known. If the response has been in a new suit at the two level, the situation is not clear since in such an auction opener may have to rebid a five card suit.

With Example 6b) opener will bid one heart, and raise a response of one spade. If the response is one notrump (forcing) opener will rebid two diamonds on his three card suit. If responder has bid either two clubs or two diamonds, opener can now bid two spades to show his shape. Since the two over one response makes the auction game forcing, opener does not need the values of a reverse to make this rebid.

With Example 6c) opener bids one spade. If responder bids one notrump (forcing) opener rebids two clubs, the lower ranking of his three card minor suits. If responder bids either two clubs or two diamonds, opener can raise unless the partnership agreement is that such a raise shows extra values. If that is the partnership agreement, opener will have no choice but to rebid two spades. If the response is two hearts, opener can rebid two notrump since his hand is balanced and he has stoppers in each of the unbid suits.

	d) Opener	e) Opener	f) Opener
♠	AK854	AQJ83	AKJ1085
♡	A97	7	K4
◇	76	Q5	AQ3
♣	Q94	KJ1086	105

Example 6d) is similar. After a *Forcing Notrump* response opener rebids two clubs on his three card suit. If the response is two diamonds, opener can rebid two notrump since his hand is balanced and he has stoppers in the unbid suits. If the response is two clubs, opener can raise only if his partnership agreement does not require extra values to go to the three level, and otherwise must rebid two spades. If the response is two hearts, opener has yet another obligation. Opener will raise to four hearts to show three card support and minimum opening bid values (this action receives full explanation when the *principle of fast arrival* is explained later in this book).

In Example 6e) opener bids one spade (one club would be correct in standard, but there is no need to bid one club when playing the Two Over One System) and after a response of one notrump (forcing) rebids two clubs. If the response is two clubs, opener can make a splinter raise by jumping to three hearts. If the response is either two diamonds or two hearts, opener can rebid three clubs since he has extra values by way of his distribution.

With Example 6f) opener is able to make a jump rebid in his spade suit to show both the extra length and the extra values he holds. This will be true after a forcing notrump response, and also after a new suit response at the two level. If the partnership has the agreement that after a two level response a jump rebid of opener's major shows a solid suit (this agreement is quite popular) then opener must simply bid two spades at his rebid, concealing both his extra length and extra strength. Your partnership should discuss the requirements for a jump rebid in this auction.

Opener Rebids After Responder Raises

Raises of minor suits in the system are **Inverted**. This means that contrary to standard, single raises are strong and jump raises are weak. When responder makes a jump raise of opener's minor suit, opener will most often have no reason to bid on. With an ordinary opening bid, opener will pass. When he has extra values, opener will either bid three notrump, or make a descriptive bid in a new suit as a try for game.

When responder has made a single raise of opener's minor suit, opener is required to bid again. Responder has shown a hand which contains no four card major suit, but has at least the values for a limit raise. Since responder's hand is unlimited at this point in the auction, opener will continue with a rebid which best describes his hand in light of the information conveyed by responder's single raise.

A complete description of opener's continuations appears in Chapter III under the discussion of **Inverted Minor Raises**.

Raises of opener's major suit are standard. They show a fit of three or more cards and the values of a good five to a bad nine in high cards. Some system practitioners use **Constructive Major Raises** which are not recommended here. A "constructive" raise requires responder to have a hand worth at least seven or eight points in support of opener's major suit in order to make a single raise.

When responder has such a hand, the agreement to use "constructive" raises does serve the partnership well. Opener will be able to make a try for game and not fear that a contract at the three level is in jeopardy since responder is known to have good values for his single raise. It is when responder has a raise that is not of the "constructive" nature that the bidding side creates unnecessary problems for itself by having agreed to use this method.

Since responder with a minimum raise of a good five to about seven points is not permitted to make that raise at once, he is required to instead make a **Forcing Notrump** response. Here, where the best idea would be to keep the opponents out of the auction by making a pre-emptive single raise, users of **Constructive Major Raises** give their opponents free rein to enter the auction and make use of the two level. Where a barricade could and should be erected, no impediment is put into the path of the opponents.

If the opponents fail to take advantage of their unwarranted opportunity to enter the auction after the forcing notrump response, users of **Constructive Major Raises** have yet another obstacle to overcome.

After opener has made his rebid, responder now takes a preference to opener's major suit. Since this auction would also occur when responder had a doubleton in opener's major suit, opener is at a loss to know whether his side does or does not have a fit in the major suit.

When opener's values would warrant a game try facing a known fit, he faces the danger that should he make a game try and discover that responder had a doubleton, he would be too high for no real reason. Conversely, if opener failed to make a try for game and responder did have a real fit for opener's major suit, a playable game would most probably have been missed.

If you feel that you must use **Constructive Major Raises**, be aware of the pitfalls that you create in order to have the advantage of knowing that responder's single raise will always be gilt-edged. The test of a convention's usefulness is to measure what is gained against what is given up. Here, our opinion is that the gain is far outweighed by the loss when this convention is adopted.

Assuming that major suit raises are standard, opener will frequently have a hand that warrants no further action, and he will pass. The exception to this general rule occurs when the partnership has agreed to play that reraises are preemptive rather than a try for game (1-2-3 stop).

If this agreement exists in the partnership, whenever the opening bidder has minimum values and more than five cards in his suit, he carries the auction to the three level in the agreed suit. A sixth card in his suit both adds to the offensive potential and subtracts from the defensive potential of the two bidding hands. An immediate call of three in the same major informs responder of the sixth card in the trump suit in opener's hand, and at the same time constructs a blockade designed to keep the opponents from entering the auction since they must do so one level higher.

Example 7:

	a) Opener	b) Responder
♠	AQ8753	KJ4
♡	6	953
♢	KJ4	Q872
♣	Q92	1083

With the hands in Example 7, opener rebids three spades after being raised to two if the partnership has agreed to play the convention known as "1-2-3 stop". The three spade bid is strictly pre-emptive and does not invite further action from the responder. Note that these hands have a reasonable play to make nine tricks in spades, but the opposing hands may be so constructed so as to be able to make four or five hearts. The preemptive three spade bid may keep them completely out of the auction.

After the single raise, particularly if it is of the "constructive" variety, opener will often know that his side has a reasonable play for game. If this is true, he should bid game directly rather than show anything additional about his hand that would be useful to the defense after game has been reached. Responder's hand is limited, so a contract higher than at the game level is out of the question unless opener has a tremendous hand and can bid slam or make a slam search after the single raise.

When game appears to be the limit of the values of the bidders, it makes no sense for opener to draw a blueprint for the defense by divulging anything additional about his hand on the way to game.

Opener may have a hand which figures to make ten tricks because of a glut of high cards. When he holds a hand in the range of 19+ points, game is probable, and he should bid it. If opener has additional length in the trump suit, that asset will also serve well at a game contract, and opener needs correspondingly less high card strength to leap to game.

Another type of hand which figures to produce a game after a single raise is one in which opener has a source of tricks in an undisclosed second suit. Rather than bid his second suit, opener should conceal this information and again bid game directly.

Example 8:

a) Opener	b) Opener	c) Opener
♠ 6	♠ 6	♠ 6
♡ AKJ95	♡ AKJ9753	♡ AJ1095
◇ AQ8	◇ A8	◇ AK1082
♣ KQ103	♣ A93	♣ K4

Example hand 8a) opens one heart and receives a single raise from responder. The power of high cards here should probably enable the bidding side to make ten tricks after hearts have been raised. Opener should jump to game.

With Example hand 8b) opener should jump to game after a single raise since he knows that at least nine tricks will come from the values he can see. Responder should be able to furnish some value to produce a tenth trick.

With Example hand 8c) When opener knows of a heart fit and some values in responder's hand, he should feel that his diamond suit will furnish tricks enough to make a game. He does not have many immediate losers and will usually find values enough in responder's hand to produce ten tricks. Opener should jump to four hearts, and never mention his diamond suit.

When opener has only a five card suit and values which fall in the range of 15+ to 19−, he should make an intelligent try for game. Although tradition has dictated that 26 points in the combined hands are necessary to produce game, the fact is that when the bidding side has found an adequate trump fit and can also discover secondary honor card fits in side suits, game will often make with much less in high card strength.

The partnership needs to have tools available which will discover high card fits in side suits, shortness facing bad holdings, and other fits which will produce tricks. To facilitate this end, after he has been raised when opener has some extra values that might lead to making a game, he should make a try for game which shows where his values are and allows responder to evaluate the cards he holds as to their usefulness.

Opener should continue by bidding the cheapest suit in which he holds moderate length (three cards or more) and some honor card holding (usually the queen or better). Responder will be able to evaluate any honor cards he holds in the game try suit as useful, and with an exceptionally good holding should proceed directly to game.

With a poor holding in the suit of the game try, responder should re-treat to three of the agreed suit, knowing that his side has several losers in the suit of the game try. With a moderate holding in the suit of the game try which might be of some help to opener, responder can make a counter try in one of the suits which remains below the level of three in the agreed trump suit.

Responder should be wary if he holds secondary honor cards (kings or queens) in any suit opener has bypassed in making his game try, for since the game try will be in the cheapest suit in which opener is attempting to find a secondary fit, he will bypass a suit in which his holding is either solid or short. When responder holds secondary honor cards facing implied shortness, he should devalue the worth of those cards.

In short, having heard opener's game try, responder may accept by going directly to game in the agreed suit, reject by returning to the agreed suit at the three level, or make a counter try for game in a suit below the level of three in the agreed major. The counter try should show some help for the suit of opener's game try but not enough to go directly to game, and offer information about help in another suit.

Example 9:

a) Opener	b) Opener	c) Opener
♠ AK984	♠ AK984	♠ AK984
♡ 6	♡ 6	♡ Q86
◇ AQ97	◇ Q86	◇ AQ97
♣ Q86	♣ AQ97	♣ 6

20

After a single raise of his one spade bid, opener with Example 9a) should not make the apparently natural call of three diamonds. If he were to do so, he would imply that cards in clubs in responder's hand were of little or no value. Since club values would be of great assistance, opener should make his game try by bidding three clubs rather than three diamonds.

With Example 9b) a game try of three clubs is again in order. Opener would welcome help in clubs, and still leaves room for responder to show fitting cards in diamonds if his club holding is tentative.

With Example hand 9c) when opener makes his game try of three diamonds after a spade raise, responder will know that values in clubs will not be useful since opener has bypassed that suit.

Example 10:

a) Responder	b) Responder	c) Responder
♠ Q103	♠ Q103	♠ Q103
♡ 984	♡ KJ104	♡ KJ104
◊ J102	◊ J102	◊ 984
♣ KJ104	♣ 984	♣ J102

All responders in Example 10 have raised a one spade opening bid and have heard opener make a try for game by bidding in a new suit. Each responder must decide what further action is appropriate.

If responder 10a) hears a game try of three clubs, he should know that his holding in clubs will produce many tricks for his side. He should jump directly to four spades. Opener's try will have been made with Example 9a) or 9b). If the game try is in either diamonds or hearts, responder 10a) should realize that his clubs will be of little use, and return to three spades. Opener's try might have been made with Example 9c) and even three spades might be in jeopardy.

If responder with Example 10b) hears a game try in clubs, he knows there will be too many losers in that suit since his holding is so poor. He should retreat to three spades. If the game try is in diamonds he should be mildly encouraged and offer a counter try of three hearts. Opener 9c) will be pleased with the counter try information and bid the game that is almost iron-clad.

Responder 10c) should reject a game try in diamonds, but if the try is in clubs he should make a counter offer in hearts. Opener 9b) would reject this counter offer, but would happily accept it if his red suit holdings were interchanged.

21

d) Responder
♠ Q103
♡ 984
◇ KJ104
♣ J102

Responder 10d) would accept a game try in diamonds, reject a try in hearts, but make a counter offer in diamonds if the game try were in clubs. Both opener 9a) and 9b) would accept after a club try and a counter offer in diamonds.

The examples quoted above demonstrate that it is not just the high cards held by the declaring side that win tricks, and that sheer numbers of high card points are not what is necessary to fulfill a game contract. More important is the location of high cards in the facing hands, and how they compliment each other. Sometimes, games will fail when the declaring side has more than 26 high card points, and on other occasions, a combined holding of less than 20 points will produce game when the proper fits exist.

When it is understood that intelligent game tries undertake to find secondary fits, it is possible for opener to make a game try by bidding the agreed suit again at the three level and in so doing to convey the message that the help he needs is in the trump suit itself. A rebid of the agreed suit at the three level should not ask responder to bid game with a maximum raise since it is fitting values rather than maximum values that opener would seek in making a game try.

Unless the partnership agreement is that a rebid of the agreed suit is preemptive (1-2-3 stop), a rebid of the agreed trump suit by opener as a game try should ask responder to bid game only if he holds good trumps. Opener will not be concerned about side suit values, for if he were, he would make a game try in a side suit.

Example 11:

a) Opener	b) Responder	c) Responder
♠ 4	♠ 765	♠ KQ3
♡ J8653	♡ KQ109	♡ Q42
◇ AKJ4	◇ 973	◇ Q973
♣ AKJ	♣ 842	♣ 842

With Example hand 11a) opener hears a single raise of his opening one heart bid and makes his most expressive game try by bidding three hearts since he needs help in the trump suit.

Responder with example 11b) hears opener's need for good hearts, and since he has good hearts he bids game. The fact that he has only five high card points is not relevant. The essence of his raise is what opener needs to make a game in hearts.

Responder with Example 11c) has a maximum with his nine point hand, but he is warned that he should not bid game. Opener has expressed a need for good heart support, and despite his maximum raise, responder does not have what is needed. Responder 11c) should pass and hope that his side will be able to make three hearts.

A modern approach to game tries has been suggested by Canadian expert Eric Kokish. Kokish suggests that rather than make an expressive game try which might help the defense after game has been reached, opener should ask responder to state where his values are. After a major suit raise, opener makes his cheapest bid to ask responder to bid the first suit in which he would have accepted a game try if opener had made one.

After a raise in spades, opener's Kokish game try is two notrump; after a raise in hearts, opener's Kokish game try is two spades. Two spades is used artificially so that responder can bid two notrump to indicate that he would have accepted a game try in spades.

Responder can jump to game to indicate that he would have accepted a game try in any suit. If instead he shows a suit in which he would have accepted a try for game, opener can evaluate not only the suit shown by responder, but can also evaluate the fact that responder may have bypassed a critical suit, indicating that he would not have accepted a try in that suit.

Opener will be able to determine from the response to his omnibus try for game whether or not game should be bid, and will have the advantage of not having told the defenders anything more than that he was interested in reaching a game. With information about declarer's hand having been withheld, the defenders will have a tougher time finding the accurate defense that might defeat a game that was bid after the concealed hand had told more about itself.

Opener Rebids to Show a Fit For Responder

Often, opener will hear a response in a suit for which he has a good fit. When this is the case, opener's rebid will nearly always be designed to show that fit while also expressing the range of his values.

The most common situation occurs when opener has bid a minor suit and responder has bid a major suit. When opener has minimum opening bid values and four cards in responder's suit, he will raise the major to the two level. Some partnerships also raise when they hold three cards to an honor in responder's major and a weak doubleton elsewhere in the hand.

The choice between raising with three card support and rebidding one notrump is strictly a matter of style. System purists continue by rebidding one notrump as an expression of size and shape. They feel that the rebid of one notrump expresses a hand which would have opened with one notrump if the partnership's agreement had been to bid one notrump in the range of 12 to 15 points. The message is strictly one to describe size and shape, and makes no reference to stoppers in unbid suits.

In uncontested auctions the need to show a three card fit has no urgency. When responder has a five card major and minimum values, after opener's rebid of one notrump, responder can opt to rebid his suit, ending the auction for his side. He knows that opener has a two or three card fit for his five card major suit.

When responder holds five cards in his major suit and values enough to seek or insist upon playing in game, he can use **New Minor Forcing** to discover the 5-3 fit when it exists.

In auctions where the opponents interfere after the response, opener needs to be able to show a fit for responder's suit even when he holds only three card support. If **support doubles** (see Chapter VII) are available, opener can distinguish between those hands where he holds three card support as opposed to four card support by using the **support double** with three cards and raising with four.

If **support doubles** are not part of the partnership agreement, opener should raise even though he has only three card support. Failure on opener's part to raise would leave responder in an impossible position, not knowing whether to compete further for fear that opener has no fit at all.

Here we see one of the basic tenets of competitive bidding. ALWAYS STRETCH TO SHOW A FIT IN COMPETITIVE SITUATIONS.

When opener has a four card fit for responder's major suit and values enough to produce game facing a minimum response, opener should jump to game in responder's suit whenever his hand is balanced. Opener will have a hand with which he planned to rebid two notrump, but the obligation to show a four card fit for responder will change his intended rebid. With a balanced hand of lesser or greater strength, he would not have opened with one of a minor suit, but instead would have bid either one notrump or two notrump at his first turn.

When opener has a four card fit for responder's major suit and values enough to produce game but is unbalanced, rather than jump to four in responder's major suit, opener should make a **splinter bid**. The **splinter bid** will take one of two forms. It will either be a double jump shift, or it will be a jump reverse.

These auctions are double jump shifts in which opener's rebid shows shortness in the suit bid, and promises a four card fit for responder's major suit: 1♣-P-1♡-P, 3♠; 1♢-P-1♡-P, 3♠; 1♢-P-1♡-P,4♣; 1♢-P-1♠-P,4♣.

These auctions are jump reverses which also show shortness in the suit bid and a four card fit for responder's major suit: 1♣-P-1♡- P, 3♢; 1♣-P-1♠-P, 3♢; 1♣-P-1♠-P, 3♡; 1♢-P-1♠-P, 3♡.

The double jump shift carries the auction to the game level, so opener must have a hand with values enough that he expects to make game even if responder has a very minimum hand for his response.

The jump reverse, however, does not necessarily commit the bidding side to the game level. After a jump reverse, it is still possible to stop at the three level in the agreed suit.

For this reason, responder must not rebid his suit at the three level unless he is willing to play in a part score rather than in a game. Opener has license to use the jump reverse when his values are only game invitational as well as when he will insist on playing in game.

When opener's values are only invitational and responder rebids his suit at the three level showing a meager responding hand, opener will pass. When responder shows a minimum and opener has sufficient values, he can continue on and bid game.

Responder must therefore realize that when his hand is suitable for game he must not make the error of merely bidding his suit again at the three level. With no interest in slam he should jump to the four level in the agreed suit, but with slam interest he should either cue bid a control, or take command of the auction and use an appropriate tool such as Blackwood or the Grand Slam Force.

Note that the jump reverse is not needed as a natural bid. If opener reverses without jumping, he shows the two suits that he has bid, and the auction is forcing. If he then rebids the reverse suit, or jump rebids it, he indicates greater length and strength holdings in his natural auction.

With the double jump shift opener can show the location of his shortness, but is unable to indicate whether it is a singleton or a void.

However, when the other type of splinter auction is available, opener can make a jump reverse to specify that his holding is a singleton, and can make a double jump reverse to indicate that his shortness is a void when the strength of his hand so warrants.

Example 12:

a) Opener	b) Opener	c) Opener
♠ A8	♠ 8	♠ AQ3
♡ KQ97	♡ KQ97	♡ KQ97
◇ AJ9	◇ AQ3	◇ AKJ97
♣ AJ103	♣ AKJ97	♣ 8

d) Opener	e) Opener	f) Opener
♠ KQ84	♠ KQ84	♠ KQ84
♡ 7	♡ 7	♡ ——
◇ A82	◇ AQ2	◇ AQ72
♣ AK975	♣ AKJ95	♣ AKJ95

Opener with Example hand 12a) bids one club and plans to rebid two notrump at his second turn. His plans change when he hears a response of one heart. Instead of bidding two notrump to show his balanced 19 count, he jumps to four hearts which shows that size but also affirms four card heart support and promises a balanced hand.

With Example hand 12b) opener again starts with one club. When he hears a response of one heart, he describes his powerful hand with a four card heart fit and shortness in spades by making a splinter double jump shift of three spades. This call forces the auction to reach four hearts, and at the same time allows responder to evaluate his cards with the knowledge of opener's shape.

With Example hand 12c) opener starts with one diamond. When he hears a response of one heart, he makes a double jump shift rebid of four clubs to show that he has four card heart support, values enough for game, and shortness in clubs.

With Example hand 12d) opener starts with one club. When he hears a response of one spade, he makes a jump reverse by bidding three hearts. This rebid shows four card spade support and heart shortness, and willingness to play at least at the three level in spades. If responder continues by bidding only three spades, opener will pass, for he has sent a complete message about his hand and must trust responder who has rejected game after having received that message.

With Example hand 12e) opener bids similarly, but this time has enough extra values to continue if responder signs off by rebidding only three spades. Opener will insist on playing in game, but he will have given responder the chance to find a slam if that contract depended on the knowledge of a perfect fit.

With Example hand 12f) after hearing a one spade response to his one club opening bid, opener makes a double jump reverse by bidding four hearts. Since a jump reverse to three hearts would have shown a singleton heart, the double jump reverse shows that opener is void in hearts, has a four card fit for spades, and that he has values enough to play in game even if responder has a bare minimum. When responder has a better hand, he will know to pursue a slam when there are no wasted heart values in his hand, since information about the heart void may be all he needs to get to that contract.

Other auctions will occur in which opener has four card support for responder's major suit, but his values are invitational rather than either minimum or sufficient to force a game. Opener will be able to make a jump raise of responder's suit to the three level.

Opener's hand will usually not be balanced, for a hand in the range with which opener would invite would have been opened with a bid of one notrump if it had been balanced. The exception occurs when opener has a good 17 or bad 18 points which would be too much for an opening bid of one notrump. Since game values are not assured, opener would make a jump raise to the three level with this balanced hand rather than jump all the way to game.

Auctions in which a jump reverse is not available leave opener with a jump raise as his only invitational call. Responder should expect that if opener's hand is distributional opener was unable to show the location of his shortness since a double jump shift would overstate his values.

Example 13:

a) Opener	b) Opener	c) Opener
♠ 7	♠ A5	♠ 72
♡ QJ83	♡ QJ83	♡ QJ83
◊ AQ5	◊ 75	◊ AQ5
♣ AK874	♣ AKJ74	♣ AK84

With Example hand 13a) opener would start by bidding one club, and if responder bid one heart opener would make a jump raise to three hearts. Although opener would like to be able to show that he had a singleton spade by making a splinter bid, that would require a jump to three spades which would force the auction to game. Opener's hand is not good enough for that action, and he must content himself with the jump raise.

With Example hand 13b) opener again starts with one club and hears a response of one heart. He should again make a jump raise to show his heart support and his good values. Note that although he had the values for an opening bid of one notrump, opener correctly elected not to make that call due to his bad doubleton in diamonds. With a semi-balanced shape he best describes by bidding suits when he has good suits and bad doubletons.

Responder should not expect opener to have a hand like Example 13c) when he opens with one club and makes a jump raise of a one heart response. Clearly, with the hand shown, opener will have started not by bidding one club, but with an opening bid of one notrump. Those who disdain an opening bid of one notrump because of the bad doubleton in spades will forever find that they are unable to describe the size and shape of the hand they hold, and they will create great guessing games for their partners. It is with semi-balanced hands that bad doubletons are deterrents to voluntary bids in notrump. With balanced hands the need to describe size and shape has priority.

When opener has bid one heart holding four spades, and responder bids one spade, the same tools are available to opener as when he opened with a minor suit, except that no jump reverse is available. Opener can still raise to two spades with minimum values, jump to three spades when he holds invitational values, and jump to four spades when his distribution is 4-5-2-2 and his values are sufficient for game. When his shape in the minor suits includes a singleton or void, he can splinter after the one spade response.

When opener has bid one spade and hears a response of two hearts, the situation is somewhat different. Responder's bid of two hearts has promised both that his values are sufficient for game facing a minimum opening bid and that his heart suit is at least five cards long.

When opener has three or four card heart support and minimum values, his heart raise should be an immediate jump to game. This raise employs the **principle of fast arrival**. Since opener knows that game values exist and that hearts should be the trump suit, he indicates that he has no interest in slam by going directly to game in hearts. Responder is warned not to go further without sufficient extra values, since opener denies more than a minimum for his opening bid.

When opener does have extra values, since the auction is already forcing to game, he can merely raise hearts to the three level to indicate his fit for responder's suit. Since opener has not jumped to game, responder understands that opener has extra values, and has some interest in either playing a slam or giving responder a chance to bid three notrump when his hand is suitable for that contract and he does not have slam values.

Opener also has the option of splintering in a minor suit when his hand looks good for slam. This will convey the location of his shortness to responder as he announces his heart fit and will allow responder to be able to evaluate fitting cards which could lead to a slam on less than the time honored 33 points between the two bidding hands. Knowledge of fits and controls can often enable a pair who bids well to reach good slams on far less in high cards than is normally deemed necessary.

Example 14:

a) Opener	b) Opener
♠ AQ72	♠ AQ72
♡ AKQ94	♡ AKJ43
◇ A3	◇ A73
♣ 72	♣ 2

Opener with Example hand 14a) will first bid one heart. If responder bids one spade opener will jump to four spades. This jump shows four card support for spades and values enough for game facing a minimum response, but denies a singleton or void in opener's hand. With side suit shortness opener would instead have splintered.

Opener with Example hand 14b) starts by bidding one heart. If responder bids one spade opener *splinters* by jumping to four clubs. This *splinter* rebid promises values enough for game, four card support for spades, and shortness in clubs.

c) Opener
　♠ AJ952
　♡ K82
　◇ 74
　♣ AJ2

d) Opener
　♠ AKJ92
　♡ K82
　◇ J4
　♣ AJ2

e) Opener
　♠ AKJ92
　♡ K82
　◇ 4
　♣ AQ92

f) Opener
　♠ AKJ92
　♡ KJ82
　◇ 4
　♣ A93

Opener with Example 14c) first bids one spade. If responder bids two hearts opener's rebid is a jump to four hearts. This is in keeping with the *principle of fast arrival*. Responder has shown a hand with at least five hearts and values enough to make game facing an opening bid. Opener's jump shows that he has three card heart support and minimum values.

With Example 14d) opener starts by bidding one spade. His hand does not quite qualify for an opening bid of one notrump due to the weak doubleton in diamonds. When responder bids two hearts, opener raises to three hearts. This gentle raise shows that opener has extra values, for if he did not have extra values he would jump to four hearts in keeping with the *principle of fast arrival*.

With Example 14e) opener again starts by bidding one spade. When responder bids two hearts opener would like to make a *splinter* bid of four diamonds, but that rebid would promise four card heart support. Opener does the best that he can by raising to three hearts to show his extra values.

With Example 14f) when opener hears a two heart response to his opening bid of one spade he continues by jumping to four diamonds. This *splinter* bid shows extra values, four card support for hearts, and shortness in diamonds.

When opener has bid either major suit and responder makes a game forcing two over one response in a minor suit, opener will often best describe his hand by raising responder's minor. A single raise to the three level should indicate good support for responder's suit since other actions are available to opener, and he should not seek a minor suit contract unless the story of his hand indicates that a minor suit contract is more likely from his viewpoint than notrump.

Opener also has the capacity to **splinter** in support of responder's minor suit after a two over one response. Systemically, since the auction is already forcing to game, it would be redundant and space consuming for opener to jump in a new suit just to show a good hand with a second suit. Therefore, a jump in a new suit as opener's rebid after responder has forced to game with a response at the two level is designated as a **splinter** in support of responder's suit.

Example 15:

a) Opener	b) Opener	c) Opener
♠ AK742	♠ AK742	♠ AK742
♡ 93	♡ Q93	♡ A93
◇ Q5	◇ 75	◇ 5
♣ KJ62	♣ KQ4	♣ K1065

With Example hand 15a) opener bids one spade and hears a two club response. Even though his values are minimum, he makes the natural call of raising to three clubs. Even when the partnership agreement is that the raise to the three level requires extra values, the fourth club is sufficient to overcome that requirement.

With Example hand 15b) opener who has bid one spade again hears a response of two clubs. With a concentration of values in responder's suit and more than a minimum opening bid, opener again raises clubs.

With Example hand 15c) opener after bidding one spade again hears a two club response. Opener's rebid is a *splinter* jump to three diamonds which shows diamond shortness as well as good values and a good fit for clubs.

Rebidding With Six-Four Hands

Opener will often be dealt a hand with a six card suit and a four card suit. Clearly, he will have opened the bidding by naming his six card suit, but at his rebid he may have a problem in determining which suit to bid at that time.

When the opening bid has been in a six card minor suit and the four card suit is a major suit, the major suit should be the choice as opener's rebid whenever it is possible for him to make that rebid. When the four card major is spades, and responder has bid one heart over one diamond or one of either red suit over one club, responder has no trouble naming spades at his rebid. If responder bids one notrump, bypassing spades, responder can rebid his six card minor suit knowing that there is no playable spade fit.

When opener's four card major is hearts and responder bids one spade, opener will be unable to name hearts at his rebid unless his hand is strong enough for a reverse. In standard bidding, opener's strength should be about an ace more than a minimum opening bid to qualify as strong enough for a reverse. With a minimum hand in this auction, opener must not rebid in hearts, but must repeat his six card minor suit.

Given the opportunity to show his four card major suit at the one level, opener should take into account the nature of the game. At match points the major suit should be shown even when it is four small cards. At IMP scoring or at rubber bridge, when the major suit quality is that bad and the minor suit is virtually solid, opener should consider repressing the bad four card major in favor of rebidding his excellent six card minor suit.

Hands with a six card major suit and another four card suit present a different problem. Since discovery of a playable major suit contract is the first goal of any auction, a rebid of the six card major is far more attractive than would be the rebid of a six card minor.

With six hearts and four spades, opener's rebid will be in hearts unless either: 1) responder bids spades allowing opener to raise. 2) Opener has the extra strength required for a reverse when responder bids one notrump (forcing). 3) Responder makes a game forcing call at the two level. This permits opener to show his shape by bidding spades at this second turn even though his hand does not have the strength for a reverse.

With six spades and four hearts, opener's rebid should be in the four card heart suit unless there is a great disparity in the quality of the two suits, and the heart suit is too poor to consider mentioning in comparison with a good spade suit.

With a six card major and a four card minor, rebid the major suit whenever its quality is so good that no support is needed. The suit should have no more than one loser even when partner has a singleton or void. When the major suit is of lesser quality, opener should bid the four card minor suit at his rebid, giving priority to the finding of a fit.

Example 16:

a) Opener	b) Opener	c) Opener
♠ Q2	♠ 7543	♠ AJ8754
♡ AJ83	♡ A5	♡ 7
◇ 4	◇ 8	◇ KQ108
♣ AQ9863	♣ AKQ1096	♣ K3

d) Opener	e) Opener	f) Opener
♠ AKJ1074	♠ KQJ6	♠ KQJ6
♡ 7	♡ AJ9842	♡ AQ9842
◇ AJ83	◇ 3	◇ 3
♣ 94	♣ Q4	♣ A4

With Example hand 16a) open one club and rebid one heart if partner responds by bidding one diamond. If he responds one heart you should make the systemic rebid of jumping to four clubs (see next section). If the response is either one spade or one no-trump, rebid two clubs. Your hand is not good enough for a reverse to two hearts.

With Example 16b) open one club and over a response of one diamond or one heart bid one spade at matchpoints. If at IMPs or rubber bridge you should most probably make a jump rebid of three clubs instead since your goal is the most likely game rather than the most score productive contract. If partner responds in spades you can jump to four clubs to show a hand with four card support and six clubs, and values enough to play a game. If partner responds one notrump showing 8 to 10 points, since you have seven apparent winners take a shot at three notrump.

With Example 16c) open one spade and rebid two diamonds if that is possible. If partner's response is two hearts rebid two spades rather than go to the three level to show your diamonds. If partner responds two diamonds, your hand is good enough for a *splinter* jump to three hearts to show heart shortness and good support for diamonds.

With Example 16d) a rebid of two spades after any response is possible because of the good quality of the suit. However, if responder happens to bid two diamonds a *splinter* jump to three hearts is a good idea.

With Example 16e) open one heart and raise if partner responds in spades. If partner's response is a *Forcing Notrump*, rebid two hearts. If partner responds in a minor suit at the two level, you can rebid two spades to show your shape since that rebid does not require the strength of a reverse.

With Example 16f) open one heart and if responder bids one spade, make a *splinter* bid by jumping to four diamonds. If partner responds one notrump your hand is good enough to reverse and make a rebid of two spades. If partner responds in a new suit at the two level, bid two spades to show your shape. You have extra values in this auction since the two spade bid did not require the strength for a reverse which you happen to have.

g) Opener

♠ AQJ1054
♡ KQ108
♢ 7
♣ 63

With Example 16g) **Open one spade and rebid two hearts. Even though the spade suit is good enough to play facing a singleton, the good heart suit should be mentioned since hearts may be a superior place to play.**

When opener has bid a six card minor suit and responder bids a major suit in which opener also had four cards, special system auctions are available. Since the distribution of such a hand will often be enough to offer a play for game, opener can make a jump rebid to the four level in his original suit to show his six-four pattern and force the auction to the game level. When the responder has meager values and the bidding side cannot make a game, it is likely that the opponents who have a double fit in the other two suits have been preempted out of a makeable game the other way.

A jump rebid to the four level has no real meaning if its sole purpose is to rebid the minor suit since a possible contract of three notrump will have been bypassed. Opener shows by this jump that in addition to his minor suit which is now known to be six (or seven) cards in length, he also holds four card support for responder's major suit and playing strength which opener feels will usually be adequate to produce game in the major suit.

When opener makes use of this jump to show his six-four pattern, his values should be concentrated in his two suits. With concentrated values opener's hand will function better to produce tricks than would be the case if his values were scattered and in his short suits. When the six card minor suit is broken, opener will probably be better off by simply raising responder's major suit to the two (or three) level rather than jumping to the four level to show his six-four pattern.

In earlier forms, other jumps to the four level were incorporated to make quality distinctions in opener's hand. Jumps to the four level in opener's original suit suggested slam, while double jump reverses showed a similar hand with interest in game but not in slam. Since progress has caused the double jump reverse to be used to show a **void splinter** instead, the gradations once available have been dropped from the system.

When opener has a six four hand that is slam oriented, he might better make use of a **splinter** bid. When opener **splinters** at his rebid he is able to get responder's reaction to the information conveyed by the splinter. If responder bids notrump to show wasted values in the splinter suit, opener can pull in his horns and settle for what appears to be the best game. If instead responder makes a positive move after hearing about opener's splinter, opener knows that his concealed source of tricks in his six card suit will be a strong asset at a slam contract.

In Splinters and Other Shortness Bids this author pointed out that there is a difference of expert opinion regarding the need to show a good side suit as opposed to making an immediate splinter bid. Quotes from Amalya Kearse and Mike Lawrence both espoused the showing of a good side suit as having priority over the making of a splinter bid, while Marty Bergen was quoted as preferring to show the good fit for partner's suit and the location of side shortness when the opportunity presented itself rather than emphasize a good side suit.

In the situation discussed above, the reasons for splintering appear to be compelling. The splinter also indicates that opener is likely to have five or more cards in his original suit, thereby lessening the necessity to rebid that suit.

Example 17:

a) Opener	b) Responder	c) Responder
♠ 3	♠ A74	♠ QJ85
♡ AQ76	♡ K983	♡ K983
◇ A9	◇ K843	◇ 843
♣ AQJ874	♣ 93	♣ 109

Opener 17a) starts by bidding one club. After a one heart response opener rebids by making a *splinter* double jump shift of three spades. This response shows the four card fit for hearts with values enough to produce game as well as a shortness control, and allows for upward evaluation by responder of honor cards in both minor suits as well as devaluation of spade cards other than the ace.

Responder 17b) should be enthused by opener's *splinter* rebid. He should take control of the auction and use *Roman Key Card Blackwood* to determine whether or not slam should be bid. When he finds three key cards and the trump queen the good six heart contract should be reached.

Responder 17c) signs off at four hearts since his minimum response suggests to him that reaching a game that should make is a pleasant surprise. He knows that his spade values will be wasted, and if his hearts were worse would elect to bid three notrump instead of four hearts.

d) Opener	e) Responder	f) Responder
♠ KJ98	♠ A763	♠ AQ73
♡ 9	♡ KQJ	♡ 954
◇ K7	◇ QJ64	◇ A853
♣ AQJ832	♣ 94	♣ K4

Opener 17d) starts with one club and after a one spade response to four clubs to show his six-four pattern. If responder has any moderate hand four spades should have a reasonable play, and with a better hand responder knows what to expect from opener as he probes further for slam.

Responder 17e) should not get excited. Despite his opening bid values, opener's rebid should show him that the two hands do not fit well, and his values will not be good for a slam contract since opener has shortness facing his secondary red suit values. He should sign off at four spades.

Responder 17f) should be more encouraged. His good spades, diamond control, and fitting honor in clubs are all known to be good values. Responder 17f) should take control and drive toward a slam by using *Roman Key Card Blackwood*.

Opener's Rebid is a Reverse

Opener's rebid in a new suit at the two level which ranks higher than the suit in which he opened the bidding at the one level is called a reverse. The description derives from the fact that opener has bid his two suits in the reverse of economical order. Had he bid those two suits in economical order, responder would be able to take a preference to opener's first suit without going beyond the two level. The reverse requires responder, if he simply wishes to return to opener's first bid suit, to do so at the three level.

Since the choice to bid suits in this order has been made, opener has promised that he has the additional values that will be needed to fulfill a higher level contract. The exact range of his promised values is subject to partnership agreement.

The **Walsh System** which was the earliest form of the two over one system now in use required that opener have game forcing values for a reverse. Later thinking has suggested that the game forcing requirement for a reverse is too confining and leaves good hands of the appropriate shape without a descriptive way to be bid. The general agreement today is that opener's reverse promises about an ace more than a minimum opening hand. Opener will have a good sixteen points or more. There is no upper limit to opener's value range, and the reverse is forcing for one round.

The reverse is also a shape showing bid. It guarantees that opener's first suit is longer than the suit of his rebid. Opener's shape in his two suits will be 4-5, 4-6, 4-7, 5-6, 5-7, or on rare occasions the rebid suit may be only three cards long when opener's values require that he make a forcing bid and he has only one long suit.

After his reverse, opener will continue as indicated after hearing responder's rebid. The complex of rebids by responder after opener has reversed that is recommended was suggested by the late Monroe Ingberman, a very highly regarded bidding theorist, and is detailed in Chapter IV.

Opener's Rebid is a Jump to Three Notrump

A jump rebid of three notrump is not needed to show any particular balanced hand, and is therefore reserved to show a special type of hand. When opener has begun by bidding one in a minor suit and after a new suit response at the one level rebids by jumping to three notrump he shows that his original suit will be a source of tricks at three notrump since it is at least six cards long and either solid or nearly solid.

Opener denies interest in responder's suit, and may even have a singleton or a void in that suit. Opener does promise that in addition to his own good suit he has stoppers in the two unbid suits. In order to hold both a near solid suit and side suit stoppers in two other suits, opener's high card content will be in the approximate range of 16 to 18 points, though there is no rigid high card point requirement.

Example 18:

a) Opener
♠ 7
♡ AQ5
◇ AKJ1084
♣ K109

With either hand in Example 18 opener will first bid one diamond.

With Example hand 18a) if responder bids one heart or one notrump or makes the game forcing response of two clubs, opener's rebid will be a jump to three diamonds. If responder bids one spade, opener will jump to three notrump to show a hand with a source of tricks in diamonds and stoppers in the unbid suits, and deny any interest in responder's suit.

b) Opener
♠ 7
♡ KQ4
♢ AKQJ63
♣ A52

With Example hand 18b) if responder bids one heart opener will make a game forcing jump shift rebid of three clubs, planning to support hearts at his next turn. If responder bids one notrump opener will raise to three notrump, gambling that responder has a spade stopper. If responder makes a game forcing call of two clubs, opener best describes his hand by jump rebidding in diamonds. If responder bids one spade, opener jumps to three notrump to show his good source of tricks in diamonds and stoppers in the unbid suits, while denying any interest in spades.

When responder hears the descriptive rebid of three notrump he understands the nature of opener's rebid. If he has no spade values facing implied shortness and fitting cards in the unbid suits, responder can visualize a slam on very little in high cards.

When responder's values are in his suit, he understands that they will not be useful cards for play at a diamond slam, but will provide needed stoppers for the notrump contract that has been reached. Responder should consider returning to his suit only when it would be self sufficient as a trump suit.

Example 19:

a) Responder
♠ 96542
♡ K86
♢ Q95
♣ A3

b) Responder
♠ A8652
♡ A93
♢ 985
♣ K3

c) Responder
♠ KQ1043
♡ J87
♢ 53
♣ Q74

d) Responder
♠ KQJ10964
♡ J87
♢ 3
♣ 42

With Example 19 hands responder has bid one spade after an opening bid of one diamond. The auction continues with a descriptive rebid by opener of a jump to three notrump.

With Example hand 19a) responder knows that his cards will be useful for a diamond slam. He indicates this fact to opener by making a cue bid of four clubs. Visualize Example 19a) as a companion hand to Example 18a).

With Example hand 19b) responder again knows that a diamond slam is extremely likely. This responder should call four diamonds and allow opener to probe for the controls in responder's hand. With good partnership agreements for slam auctions it may even be possible to reach a grand slam.

With Example hand 19c) responder should realize that his spade holding will provide the needed stoppers for play at three notrump. With no reason to seek another contract, responder will pass.

With Example hand 19d) responder will realize that his hand will do nothing more than provide stoppers in spades if he passes. Opener will have many hands that do not have nine tricks in notrump, but at a contract of four spades responder's excellent suit will win six tricks. Since four spades should be a better contract than three notrump, responder should correct to that contract.

General

As has been explained, more information on opener's rebids appears in discussions of specialized responses such as **Forcing Notrump, Drury,** and **Inverted Minor Raises** in Chapter III which follows. Where no special systemic method has been presented, bidding is primarily as in standard methods.

Rebids in notrump reveal balanced hands or semi-balanced hands with good doubletons. Rebids in a higher ranking suit at the one level do not necessarily speak of shape but comprise part of the major suit search which is part of most intelligent auctions.

Rebids in lower ranking suits at the two level show either minimum or intermediate strength hands which are unbalanced or semi-balanced with honors concentrated in long suits.

Jump shift rebids by opener are forcing to game, and reverses are forcing for one round.

Rebids of five card suits are not voluntarily made except in special systemic circumstances, although an involuntary rebid of a five card suit may occur when no other action is suitable.

Hands with four diamonds and five clubs are opened with one diamond and a planned rebid of two clubs when they are minimum unless the diamonds are poor and the clubs are good. In that case clubs are opened and rebid unless a good doubleton in one major permits a rebid of one notrump when partner responds in the other major.

Hands with four diamonds and five clubs which are better than minimum (16+) qualify for a reverse unless they are seriously flawed by ragged suits, in which case two good major suit doubletons qualify the hand for a one notrump opening bid.

When opener rebids two notrump after a two over one response he will have one of two value ranges. He is permitted to make this rebid with minimum values if it is descriptive and he is balanced with stoppers in the unbid suits.

Opener may also have a much better hand in the range of eighteen or nineteen points. When he has this better hand and has bid two no-trump at his second turn, his third call will a quantitative bid of four notrump.

If opener had instead bid three notrump after the two over one response he would show a hand in the fifteen to seventeen range that was balanced but not appropriate to an opening bid of one notrump.

CHAPTER III
RESPONDING TO
OPENING SUIT BIDS

Responses to opening suit bids are not always the same in the Two Over One bidding style as they would be in standard bidding. The response that seems natural and obvious will sometimes not be systemically correct, and responder must be careful not to speak before being sure that his call is correct in the system.

Responder's estimate of the worth of his hand will be aided by the counting of high card points, but point ranges in themselves do not necessarily determine the worth of the hand. One must be able to judge when his hand is "good" for the high card count it presents, and also when it is "bad" within those same high card count confines.

To emphasize the need for the bidder to do more than just count points, reference to ranges will often include plus or minus signs. The designation 9+ will refer to a hand with nine high card points that is really better than might be expected, while 9− will indicate that the hand contains a poor nine high card points. All hands of a stipulated point count are not necessarily created equal, and the bidder must use his understanding of what creates a good or bad hand within the confines of a stipulated point range.

Those factors which improve a hand beyond its point count are such things as honor cards that are combined rather than isolated, inclusion of good spot cards, and distributional merit rather than absence of long suits. These plus factors can cause a hand to be worth several points more than what a simple count of high cards might indicate.

Similarly, when honor cards are sprinkled throughout the hand and not combined in any one suit, when the hand has very small spot cards rather than tens, nines and eights, and when it is balanced rather than distributional, such a hand may be worth much less than the value assigned to it by the counting of its high card points.

This chapter will include several specialized responses which are linked to continuation sequences. Rather than present piecemeal portions of these specialized sequences, discussions of **Inverted Minor Raises, Major Suit Raises** other than the simple single raise, the **Forcing Notrump,** and **Drury** will include those continuations. Some of the continuation discussions were postponed from the preceding chapter and include rebids by the opening bidder. That postpone-

41

ment was deliberate so that each presentation could be more cohesive.

Preemptive Jump Shift Responses

The use of preemptive jump shift responses is not necessary to the system, but because they compliment other system components, they are adopted by most system users and are recommended here. In auctions that start with a minor suit opening bid, preemptive jump shifts are useful and effective, and do not interfere with other systemic devices. The only loss is that of giving up strong jump shifts, a tool that some bidders prefer to have available. An important gain is the ability to make a preemptive jump response when jumps to the three level are not preemptive, but are used as splinters.

In auctions that begin with a major suit opening bid, preemptive jump shifts are more difficult to use since, with one exception, they require responder to bid at the three level, and often other systemic devices replace them in certain auctions. Preemptive jump shifts at the three level require good suits, and slightly more in high card strength than do preemptive jump shifts at the two level.

The jump shift shows a suit of six or seven cards and very little in high card strength. Ideally, most of the limited high card strength should be within the suit of the jump shift.

The high card strength for a jump shift at the two level should be roughly between two and five high card points, though tactically one might have less in high cards with a suit longer than anticipated for the level at which the jump shift is made. Auctions in which responder fails to make a jump shift, then repeats his suit at the cheapest level now become more sharply defined due to the omission of the jump shift. In such an auction responder's minimum will be a very good five points in addition to his long suit.

A systemic device now widely used is a double jump shift to a higher ranking suit in response to a minor suit opening bid to show a **splinter** in support of opener's minor suit. Since an auction such as 1♣-P-3♠ shows a **splinter** raise for clubs rather than a preemptive jump shift in spades, responder needs to have the preemptive jump shift at the two level available to him in order to be able to preempt the auction without having to leap all the way to the four level.

When responder to an opening minor suit bid makes a **splinter** jump it is not clear whether the eventual contract will be in opener's minor suit or in notrump. For this reason when responder does **splinter** he needs to have full opening bid values, since a contract of three notrump will need more high cards than would a suit contract based on lots of trumps and good fits.

42

Example 20:

a) Responder
♠ 3
♡ KJ10962
◊ J54
♣ 765

b) Responder
♠ 8
♡ KQJ763
◊ Q95
♣ 1087

c) Responder
♠ 9
♡ KQJ843
◊ K62
♣ 1083

d) Responder
♠ AQ5
♡ 3
◊ KJ864
♣ K954

Example 20a) is a textbook jump shift response after an opening bid of one in either minor suit. Responder describes his hand perfectly by jumping to two hearts. If the opening bid is one spade, responder must make a *Forcing Notrump* response and hope to bid two hearts at his second turn. He cannot jump to three hearts since that call is systemic and shows a raise for spades.

Example 20b) is far too good for a preemptive jump shift response after a minor suit opening bid. Responder bids one heart and plans to bid hearts as cheaply as possible at his second turn. If the opening bid has been one spade, responder with this hand first bids a *Forcing Notrump*, and plans to rebid two hearts at his second turn.

Example 20c) shows a good nine points which makes the hand good enough to invite a game. In response to an opening minor suit bid responder bids one heart, then jumps to three hearts at his rebid to show this good suit with invitational values. If the opening bid is one spade, responder must again content himself with a *Forcing Notrump* response since his invitational hand is not good enough for a game forcing two over one response. To show the invitational nature of his hand, he jumps to three hearts at his second turn. If opener rebids two spades, responder's rebid of three hearts will not be a jump, but will show this hand.

With Example 20d) responder can make a *splinter* jump of three hearts in response to an opening bid of one diamond. Although a *splinter* in response to an opening major suit bid can be made with less in values, that is because the major suit will certainly be the trump suit. Here, since the contract will often be three notrump responder needs full opening values in addition to a fit which should be five cards long as well as the short side suit identified by the *splinter* jump.

43

e) Opener
♠ J2
♡ KQ109
◇ A753
♣ QJ3

f) Opener
♠ K106
♡ 1095
◇ AK753
♣ A3

Opener with Example 20e) hears responder splinter to three hearts and bids three notrump with heart values that are wasted for suit play but will be stoppers for a notrump game.

Opener with Example 20f) who hears responder splinter in hearts has no wasted heart values and good control cards. He next cue bids four clubs and if responder cue bids the ace of spades the slam based on perfect fits will probably be bid.

Responses to Minor Suit Opening Bids

1) General

When the opening bid has been in a minor suit, the search for a playable major suit contract begins with the first action by responder. Systemically, whenever responder's hand is limited to less than the values for an opening bid, he tends to respond in a major suit even when longer suits are available. Only when responder has full opening bid values of his own will he bid naturally to show his hand pattern, and bid a longer minor suit ahead of a four card major suit when he has both. This practice of bypassing longer minor suits to bid four card majors on limited hands is controlled by systemic safeguards, and is not recommended to those who play an otherwise standard bidding approach.

In responding to an opening minor suit bid, when it is correct to bid a four card major, responder should do so without regard for the quality of the suit. If responder fails to bid his four card major suit at the correct time in the auction, opener will draw systemic inferences, and will often be compelled to supress his own four card major.

2) The One Diamond Response to One Club

When responder bids one diamond in response to one club his call is assumed to be natural. On rare occasions responder will temporize by bidding one diamond when he has no four card major and his high card strength is not sufficient to respond one notrump (many play that a response of one notrump to the opening bid of one club requires 8 to 10 HCP). Responder might, in this case, have a 3-3-3-4 hand pattern. Even more rare might be responder's decision to temporize with a 3-3-2-5 pattern rather than make an inverted club raise that would

44

require him to jump to the three level with his balanced hand. However, responder will nearly always have a diamond suit and opener will assume the response to be natural.

Responder's call of one diamond denies that he holds a four card major suit unless he also has at least five diamonds and the values of an opening bid. When responder does hold a hand with five or more diamonds as well as a four card major and opening bid values, he is prepared to show the major suit at his second turn. When the auction proceeds in this fashion, opener will know that responder has values enough to force game and is bidding naturally.

When opener hears the one diamond response he continues with the expectancy that responder does not have a four card major suit. With this as his premise, opener rebids one notrump with any balanced minimum hand, and will conceal one or both four card majors when they are a part of that balanced minimum.

In auctions that begin in this fashion, when responder passes or raises notrump to a level in keeping with the values he holds, the defense must begin without information that will have been conveyed by any standard auction. With information about opener's major suit holdings having been concealed, the blind start of the defense may be of great assistance to the declaring side.

Opener's rebid after a one diamond response will not always be in notrump, for on many occasions he will have been dealt an unbalanced hand. When his hand is unbalanced, opener will continue to bid descriptively, and if his choice is a rebid in a major suit, responder knows that opener's hand is unbalanced, and therefore unsuited to a rebid of one notrump.

When responder does have the hand with five or more diamonds as well as a four card major suit and opening bid values, after opener's natural rebid responder shows his four card major suit. Most often this will produce an auction in which responder reverses to show his major suit after a rebid of one notrump by opener.

When opener has rebid in a major suit, confirming a hand that is unbalanced, if responder raises that major suit to the three level, he confirms that he holds four cards in opener's major suit, thereby guaranteeing values enough to produce game and showing at least five diamonds. If responder instead raises opener's major suit to the two level he shows a hand with three card support for the major suit and game invitational values.

When opener rebids in a major suit to show an unbalanced hand and responder holds the other major suit, one such auction requires a different definition. When opener rebids one spade and responder continues to two hearts, the auction is usually natural showing that responder has a four card heart suit and longer diamonds with good values. However, responder may have a hand with which he holds long diamonds or support for one of opener's suits and has the need to create a forcing auction. Two hearts therefore should be considered to be **Fourth Suit Forcing** which is artificial and creates a subsequent auction which is forcing rather than merely invitational.

When opener continues by bidding one heart, to show a four card spade suit responder must jump to two spades. If responder were to bid only one spade in this auction, that call would not show spades, but would be **Fourth Suit Forcing**. Responder needs to be able to make the distinction between those hands where he truly holds a four card spade suit in addition to five or more diamonds and game forcing values, and those hands with which he simply needs to create a forcing auction by bidding artificially in the fourth suit.

If responder is a passed hand, he must take into account that opener may have opened a light hand with the intention of passing any response. For this reason, when responder is a passed hand it is not possible for him to temporize on a short diamond holding since he does not wish to play a diamond contract if opener should elect to pass. As a passed hand, responder must therefore respond with one notrump holding a hand in the range of a good five to ten points and a balanced hand unsuited to a club raise.

In summary, a one diamond response to the opening bid of one club shows any hand that is primarily one suited in diamonds, a hand which contains a four card major only when it has opening bid strength and diamonds are five cards or longer, a hand that may otherwise be two suited only if the second suit is clubs, or a hand which visualizes a contract by opener since it is balanced and minimum, but is not strong enough to respond one notrump since that shows eight to ten points when responder is unpassed.

Example 21:

a) Responder	b) Responder	c) Responder
♠ AJ82	♠ AJ82	♠ AJ82
♡ 5	♡ 5	♡ K5
◇ Q109863	◇ 86	◇ Q10843
♣ 86	♣ Q109863	♣ K6

d) Responder
- ♠ KQ103
- ♡ A4
- ◇ 74
- ♣ KQ1097

e) Responder
- ♠ K85
- ♡ Q103
- ◇ KJ62
- ♣ 943

With Example hand 21a) responder systemically bids one spade when partner has opened in any of the three lower ranking suits. If the opening bid has been one club, he bypasses his six card diamond suit to do so since systemic methods will enable him to show his diamond suit later if that becomes a matter of consequence (see Chapter IV).

With Example hand 21b) responder again bids one spade, but this time he does so without bypassing any suit. Again, if the auction progress in such fashion that the six card club suit needs to be shown, a systemic auction will allow that to occur (see Chapter IV).

With Example 21c) responder will make a systemic raise (discussed later in this Chapter) to an opening bid of one spade, or respond one spade to an opening bid of one diamond. If the opening bid has been either one heart or one one club, responder bids diamonds first and plans to show his spade suit later. With the values of an opening bid, responder can show his suits in natural order.

With Example 21d) responder would again make a systemic raise after an opening bid of one spade or would bid one spade in response to an opening bid of one club. If the opening bid were either one diamond or one heart responder would first bid two clubs, then show his four card spade suit at his second turn. His full opening bid values entitle him to bid his suits in natural order.

With Example 21e) responder would make a single raise of an opening bid in either major suit, but would respond one notrump to an opening bid in either minor. Responder to an opening one diamond bid has little choice, but responder to an opening bid of one club is happy to bid one notrump to describe his hand in the 8 to 10 range that has good tenaces to protect.

f) Responder   g) Responder
    ♠ J85   ♠ J85
    ♡ A43   ♡ 943
    ◊ A872   ◊ Q87
    ♣ 943   ♣ K943

Example 21f) should again raise a major suit opening bid to two and respond one notrump over the opening bid of one diamond. His hand is not suited to a diamond raise and his balanced pattern is more oriented to play in notrump than to play in a suit. If the opening bid is one club, responder should bid one diamond rather than one notrump. Although he has the values required for a one notrump response, he has no tenaces to protect, and notrump should be declared from the other side of the table if that becomes the eventual contract.

Example 21g) would again raise an opening bid in either major suit, or would bid one notrump in response to one diamond. If the opening bid is one club, responder should not bid one notrump, but should temporize by bidding one diamond. He does not have the strength for a one notrump response if he is an unpassed hand since that shows 8 to 10 high card points. If he is a passed hand, responder has no choice but to bid one notrump despite his miserable hand, for he does not want to play in one diamond if opener should pass his response which is now not a forcing call.

3) The Three Club Response to One Diamond

The jump shift response of three clubs to an opening bid of one diamond is neither preemptive nor strong. It systemically shows a hand with a six card club suit and game invitational values (9+ to 12-points). Were this auction not to be available, responder would have to bid two clubs, then rebid three clubs to cancel the game force established by the original two over one response.

A distinct advantage to the system presented in this book is that the two over one response is never diluted. Other presentations that purport to deal with two over one are replete with exceptions, and system users have to carefully memorize all of the continuation sequences that are the exceptions. They have to learn the situations in which after a two over one response the auction ceases to be game forcing after certain rebids by either opener or responder.

Not so the way we believe a Two Over One System should be constructed. Our presentation is based on the premise that a Two Over One response forces the auction to three notrump or four of a suit. In minor suits, the auction can stop below game (at the four level) but only if a total misfit is deemed to exist and responder has minimum values for his original two over one response.

Since with invitational values and a good club suit responder will jump directly to three clubs in response to one diamond, it follows that when he bids two clubs and then rebids three clubs, he is describing a hand that might possibly play a club slam.

Example 22:

a) Responder	b) Responder
♠ 54	♠ A4
♡ K93	♡ KQ3
◇ Q8	◇ 86
♣ KQ10962	♣ KQ10962

With Example 22a) responder to an opening major suit bid would use a *Forcing Notrump* response. If the opening bid was one heart he would be preparing a delayed limit raise to show three card trump support and a balanced hand. If the opening bid had been one club, responder would make an *Inverted Minor Raise* to two clubs. In response to an opening bid of one diamond the systemic call is a jump to three clubs which promises a six card club suit with game invitational values (9+ to 12-).

With Example 22b) the correct response to any opening suit bid is two clubs. If the opening bid was one club this is an *Inverted Minor Raise* but after any other opening suit bid it is natural and forcing to game. If the opening bid was one heart, responder will show his heart support at his second turn, but if the opening bid was either one diamond or one spade, responder's rebid will be three clubs to show his good suit. Since the two club response was game forcing, the three club rebid is forcing and descriptive. If the opening bid has been one club, responder may not bid three clubs at his second turn as that call would be non-forcing, showing only a limit raise for clubs.

4) Two and Three Notrump Responses to One Diamond

An awkward hand with which to respond to a one diamond opening bid is one which is in the invitational range (9+ to 12-), has no four card major, and is not suited to an **Inverted Minor Raise**. When that hand is otherwise balanced, the systemic response is a jump to two notrump. This limited jump is descriptive and non-forcing. Only in response to a one diamond opening bid is this jump to two notrump necessary, since in response to one club it is possible to mark time by bidding one diamond with an awkward hand.

The corollary to this non-forcing two notrump response to the opening bid of one diamond is that a jump to three notrump shows a balanced hand without a four card major and 12+ to 15- points. These responses are needed only when the opening bid has been one diamond, but for the sake of uniformity some system users play them in response to both minor suits rather than just after one diamond.

Example 23:

a) Responder	b) Responder
♠ Q53	♠ K5
♡ KJ3	♡ KJ3
◇ Q94	◇ KQ84
♣ K1065	♣ Q1065

With Example 23a) responder would make a *Forcing Notrump* call to an opening bid in either major suit, planning to make a delayed limit raise at his second turn. In response to one club responder could jump to two notrump if that were only invitational, but if two notrump in response to one club is forcing responder should temporize with one diamond, then bid two notrump at his next turn. If the opening bid has been one diamond, responder jumps to two notrump to describe his balanced invitational hand, and in this case is pleased that he has tenaces in all suits.

Responder with Example 23b) would bid two notrump in response to one club if that call were agreed to be forcing. Responder has values appropriate for a notrump game and the notrump jump is more descriptive than would be an *Inverted Raise* to two clubs. If the opening bid were in a major suit, responder would bid two clubs, a natural game force. If the opening bid has been one spade responder's most likely rebid will be in notrump. If the opening bid has been one heart, responder will show his heart support at his rebid. If the opening bid has been one diamond, responder could force to game by bidding two clubs, but a jump to three notrump showing 12+ to 15- with a balanced hand is far more descriptive. Responder has the tenaces and secondary honor cards that make notrump play well, and lacks the controls that would suggest a slam.

5) Inverted Minor Raises

Inverted Minor Raises are so named because the single raise is strong and forcing, and the jump raise is weak and preemptive. This inverts the meaning of these bids from the way they are used in standard bidding where the single raise is weak and the jump raise is stronger. The philosophy for the system is well suited by a tool of this nature since instant preemption is complimented by a slow auction which allows for a greater exchange of information whenever responder has a good hand.

a) The jump raise of a minor suit opening bid denies a four card major and promises length in support of opener's minor suit. If the opening bid has been one club, the jump raise requires a minimum of five card support since opener will often have bid a three card club suit.

If the opening bid has been one diamond opener will nearly always have a four card or longer suit, so responder might jump raise with good four card support, major suit shortness, and the feeling that pre-emption would be better than an awkward response in notrump. In this situation responder will almost always have five clubs as well due to his extreme shortness in the major suits. Most often, though, when responder makes a jump raise in diamonds, he will have five card or longer support.

The strength required is that of a normal response, about a good five to a bad nine points, but the more cards responder holds in opener's suit the more he should be inclined to respond preemptively even with less in high cards. When responder has made the preemptive jump raise, opener is warned to bid no further unless his hand suggests that a game in notrump or the agreed minor suit is possible.

Example 24:

a) Responder	b) Responder	c) Responder
♠ 63	♠ 643	♠ Q64
♡ 8	♡ 8	♡ J85
♢ KJ9754	♢ KJ95	♢ KJ975
♣ Q876	♣ Q8765	♣ 76

With Example 24a) if the opening bid has been one diamond responder has a classic hand for an *Inverted* jump raise to three diamonds. He has no four card major, minimum response values, good shape, and lots of diamonds.

With Example 24b) if the opening bid has been one club, responder has an easy jump raise to three clubs. If the opening bid has been one diamond, no call is good, but responder might try an inverted jump raise since opener is favored to have at least four diamonds.

With Example 24c) when the opening bid has been one diamond responder should bid one notrump. With moderate values including a face card in each major suit and a balanced hand, even though he does have five card diamond support, responder best describes his hand this way rather than with a jump to three diamonds.

b) The single raise of a minor suit opening bid shows a good nine points or more (there is no top limit to its strength), four or more cards in the suit that is being raised, denies a four card major suit, and is forcing for one round.

Responder may have a limit raise for this response. By definition a limit raise is a hand with a good nine to a bad twelve points with at least four card support for the minor suit and no four card major. Responder will invite, but not insist upon reaching a game. After opener's rebid, responder must be careful that his next call does not carry the auction beyond the agreed suit at the three level, for if he exceeds that level he promises that his **Inverted Raise** was made with game forcing values.

Responder might continue by showing a stopper in an unbid suit at his second turn, or he might simply return to the agreed suit at the three level to indicate a distributional raise with no feature to show within the available bidding space. He also has the option to bid two notrump to indicate that his hand is reasonably balanced, all suits are known to be stopped, and that his hand is only in the invitational range.

When responder has made an **Inverted** raise with a hand that has game forcing values, he must be sure to show those values by not making a bid that might be passed by opener. He must avoid the bids of two notrump and three of the agreed suit, both of which would limit his values to the invitational (9+ to 12-) range.

He may bid to show feature holdings in new suits below the level of three in the agreed minor since all such new suit bids are forcing, or he may push the auction beyond three of the agreed minor suit which will indicate that his values are great enough to force to game. When responder's values are so substantial that he visualizes the possibility of slam, he must again be sure not to make a bid that may be passed by opener until his slam suggestion has been conveyed.

Example 25:

a) Responder
♠ K95
♡ Q108
◇ A987
♣ Q65

b) Responder
♠ KJ5
♡ 943
◇ AQJ4
♣ 732

c) Responder
♠ KJ5
♡ 943
◇ AQJ4
♣ K103

d) Responder
♠ KJ5
♡ 4
◇ AQJ43
♣ A1095

e) Responder
♠ Q65
♡ 4
◇ AQJ865
♣ J73

f) Responder
♠ AQ5
♡ AK4
◇ AQJ85
♣ 85

With all Example 25 hands you are responding to an opening bid of one diamond.

With Example 25a) do not make an *Inverted Minor Raise*. Your hand is best described by an immediate jump to two notrump which is invitational. You have good tenaces in the unbid suits and a balanced hand which is best described by this bid in notrump.

With Example 25b) raise to two diamonds. If opener continues by bidding two hearts to show a value in that suit, you can bid two spades. If opener continues by bidding either two spades or three clubs, bid three diamonds to show no extra values or feature that you are able to show. If opener bids two notrump you can pass with your balanced hand. Opener has shown a minimum with both majors stopped, and your best contract is to play for eight tricks in notrump.

With Example 25c) raise to two diamonds. If opener bids two hearts you can jump to three notrump to show your values and that the unbid suits are stopped. If partner bids two notrump raise to three. If opener continues by bidding in either black suit he tends to deny a value in any suit he has bypassed, or he is bidding to show shape. If he bids two spades bid three clubs to show your values there. If he bids three clubs bid three spades to show your value there. In each case opener's next bid will tell you enough more about his hand that you will have a good idea of what to do.

With Example 25d) do not make an *Inverted Minor Raise* in diamonds. With this hand the best description is a *splinter* jump to three hearts. If opener next bids three notrump he will have concentrated values in hearts, and you should pass. If he makes any other call you can show your black suit values and your side might easily be able to reach a diamond slam.

With Example 25e) raise to two diamonds, then bid diamonds again at the cheapest level. You want to show that your values are limited and that the essence of your hand is just diamonds. Opener will play you for an invitational (9+ to 12-) hand with long diamonds.

With Example 25f) raise to two diamonds. If partner next bids two spades, two notrump or three clubs, bid three hearts. If he bids two hearts bid two spades and bid hearts at your next turn. You are eager to reach slam with this powerful hand and must listen to opener's description while making your own forcing descriptive bids. The bids that you hear from opener will guide you to the best contract.

c) Opener's rebids after the forcing single raise are as follows: With a balanced minimum which contains stoppers in both major suits, opener continues to two notrump. Responder is warned of the minimum nature of opener's hand, and that there is a possibility that opener does not have a stopper in the unbid minor. With less than game going values responder can pass or correct to the agreed minor suit at the three level.

If opener instead bids three notrump he shows a hand which would have made a jump rebid of two notrump after a one level response. His hand will be balanced and too good for an opening bid of one no-trump but not good enough to have opened with two notrump (18+ to 20-). When opener has a hand good enough to get to game facing an **Inverted Raise** with a balanced 14 or 15 points, he must temporize by showing a stopper, but must be sure that three notrump is reached.

With other minimum balanced hands, opener continues by bidding "stoppers up the line". After an **Inverted Raise** in clubs, if he continues by bidding two hearts he denies a diamond feature and shows one in the heart suit. If he has a minimum (12 or 13 points) he will not also have a spade stopper, for with a spade stopper as well he would instead have bid two notrump. With a better hand (14 or 15 points) he might also have a spade stopper but be unable to bid any number of notrump at that turn.

When opener bids a new suit at the three level after an **Inverted Mirror Raise**, with a single exception his bid will be a jump. The exception is a rebid of three clubs after an **Inverted Raise** in diamonds. Regardless of whether the rebid is or is not a jump, opener's rebid shows shortness in the suit of his rebid. It is a **splinter** rebid showing a singleton or void in the suit of his rebid.

Responder knows to rebid three notrump whenever he holds a concentration of values in opener's known short suit since those values will not facilitate play at slam but will promise good stoppers where stoppers are needed for play in notrump.

When opener's **splinter** rebid at the three level finds responder with no wasted values facing the announced shortness, responder should continue toward a contract in the agreed minor suit. His subsequent bids should show the location and extent of his values. With no wasted values in responder's hand facing shortness in opener's hand, the values that are present should be enough at least for a game, and will often be good enough to produce a slam.

Opener also may wish to take immediate charge and ask for controls. For this purpose, opener jumps to four in the agreed minor suit which functions as **Roman Key Card Blackwood** (see Chapter VIII). This treatment was suggested by Ron Feldman of Berkeley. California, and allows for the exchange of control information while permitting a stop at five of the agreed minor suit, a luxury often denied when the control asking bid must be four notrump.

Another systemic device available to opener after the **Inverted Raise** is an **Asking Bid** which can be used to seek controls in a specific suit. The **Asking Bid** is a double jump shift in a new suit (see Chapter VIII) in this auction.

If opener has an unbalanced minimum, after the **Inverted Raise** he can best describe his hand by re-raising the agreed suit to the three level. While this re-raise does not deny stoppers in outside suits for use in play at notrump, the description of an unbalanced hand serves better to warn responder that opener's hand is more suited to play in a suit than for play in notrump.

Example 26:

a) Opener	b) Opener	c) Opener
♠ AQ83	♠ Q1083	♠ AQ8
♡ KJ2	♡ AQ2	♡ J72
◇ Q8	◇ Q8	◇ Q8
♣ Q754	♣ K754	♣ KJ754

With all Example 26 hands you have opened with one club and responder has made a strong and forcing response of two clubs.

With Example 26a) the road to three notrump looks attractive, but you cannot bid notrump at this time. Two notrump would show minimum values and responder might pass. Three notrump would show that you have a hand of 18 or 19 points. You must temporize at this turn by bidding your nearest stopper, then show your values and desire to play three notrump by making that call at your next turn unless there is an unexpected development in the auction which leads in a different direction.

With Example, 26b) you can describe your minimum with stoppers in both majors by rebidding two notrump.

With Example 26c) bid two spades to show a stopper in that suit while denying stoppers in the red suits.

d) Opener
- ♠ K62
- ♡ 5
- ◇ QJ3
- ♣ AQ9864

e) Opener
- ♠ AK2
- ♡ 5
- ◇ A943
- ♣ KQJ106

f) Opener
- ♠ AQ4
- ♡ K6
- ◇ K3
- ♣ AQJ963

g) Opener
- ♠ A
- ♡ AQ4
- ◇ 743
- ♣ AKJ1062

With Example 26d) you should limit your hand and show long clubs by rebidding three clubs. If partner has a limit raise you are high enough. Three hearts would show your singleton heart, but would be an overbid of your values.

With Example 26e) after partner's *Inverted Minor Raise* you should show your shortness by jumping to three hearts. If partner continues by bidding three notrump you will be warned that he has heart values which will not be useful for play at a club slam and will be good stoppers for notrump, but if his next bid is in any other suit, a club slam is a good prospect.

With Example 26f) when partner has made an *Inverted Raise* in clubs, you have visions of slam and want to determine what controls he has. A jump to four clubs in this auction is *Roman Key Card Blackwood* in clubs. If partner shows three key cards you can ask him for the spade king to reach a grand slam. If he has only two key cards a small slam in clubs should be safe.

With Example 26g) after the strong raise to two clubs you need to know about diamond controls in order to try a slam. A double jump shift to four diamonds is an *Asking Bid* (see Chapter VIII) which will secure for you the information you need about partner's controls in the diamond suit.

Responses to Major Suit Opening Bids

General

When opener has bid a major suit in first or second seat, he guarantees a suit at least five cards long. In third or fourth position opener will bid as he would in first or second seat whenever he has full opening bid values and feels that game is still possible even though partner has passed.

When opener elects to bid with less than expected opening bid values in either third or fourth position, he is permitted to bid a good four card major suit. When he has two four card majors and elects to open with his light hand he will prefer to open in hearts rather than spades. This choice allows both majors to be bid at the one level when responder has spades.

When he is a passed hand responder's procedures will change since he is aware that opener's requirements are quite different than they were in first or second position.

The Single Raise

In Chapter II opener's rebids after a single raise were discussed and at that point the nature of the single raise was covered in depth.

The Forcing Raise

Many varieties of forcing raises are employed by system users. Perhaps the most frequently used agreement is the **Jacoby Two Notrump**. When the partnership has agreed to use this convention responder will make a jump response of two notrump after a major suit opening bid to confirm that he holds a hand which is worth a forcing raise, promising a four card fit for opener's major suit. By bidding two notrump responder takes charge of the auction and asks for a further description of the opener's hand.

When opener has an ordinary minimum opening bid without a singleton or void in any side suit, he describes that hand by immediately jumping to game in the agreed major suit. This is an application of the **principle of fast arrival** since opener knows that his side is committed to at least a game in the agreed major suit, and opener has no values which would suggest getting to a higher level contract.

When his hand includes a singleton or void opener shows that shortness by bidding the short suit at the three level. When his shortness is a void he plans to bid the shortness suit again at the four level if the auction allows him to do so.

When opener has a hand with 14 or 15 points with no side shortness to show he continues by bidding three notrump. He will nearly always have 5-3-3-2 distribution.

With no side shortness and 16 or more points he continues by bidding his suit again at the three level.

When opener has a good second suit of five cards he shows that suit after the **Jacoby Two Notrump** response by jumping to the four level in the second suit. If the second suit is of poor quality opener treats it as though it were only four cards long and instead of showing it bids his short suit at the three level.

Example 27:

a) Opener	b) Opener	c) Opener
♠ AJ853	♠ AJ853	♠ AJ853
♡ Q94	♡ KQ94	♡ KQ94
◇ K6	◇ 6	◇ --
♣ K102	♣ K102	♣ K1062

d) Opener	e) Opener	f) Opener
♠ AKJ83	♠ AKJ853	♠ AJ853
♡ K9	♡ K9	♡ 9
◇ Q63	◇ Q63	◇ KQ1086
♣ Q98	♣ K8	♣ K8

With Example hand 27a) opener bids one spade and hears a *Jacoby Two Notrump* response. With an ordinary minimum opening bid opener jumps to four spades as his rebid. He invokes the *principle of fast arrival* to show this ordinary hand.

With Example hand 27b) after the *Jacoby Two Notrump* response to his one spade opening bid, opener conventionally bids three diamonds to show his singleton.

With Example hand 27c) the auction is similar, but if given the opportunity opener will next bid four diamonds to indicate that his shortness is a void rather than a singleton.

With Example hand 27d) when opener hears a *Jacoby Two Notrump* response to his opening bid of one spade he shows his extra values and denies holding a singleton or void by rebidding three notrump.

With Example hand 27e) in the same auction opener instead rebids three spades to show sixteen or more points.

With Example hand 27f) opener jump rebids four diamonds after hearing a *Jacoby Two Notrump* response to show a good second suit of five cards. (An earlier version of the convention used the immediate jump to four of a new suit to show a void rather than a second five card suit. The revised version allows both good second suits and voids to be shown.)

When the partnership has agreed to use the **Jacoby Two Notrump** it will usually also agree to use **splinter** raises. When responder wishes to convey the nature of his hand to opener and let opener take charge of the auction, his hand will be limited to the point that conveyance of information becomes more practical than the seeking of information.

Responder will have four card support for opener, shortness in the suit in which he makes the **splinter** bid (a singleton or void), and high card values in the range of about 10 to 13 points.

The **splinter** bid will take the form of a double jump shift in response to the opening bid. When the opening bid has been one spade the **splinter** will be a jump to the four level in any of the three remaining suits. When the opening bid has been one heart the **splinter** will be a jump to three spades or four of either minor suit.

Use of the **Jacoby Two Notrump** coupled with splinter jumps by responder is quite popular because in addition to being sound from a conceptual viewpoint they are widely understood by system players. Less widely known and requiring more study is the complex recommended which follows. It is recommended since it enables responder to describe a greater range of hands when responding to an opening major suit bid and wishing to show some variety of forcing raise.

The primary function of a major raise structure focuses on its capacity to find good slams. When responder greatly increases the information he can convey in presenting a forcing major suit raise, the ease of reaching makable slams increases proportionately.

The major raise structure to be presented here is completely cohesive and contains several components. It includes limit raises, game forcing limit raises, game forcing raises with balanced hands, and game forcing raises with unbalanced hands.

Game Forcing Raises With Balanced Hands

When responder's hand is balanced, in the range of a good twelve to a bad fifteen points, and includes four card (or longer) support for opener's major suit, responder identifies his hand type by the use of **Inverted Trump Swiss.** Responder uses a jump to four of a minor suit to show this hand type.

The choice of minor to which responder jumps is dictated by the quality of his trump support for opener. A jump to four clubs promises that responder's trumps are good. He holds two of the top three honors whenever his support is four cards long, and promises either the ace or king when his support is five cards or longer. Knowledge of the quality of responder's trump holding can be of great help when opener has enough in extra values to initiate a further slam search.

When responder has the same hand but with trumps of lesser quality he jumps to four diamonds. Again he shows that he has a good twelve to a bad fifteen in high cards, a balanced hand, and four card (or longer) trump support for the opening major suit bid. The sole difference is that he indicates that the quality of his trump holding is less than two of the top three honors if it is four cards long, and does not contain either the ace or king if it is longer.

Example 28:

a) Responder	b) Responder	c) Responder
♠ 94	♠ 94	♠ A3
♡ K843	♡ KQ83	♡ K9654
◇ AJ2	◇ A52	◇ A52
♣ KQ106	♣ KJ106	♣ K106

All hands in Example 28 are responding to an opening bid of one heart.

Responder with Example hand 28a) jumps to four diamonds to show his balanced raise with four card support in the range of 12+ to 15- points. His choice of four diamonds indicates that his trump holding is not outstanding.

Responder with Example hand 28b) jumps to four clubs to show his balanced raise with four card support in the range of 12+ to 15- points. His choice of four clubs also conveys the information that he has good trump support. In this case he holds four card support with two of the top three honor cards.

Responder with Example hand 28c) also jumps to four clubs and conveys the same message as responder 28b). This time the good trump holding is five headed by the king. When opener knows that responder has either of the trump holdings described by the jump to four clubs and holds either the king or the ace in his own opening hand, he knows that there will be no losers in the trump suit.

Note that these **Inverted Trump Swiss** bids use jumps that are often otherwise used as splinter bids. This does not mean that splinter bids are to be abandoned, for splinters are among the most descriptive of available bidding tools.

When **Inverted Trump Swiss** is part of the agreed major suit raise complex, splinters are still present, but they occur in disguise. Instead of jumping to the suit of his splinter, responder makes a bid which announces that he has four card or longer support for opener, values that fall within a certain range, and that he has shortness somewhere in another suit.

Using this basic approach the bidding side gains a distinct advantage. Whenever opener, after hearing the response and the special message that it conveys, visualizes the possibility of a slam, he can inquire and find out the location of responder's shortness. In some instances opener can also learn whether responder's shortness is a singleton or whether it is a void. Opener can seek this information if he needs to have it.

Often opener will have an ordinary hand with no desire to seek a slam. Armed with the knowledge that responder has a forcing raise, opener simply invokes the **principle of fast arrival** and bids game in the agreed major suit. Since he has no need to know the location of responder's shortness, he does not ask responder to disclose that information.

The result of such an auction will be that the defense must make the opening lead without having been informed as to the location of responder's shortness. They know to expect shortness in some side suit in the dummy, but they will not know in which suit until after the opening lead has been made.

Forcing Raises With Unbalanced Hands

When responder's range is a good twelve to a bad fifteen points and he holds four card or longer trump support for opener's major suit, and he also has a singleton or void in some side suit, his response is a double jump shift in the denomination directly above the suit of the opening bid. When opener has bid one heart responder bids three spades. When opener has bid one spade responder bids three notrump. Both of these bids are completely artificial and have the purpose of sending a message about the nature of responder's hand.

When opener hears this message bid he knows the hand type that responder has named. He knows that responder has a four card fit for his major suit with 12+ to 15-points and some side suit shortness. Armed with this information, when opener has no desire to proceed toward a slam, he has no need to find out where responder's shortness is. He simply bids game in the agreed major suit.

Again the defense must begin without knowing the location of the short suit that will come down in the dummy. If direct splinters had been used the defense would have been in a better position from which to make an informed opening lead, but the use of this conventional approach which announces a splinter without identifying its location leaves the opening leader in the dark when opener signs off at a game contract.

When responder has made this "message" response and opener upon hearing the nature of responder's hand has any desire to seek a slam, he can proceed to ask responder for the location of his short suit. He does this by making the cheapest available bid.

When opener has bid one spade and the response has been three no-trump, opener's continuation of four clubs is artificial and asks responder to divulge the location of his short suit. Responder then continues by bidding four diamonds if his shortness is in that suit, four hearts to show shortness in hearts, or four spades to show that his shortness is in clubs (the suit in which opener had to artificially ask).

If opener's first bid has been one heart and responder has bid three spades, when opener needs to know the location of responder's shortness he continues by bidding three notrump artificially to ask the location of that shortness. Responder then bids four clubs when his shortness is in that suit, four diamonds to show shortness there, or four hearts to show that his shortness is in the remaining side suit, spades.

Having determined the location of responder's shortness opener might feel that the hands do not fit well enough to have a good play for slam. If so, he will be able to stop at game in the agreed major suit. When instead opener feels that the information he has gained is positive enough to justify further slam exploration, he is well placed to continue.

Example 29:

a) Responder
♠ AJ3
♡ KQ94
◇ 6
♣ K9842

b) Responder
♠ 6
♡ KQ943
◇ AJ3
♣ K984

c) Responder
♠ AQ104
♡ 7
◇ KJ86
♣ QJ103

d) Responder
♠ QJ103
♡ AQ104
◇ KJ86
♣ 7

With Example hand 29a) you have heard an opening bid of one heart and have jumped to three spades to show a forcing raise with some side shortness. If opener next bids three notrump to inquire, bid four diamonds to locate your singleton.

With Example hand 29b) the auction has begun with the same first three calls. You will next bid four hearts to indicate that your shortness is in spades.

With Example hand 29c) you have heard an opening bid of one spade and have responded with a leap to three notrump to show a

62

forcing raise with some shortness. If partner next bids four clubs to inquire, bid four hearts to locate your singleton.

Example hand 29d) qualifies as a forcing raise for an opening bid in either major suit. If partner has bid one spade jump to three notrump, and over partner's inquiry of four clubs bid four spades to indicate that your shortness is in clubs. If the opening bid has been one heart jump to three spades, and if partner inquires by bidding three notrump bid four clubs to show the location of your shortness.

Example 30:

a) Opener	b) Opener
♠ KQ4	♠ KQ4
♡ AJ632	♡ AQJ62
◊ Q97	◊ A9
♣ 82	♣ 852

Opener with Example hand 30a) has bid one heart and has heard a response of three spades. He knows that responder has a four card heart fit with 12+ to 15-points and shortness in some side suit. This opener does not have any ambition for slam since his values are minimum and it is likely that responder's shortness will devalue his secondary honor cards in either spades or diamonds. Opener should not seek the location of responder's shortness since that information would only help the opening leader. Opener should sign off by bidding four hearts.

Opener with Example 30b) hears the same response but has interest in knowing where responder's shortness is located. He continues by bidding three notrump to ask where the shortness is. If responder continues by bidding four hearts to show shortness in spades, opener will devalue his spade honors and pass, playing at game in hearts. If responder instead shows shortness in clubs, opener will continue toward a likely slam. He knows that responder's high cards will be in the suits where they will compliment his own high cards, and that there will be a maximum of one loser in clubs.

There are other unbalanced hands with which responder will wish to force to game. The hand which has four card support for opener, some singleton or void, and values of a good nine points to a bad twelve points is considered to be a "game forcing limit raise". Even when opener has a minimum opening hand, responder's good support and ruffing values will nearly always provide enough to make a game, and game should always be reached.

To show hands of this nature responder makes an "under jump shift". His response is a jump shift to the suit which ranks directly below the major suit bid by opener. When opener has bid one spade this response will be a jump to three hearts. When opener has bid one heart responder's call to show this hand is three diamonds. Both jumps are completely artificial, saying nothing about the suit to which the jump is made. Each such conventional response simply sends a message about a specific hand type.

When opener hears this "under jump shift" response he recognizes the message that responder has sent. When he has no desire to play in slam after having received this message opener simply signs off by jumping to game in the agreed major suit. Opener is aware that responder's values, trump support and distribution will be ample to produce a game even though the bidding side may have only about half of the high cards in the deck.

When opener makes this decision the opening leader will once again be deprived of information which might have helped him make the best first play for his side. Although he knows that dummy will have shortness in some suit, he does not know which suit until after the opening lead has been made.

When opener feels that a slam is possible after the message conveyed by responder's "under jump shift" he again has the facility of asking for more information about responder's shortness. He inquires by repeating the agreed suit at the three level.

When responder hears opener repeat the agreed trump suit at the three level rather than jump to game, he must realize that opener has made a try for slam. Although the rebid of the agreed major suit at the three level sounds as though opener is weak and is trying to sign off, the opposite is true. Opener has made the strongest call available to him and responder is obliged to continue by answering the question asked by opener's rebid.

Responder continues by telling two things about his hand. He is able not only to show where his shortness is, but he will also identify that shortness as to whether it is a singleton or a void. Responder's ability to make this distinction can be of great value when a slam depends upon perfect fits rather than a preponderance of high cards.

When opener has rebid three of the agreed major suit to ask about responder's shortness, if responder continues by making the cheapest available call, he indicates that his shortness is a void, but does not yet divulge its location. If the auction has been 1♠-P-3♡-P, 3♠-P-3NT, or 1♡-P-3◇-P, 3♡-P-3♠, by making the cheapest available call in response to opener's question responder has indicated that his short suit is a void.

If responder instead bypasses the cheapest available call and bids any other denomination cheaply, he both shows that his shortness is a singleton and pinpoints its location. In the auction 1♠-P-3♡-P, 3♠-P, a bid of three notrump would show some void, while a bid of four clubs shows a club singleton, four diamonds shows a singleton there, and four hearts shows a singleton in that suit. When the auction has been 1♡-P-3♢-P, 3♡-P, since the cheapest bid of three spades announces that responder has some void, the replacement bid of three notrump shows a singleton spade, while four clubs or four diamonds shows a singleton in the suit bid.

When responder has indicated that his shortness is a void, opener can again continue to ask for the location of the void suit. He does this by making the cheapest available bid.

When the auction has been 1♠-P-3♡-P, 3♠-P-3NT-P, opener's continuation of four clubs asks for the location of responder's void. When responder next bids either four diamonds or four hearts, he locates his void in that suit. When he instead bids four spades, he shows that his void is in clubs, the suit in which opener has asked.

When the auction has been 1♡-P-3♢-P, 3♡-P-3♠-P, opener's continuation of three notrump asks for the location of responder's void. Responder locates his void in clubs or diamonds by bidding that suit at the four level, but with a void in spades responder bids four hearts. This auction keeps the bidding side at the level of game in the agreed suit, which is important if the location of the void is not a useful asset for slam and getting beyond the level of game would be dangerous.

The concept of both over and under jump shifts, which adds a marvelously revealing dimension to the structure of major suit raises, is the brainchild of Los Angeles expert Bill Schreiber.

Example 31:

a) Responder
♠ K963
♡ 8
♢ A1076
♣ K943

With Example hand 31a) in response to an opening bid of one spade jump to three hearts to show your hand with four card trump support, 9+ to 12- in high cards and some side shortness. If partner bids three spades to ask about the location of your shortness bid four hearts to show a singleton heart.

b) Responder
♠ 8
♡ K963
♢ A1076
♣ K943

c) Responder
♠ A1074
♡ K963
♢ A1076
♣ 8

d) Responder
♠ --
♡ K983
♢ A1074
♣ K9432

e) Responder
♠ K9632
♡ K943
♢ A1076
♣ --

f) Responder
♠ A1074
♡ K983
♢ --
♣ K9432

With Example hand 31b) in response to an opening bid of one heart jump to three diamonds. If partner asks about your hand by bidding three hearts, bid three notrump to show a singleton spade. Do not bid three spades as that would show an undisclosed void in your hand.

With Example hand 31c) in response to an opening bid of one spade jump to three hearts, but if the opening bid is one heart jump to three diamonds. If partner repeats the suit of his opening bid to ask about your shortness bid four clubs to show a club singleton.

With Example hand 31d) if partner opens with one heart jump to three diamonds. If partner next bids three hearts to ask about your hand bid three spades to indicate that you have a void somewhere. When partner then continues to three notrump to ask where your void is, bid four hearts to indicate that it is in spades.

With Example hand 31e) if partner has opened one spade respond by bidding three hearts. If partner then bids three spades to ask about your hand bid three notrump to indicate a void somewhere in your hand. When partner then bids four clubs, bid four spades to indicate that your void is in clubs.

If partner has instead opened with one heart respond by jumping to three diamonds. If partner bids three hearts to ask about your shortness bid three spades to announce some void. When partner continues by bidding three notrump to ask where your void is located bid four clubs to show your void there.

With Example hand 31f) if partner opens in either major suit make an "under jump shift" to show the nature of your hand. If partner then continues by repeating his original suit to ask about your shortness you will make the cheapest available call to indicate that your shortness is a void. When partner again makes the cheapest bid to ask where your void is you will bid four diamonds to locate it for him.

When the complex which employs over and under jump shifts and **Inverted Trump Swiss** has been agreed, the partnership has powerful weapons indeed. Responder in each of the auctions will have been able to convey substantial information to opener about the nature of his hand. He will have been able to show the extent of the fit that he has for opener, and not only whether or not he holds shortness, but also where and often what that shortness is when opener needs to know. When opener does not have the need to know because slam is not suggested by his hand, the defenders also do not know the location of dummy's shortness until they have made the opening lead.

Using this complex, responder who has a limited hand conveys information to opener instead of asking for information about opener's hand as he would do if the agreed major raise structure were the **Jacoby Two Notrump**. Our feeling is that responder should tell rather than ask with minimum game forcing hands when he has a good fit for opener's major suit.

There does come a point when responder's values are so great that he should take charge of the auction and ask about opener's hand rather than tell about his own. Instead of using the **Jacoby Two Notrump** with all hands that have game forcing raises, we suggest that the complete major raise structure which has been presented here be augmented by the use of the **Jacoby Two Notrump**. Responder tells about his hand when his maximum is a poor fifteen points, but with a good fifteen points or more responder takes charge and asks about opener's hand via the **Jacoby Two Notrump**.

This arrangement assures that the hand that seeks information will be the hand better suited to determining the level that will be sought by the partnership since it will be the stronger hand of the two. When the stronger hand seeks information and the lesser hand tells all it can about itself it is more likely that all of the partnership assets can be known by the holder of the stronger hand than it would be if the weaker hand asked and the stronger hand tried to tell all about itself.

When the partnership agreement is that the **Jacoby Two Notrump** will be used only when responder has a very strong hand (a good fifteen points or more) opener is better placed than otherwise. He knows all of the conventional bids that will describe his hand when responder has made use of the **Jacoby Two Notrump** but he also knows that responder's extra values make slam very likely when his own opening hand is better than minimum.

When responder uses the **Jacoby Two Notrump** and hears opener sign off by jumping to four of the agreed major suit, with his super values responder has one more descriptive try for slam available to him. If responder continues by bidding in any new suit he shows shortness there (a singleton or a void) and asks opener to make one more evaluation in light of that information. Opener then knows that even though he has minimum values slam is still possible if he has no wasted values facing responder's shortness.

Example 32:

a) Responder	b) Opener	c) Opener
♠ KJ87	♠ AQ1042	♠ AQ1042
♡ AQ3	♡ K6	♡ K42
◇ 5	◇ KJ3	◇ 763
♣ AQ942	♣ 753	♣ K5

Responder with Example hand 32a) makes a *Jacoby Two Notrump* response to an opening bid of one spade. When opener shows an ordinary hand with no side shortness by next bidding four spades, this responder makes one more effort by bidding five diamonds to show his shortness.

Opener with Example hand 32b) is not happy with this turn of events since he knows that his diamond values are not working. He signs off at five spades.

Opener with Example hand 32c) likes what he hears. Since responder is short in diamonds all of his high cards should mesh with opener's and a slam in spades should be a cinch.

Limit Raises

Other hands in which responder has a good nine to a bad twelve points with support for opener's suit are not so good that he can insist on playing in game. Limit raises, except as noted in the previous section, are invitational in value, but system auctions are designed to tell opener as much as possible about the nature of the limit raise in responder's hand.

Responder's direct jump to three in opener's major suit promises one of two types of hand. In addition to a good nine to a bad twelve in high cards, responder will either have four card trump support without side shortness, or he will have three card support with a side singleton or void. In both of these cases responder's hand is good enough to invite a game, but not good enough to insist upon playing game.

When opener hears the direct limit raise from responder he will be able to bid on quite often, even though he has minimum high card values. If opener has distributional values with his high card minimum and bids a game he will often be able to make ten tricks since his dummy either will also be distributional or will have an extra trump.

If opener does not have extra values either in high cards or distribution he will pass and play a contract at the three level. Both hands will have bid their limit, and without some extra value opener knows not to expect that game will make.

With better than a minimum hand and some interest in slam, opener may probe further about the nature of the limit raise by using the **Mathe Asking Bid**. The **Mathe Asking Bid**, a creation of the late Los Angeles expert Lew Mathe, uses an artificial bid in the cheapest denomination after a limit raise to ask responder to show shortness if he has it. After a limit raise in hearts that call would be three spades. After a limit raise in spades that call would be three notrump.

Since responder is known to have either a four card trump fit or shortness in some side suit, opener could never want to play three notrump, which releases that call to be used artificially. When opener does use the **Mathe Asking Bid** responder bids the suit of his shortness when he has made his limit raise with three card trump support, but returns to the agreed major suit at the four level when he holds four card trump support with no side shortness.

When the limit raise has been in hearts and opener's **Mathe Asking Bid** is three spades, responder bids three notrump to show that his shortness is in spades. If opener instead bids three notrump over three hearts, he has elected to cue bid and is showing the ace of spades.

Example 33:

a) Responder
♠ 82
♡ K963
♢ A107
♣ K843

With Example hand 33a) make a jump raise of a one heart opening bid. If opener next makes a *Mathe Asking Bid/* by calling three spades, bid four hearts to show that you have no side shortness, and thereby inform opener that you do have four card trump support.

b) Responder	c) Responder	d) Responder
♠ 8	♠ QJ6	♠ QJ3
♡ K93	♡ K873	♡ K9873
♢ A1074	♢ 7	♢ 75
♣ K9432	♣ KJ654	♣ KJ5

With Example hand 33b) after you make a jump raise to three hearts when the opening bid has been one heart, if opener continues by making a *Mathe Asking Bid* of three spades, bid three notrump to show that you have shortness in spades and only three card trump support.

With Example hand 33c) make a limit jump raise after an opening bid of one spade and if partner makes a *Mathe Asking Bid* of three notrump show your singleton and three card trump support with a rebid of four diamonds. If the opening bid has been one heart do not jump to three hearts. This hand is too good for a standard limit raise with its four card support and side shortness in addition to good limit raise values. Make an "under jump shift" of three diamonds to announce this hand, and if opener continues by bidding three hearts to ask about your side shortness bid four diamonds to show that you have a diamond singleton.

With Example hand 33d) some would make an immediate jump to game facing a one heart opening bid. With ten points and a fifth trump it is most likely that game should be reached, but a jump to four hearts would suggest a much weaker hand, and opener might pass and miss a slam if this hand were to make a limit raise. We suggest a *Forcing Notrump* response followed by a jump to four hearts to indicate that in addition to trump length the responding hand has reasonable values.

4) Drury

When responder has passed and opener bids a major suit in third or fourth seat, if responder has a hand which qualifies as a limit raise for opener's major suit, he must be cautious. Facing a passed partner, opener may have considerably less in values than he would be expected to hold in first or second seat.

Also, his major suit which was guaranteed to be five cards or longer in first or second seat might now be only four cards long. If responder were to precipitously jump to the three level to show his limit raise for opener's major suit when opener could both be light and have a four card suit, the bidding side would often be too high.

The solution to this problem lies with the **Drury** convention. When **Drury** is used, responder who has previously passed artificially bids two clubs in response to opener's third or fourth seat major suit opening bid to show a hand which contains a limit raise and to seek further information about the nature of the opening bid.

In its original form, **Drury** simply asked the opening bidder about the quality of his hand and did not necessarily promise a fit for opener's suit. Modern theory holds that unless responder has a fit for opener's major suit he has no reason to believe that game is still within the realm of probability. Thus the modern application of **Drury** includes the provision that responder must hold a limit raise for opener's major suit.

When responder bids two clubs, the **Drury** convention, opener knows the nature of responder's hand and proceeds accordingly. When opener has a hand that wants to play in game facing a limit raise, he jumps directly to game in the major suit he has opened. When his hand does not warrant being in game facing a known limit raise but otherwise has full opening bid values, opener announces that fact to responder by rebidding his suit at the two level. When opener has opened light and might have only a four card suit, opener announces that fact to responder by artificially rebidding two diamonds.

Opener's other rebids are natural. When opener has first bid one spade and after a **Drury** response continues by bidding two hearts, he shows that in addition to having five spades he also has four or more hearts. This caters to the fact that responder might have a three card fit for spades but also hold four hearts.

When this is the case the bidding side will prefer to play the four-four fit in hearts rather than the five-three fit in spades as the trump suit. Opener's rebid of two hearts denies the values to be in game facing a passed responder, and responder may pass the two heart rebid. Rebids in other suits are natural and suggest the possibility of slam.

When opener has hearts as well as spades and game forcing values he cannot just bid his heart suit at the two level. After responder makes his **Drury** bid of two clubs when opener has four hearts with game forcing values he continues by jumping to three hearts. When he has five hearts he instead jumps to four hearts to give responder a choice of games.

After **Drury** has been used, when opener shows full values and that his suit is guaranteed to be five cards long by rebidding his major at the two level, responder will pass unless his hand includes a distributional feature. If responder continues, making a try for game, that try will be in a short suit. Responder will bid a suit in which he holds a singleton or void. When responder shows where his shortness is, opener will be able to make instant evaluation in all suits.

When opener has wasted values facing responder's announced shortness he signs off by returning to the agreed major suit at the three level. When opener's values fall in the remaining suits rather than opposite responder's shortness, he knows that the hands fit well and will bid game in the agreed suit.

When opener holds a hand facing responder's **Drury** bid of two clubs that is borderline, rather than guess whether or not to bid game he can set the stage to make a short suit game try of his own. Opener does this by making a false signoff, bidding two diamonds to show less that a real opening bid and force responder to sign off at two of the agreed major suit. After responder has done what he must, opener exposes his own previous untruth by continuing to bid in the suit of his shortness. Responder then realizes that opener did not really have a poor hand, but simply arranged to make a short suit game try of his own by requiring responder to sign off. These agreements allow for a short suit game try after **Drury** by either bidder.

A **Drury** variation which is very popular is called **Reverse Drury**. Those who play this variation reverse the meaning of the rebid of opener's suit at the two level and his artificial rebid of two diamonds. They play that opener's return to his original suit shows a hand that would not have been opened in first or second position and might have been opened with a four card major, and also that opener's artificial rebid of two diamonds shows full opening bid values and promises a five card major suit, but denies the ability to go to game facing a known limit raise. When these two bids have their meanings reversed there is more room in which game tries can be made when opener has full values.

Another **Drury** variation which has great merit is **Two Way Drury**. In this variation responder uses two clubs as **Drury** when his support for opener's major suit is exactly three cards in length. When responder holds four card or longer support his **Drury** bid is two diamonds instead of two clubs.

When responder can use either of these artificial calls to show his passed hand limit raise for opener, the distinction between the expression of three card support or longer trump support can allow the opener to make choices that otherwise would not have been available. Knowledge of a nine card fit rather than one of only eight cards can encourage the opener to bid a marginal game which would not be a good risk if responder held only three card trump support.

When responder has bid two diamonds as **Drury** opener will return to his suit when he has less than full values, but will bid two notrump to announce a full opening hand that can't quite jump to game. Responder can then continue by showing a short suit if he has one. If opener bids another suit directly over the two diamond **Drury** call he is making a short suit game try.

Drury also functions in competition. When opponents overcall in spades or in notrump, or make a takeout double, the response of two clubs is still available. If responder makes that call he still shows a limit raise for opener's major suit. If the overcall has been in clubs, responder can use two diamonds as all-purpose **Drury**, not necessarily promising more than three card support for opener's major suit.

Responder still has the option to make an "under jump shift" in response to a major suit opening bid in third or fourth position. If he does opt for this action, responder will have four card or longer support for opener's major suit and his shortness will always be a void. Were that shortness to have been a singleton instead, responder would have used **Drury** then made a short suit game try if opener showed full values.

In this situation if responder has made an "under jump shift" and opener rebids his original suit, he is signing off. If he wants to know the location of responder's void suit, he bids the next higher denomination above the agreed suit, and responder obliges by showing the location of his void.

A necessary adjunct to **Drury** is a method for responder to show minor suits when he has no interest in playing in opener's major suit. A passed responder's jump to three clubs after a third or fourth seat major suit opening bid shows shortness in opener's major suit, a good club suit usually six cards in length, and game invitational values (9+ to 12−).

This is similar to the hand that would make a jump response to three clubs facing an opening bid of one diamond, except that responder in this case must also be short in opener's major suit. When **Two Way Drury** is the partnership's agreement, a jump to three diamonds has the same meaning if the opening bid has been one spade.

If the opening bid has been one heart, a jump to three diamonds is an "under jump shift" so responder must show his heart shortness, invitational values (9+ to 12−) and good diamond suit in another way. He uses a jump to two notrump, which ostensibly shows both minor suits and asks opener to pick one of them. If opener chooses clubs responder corrects to diamonds to show the nature of his hand. If opener instead bids three diamonds responder can take a stab at three notrump knowing that diamonds will furnish a lot of tricks.

Example 34:

a) Responder
♠ 82
♡ K963
◇ A107
♣ K843

b) Responder
♠ 8
♡ K93
◇ A1074
♣ K9432

c) Responder
♠ QJ6
♡ K873
◇ 7
♣ KJ654

d) Responder
♠ QJ3
♡ K9873
◇ 75
♣ KJ5

e) Responder
♠ K963
♠ 8
◇ A1076
♣ K943

f) Responder
♡ 8
♡ K963
◇ A1076
♣ K943

g) Responder
♠ A1074
♡ K963
◇ A1076
♣ 8

h) Responder
♠ --
♡ K983
◇ A1074
♣ K9432

i) Responder
♠ K9632
♡ K943
◇ A1076
♣ --

j) Responder
♠ A1074
♡ K983
◇ —
♣ K9432

Example 34 revisits all of the limit raises that were shown in Examples 31 and 33 in this Chapter and faces them from the viewpoint of a passed responder.

With Example hand 34a) if opener has bid one heart, bid two diamonds if you have agreed to use *Two Way Drury* but otherwise bid two clubs. If opener signs off, go quietly.

With Example hand 34b) bid two clubs in response to a one heart opening bid. If opener signs off but shows full values, continue by making a short suit game try of two spades.

With Example hand 34c) use *Drury* in response to an opening bid in either major suit. If *Two Way Drury* has been agreed bid two diamonds if opener has bid one heart. If opener shows full values in either case but does not go to game, make a short suit game try in diamonds.

With Example hand 34d) make a *Drury* call in response to an opening bid in either major suit. If *Two Way Drury* has been agreed, your response will be two clubs if the opening bid is in
74

spades or two diamonds if it is in hearts. If opener signs off you will respect his decision since you have no short suit in which to try for game.

With Example hand 34e) make a *Drury* call of two diamonds in response to an opening bid of one spade if that is possible in your agreement, otherwise bid two clubs. If opener shows full values but does not go to game continue by showing your shortness in hearts.

With Example hand 34f) show a four card limit raise for partner's opening bid of one heart. If he bids two notrump to show full values you will bid three spades knowing that you have forced the auction to game. Although that may be a difficult contract to make, on some occasions the knowledge that you have spade shortness may enable opener to get to a good slam in hearts. Even when his values are not enough to cause him to bid game knowing of your limit raise, when he hears of spade shortness and four card trump support he may have a perfect minimum (e.g. ♠ 9732 ♡ AQ854 ◇ 4 ♣ AQ2).

With Example hand 34g) you can show a four card limit raise for either major suit. If opener continues to two notrump to show a full opening hand but deny the ability to bid a game, you will make a short suit try in clubs.

With Example hand 34h) if partner opens with one heart in third or fourth seat you can make an "under jump shift" of three diamonds. (This is not to be confused with a descriptive minor suit jump that shows heart shortness, game invitational values and a good diamond suit. With that hand responder must instead bid two notrump.) If opener next bids three hearts he wants out and you should pass. If opener continues by bidding three spades he is asking for the location of your void. You will bid four hearts to show that your void is in spades.

With Example hand 34i) you can make an "under jump shift" in response to a third or fourth seat opening bid in either major suit. If opener returns to his suit you might still bid game if that suit is spades since you have an extra trump and game may make on very little in values. If opener instead bids the denomination above the suit of his opening bid, show your club void.

With Example hand 34j) bid similarly. Make an "under jump shift" in response to a third or fourth seat opening bid of either major and show your void in diamonds if opener asks where it is.

The One Spade Response to One Heart

Requirements for a one spade response to the opening bid of one heart will vary depending upon whether the partnership has agreed to use **Flannery**. Those who have agreed to use this convention usually require that responder have five or more spades in order to bid that suit as a response to a one heart opening bid.

Although this is moderately playable, when the opening bidder has six hearts and four spades and has opened with one heart, if the agreement is that responder cannot bid a four card spade suit, the four-four fit in spades will often not be found when it exists. For this reason, even partnerships that use **Flannery** should respond by bidding a four card spade suit when the opening bid has been one heart.

If **Flannery** has not been agreed the opening bidder may well also hold four spades when his opening bid has been one heart. When this possibility exists responder must bid one spade if the spade fit is to be found.

When responder has a minimum hand with three good spades and a singleton heart, his best bridge bid in response to the opening bid of one heart is probably a response of one spade. When opener has four card spade support and raises, a good three-four fit will have been found which will probably play as well as any contract. When opener does not have four spades but does have a balanced hand he can rebid one notrump and play there. Note that it is not possible to reach a contract of one notrump otherwise, for if responder bids one notrump instead of one spade, that call is forcing and requires opener to continue to bid.

Do not get the mistaken idea that one spade is used as a relay so that one notrump can be played. When responder bids one spade he holds spades, even if only a good three, and suggests that a contract in spades will be fine when opener has four card support and can raise. Systemically a raise with only three card spade support is not possible.

Responder should be sure to raise hearts when he has a minimum response in the range of 5+ to 9- even though he might hold a four or five card spade suit. If he instead bids spades he will never be able to adequately show that he has heart support. If he returns to hearts at his next turn opener will believe that he is taking a preference with a doubleton, and if he bids hearts at a higher level in order to convey that he has real heart support he will overstate his value range.

There is a school of thought that believes that spades should be bid in this situation. Advocates of the bidding of spades rather than the rais-

d) A raise of the **Forcing Notrump** to two notrump shows a balanced 18 or 19 points and is almost forcing. If responder has a balanced bare minimum response he is permitted to pass since game is not likely and no better contract seems apparent.

e) If opener makes a jump raise to three notrump after responder's **Forcing Notrump** he shows good values (about 16 to 18 points) and indicates that his major is a solid six card suit. The rest of his hand should also be balanced.

f) With all other hands opener will rebid in a new suit at the two level. Opener's values might be those of a minimum opening bid, but it is possible for opener to have a better hand. Opener's value range is from the expected minimum for an opening bid all the way up to a hand that would qualify for a jump shift rebid. When his hand does include extra values opener has no way to show them at the time of his rebid.

The opportunity for opener to show those extra values when he holds them will come later in the auction. If responder's rebid is invitational opener will accept the invitation, but if responder attempts to sign off with his rebid and opener has extra values, opener will not accede to the signoff attempt, and will continue to bid naturally as he shows his extra values.

Opener's new suit rebid at the two level will be in a suit that is lower ranking than his original major suit. If the opening bid has been one spade and opener rebids two hearts, he promises that his heart holding is four cards or longer. When opener rebids in a minor suit at the two level, that suit may be shorter than four cards when a real second suit is not present.

When opener has 5-3-3-2 distribution he rebids in his lower ranking three card minor suit. Since responder knows that this suit might be shorter than four cards he will alert.

With hands of 4-5-2-2 distribution when the opening bid has been one heart opener will have to rebid in an even shorter suit. Since he cannot reverse and bid spades without extra values, and a rebid of the five card heart suit is not systemically permitted, opener will rebid two clubs on his doubleton. Only in the auction: 1♡-P-1NT-P, 2♣ will the rebid possibly be a two card suit, and if questioned opener must be sure to inform his opponents of this possibility.

If the prospect of bidding two clubs on a doubleton and playing there appears a bit frightening, those fears will be dispelled if one looks to the pattern of the hand responder must have in order to pass. Responder will have a singleton or void in hearts since with a doubleton he would take a heart preference rather than pass. Responder will also have fewer than four spades since he did not respond by bidding one spade over the one heart opening bid (with a singleton heart he might even have bid one spade on three). With a maximum of four major suit cards responder must have at least five cards in one of the minor suits. If clubs are shorter than five, responder will have a diamond suit at least five cards long that he will be able to bid.

Opener's rebid of two clubs after an opening bid of one spade can show a hand with five-five in the black suits. In "standard" bidding it is necessary to open with one club with that distribution in order to bid both suits without letting the auction get out of hand. However in the system responder will not bid two of a red suit in response to one spade unless he has game going values. If responder has made a two over one response in a red suit, opener must have extra values either in high cards or in distribution to bid three clubs. The five-five shape provides the extra distributional values that allow opener to show both suits and rebid his club suit at the three level.

Example 36:

a) Opener	b) Opener	c) Opener
♠ J4	♠ J54	♠ QJ65
♡ KQ1087	♡ KQ1087	♡ AQ874
◇ AJ3	◇ QJ6	◇ J3
♣ QJ6	♣ A3	♣ K3
d) Opener	e) Opener	f) Opener
♠ K4	♠ K4	♠ AK
♡ AQJ1096	♡ QJ7643	♡ AQJ63
◇ 5	◇ 5	◇ A53
♣ QJ43	♣ AQJ3	♣ 986
g) Opener	h) Opener	i) Opener
♠ K4	♠ 4	♠ AQ984
♡ AKQJ63	♡ AQJ63	♡ 7
◇ Q7	◇ AKJ4	◇ K3
♣ J95	♣ A95	♣ KJ1096

With Example 36 hands a) through h) you have opened with one heart.

With Example hand 36a) if responder bids one spade, rebid one notrump. If his response is one notrump (forcing) rebid two clubs, your lower ranking three card minor suit.

With Example hand 36b) again rebid one notrump if the response is one spade. If the response is one notrump (forcing) rebid two diamonds on your three card suit.

With Example hand 36c) if responder bids one spade raise to two. If the response is one notrump (forcing) rebid two clubs on your doubleton. You cannot be in trouble if partner bids correctly, and will play in clubs only when that is your longest fit.

With Example 36d) over partner's response of either one spade or one notrump (forcing) rebid two hearts. Although you have a second suit that suit is a minor, and your heart suit is good enough to play facing a singleton or void in partner's hand.

With Example hand 36e) over partner's response of one spade or one notrump (forcing) rebid two clubs. Your six card suit is not good enough to rebid and you may have a fit in clubs. You will play in hearts if partner returns you there.

With Example hand 36f) if partner responds one spade, jump rebid two notrump. If partner's response is one notrump (forcing) raise to two. This raise shows a balanced hand with 18 or 19 points.

With Example hand 36g) if partner responds one spade jump rebid your heart suit at the three level. If partner responds one no-trump (forcing) jump raise to three notrump. This jump rebid shows a solid six card heart suit and about sixteen points.

With Example hand 36h) whether partner's response is one spade or one notrump (forcing) you have the values to make a jump shift rebid of three diamonds.

With Example hand 36i) you have opened by bidding one spade which is correct in the system. If partner responds one notrump (forcing) you have an easy two club rebid. If partner's response is two clubs you will show your excellent support with a *splinter* rebid of three hearts. If partner's response is in a red suit at the two level he has shown game forcing values. Your distribution entitles you to rebid your club suit at the three level, but if clubs were only four cards long you would need extra high card values for that rebid. With minimum values you would instead rebid two spades.

2) Responder's Rebids in Forcing Notrump Auctions

a) When opener has rebid his suit responder should nearly always pass when he has minimum values. He knows that opener's suit is at least six cards long, and even when he has a singleton or void in opener's suit responder dares not try to correct unless he has a suitable hand. If responder introduces a lower ranking suit at the three level opener should be warned that responder has no fit for the rebid major suit and is attempting to get to a more playable spot. Responder may have minimum response values but is showing a good suit while denying a fit for opener's major suit.

When responder has invitational values (9+ to 12-) and a doubleton in opener's rebid major suit, he should raise to the three level. Two card support will suffice and responder's values are such that he should invite opener to bid a game in his major suit.

When responder has the same invitational values (9+ to 12-) with a three card fit for opener's major suit he should raise to game. Responder will have planned to show his balanced limit raise with three card support by jumping to three of opener's major suit at his rebid, but when opener shows a sixth card in his suit, the combined values are adequate for game.

When responder has invitational values (9+ to 12-) with all of the other suits stopped and a singleton in opener's rebid major suit, he can continue by bidding two notrump. With a doubleton in opener's major suit the same action is possible, but responder should be sure that notrump will play better than the six-two major suit fit.

Example 37:

a) Responder
♠ 5
♥ 63
♦ Q42
♣ KQ108532

b) Responder
♠ 5
♥ K3
♦ Q42
♣ Q1087532

c) Responder
♠ 97
♥ KJ4
♦ AQ52
♣ 9873

d) Responder
♠ 5
♥ KJ93
♦ K1087
♣ KJ104

e) Responder
♠ 53
♥ KJ93
♦ K1087
♣ KJ10

f) Responder
♠ Q3
♥ Q93
♦ K1087
♣ KJ104

With Example hand 37a) if opener has bid one spade and rebid spades after your *Forcing Notrump* response, bid three clubs. Your hand will not be useful at a spade contract, but if clubs are trumps your side will probably fare well. If your system permits, you might have considered a preemptive jump shift of three clubs as your original response. A jump shift to the three level will need a hefty suit such as this one.

With Example 37b) if opener has bid one spade and rebid two spades after your *Forcing Notrump* response you should pass. Do not try to improve the contract when your suit is as broken as this club suit is.

With Example hand 37c) if opener has bid one spade and rebid two spades after your *Forcing Notrump* response, raise him to three spades. Your invitational values and doubleton spade are quite enough for this action. If instead opener has bid and rebid hearts, raise to game at your second turn. You had planned to jump to three hearts if opener had rebid in a minor suit at the two level to show your balanced three card limit raise. Since opener has extra length in hearts your values should be enough to produce game.

With Example hand 37d) when opener has bid and rebid spades after your *Forcing Notrump* response, continue by bidding two no-trump to show your values and deny the desire to play in spades.

With Example hand 37e) despite a doubleton spade you can take the same course of action as with 37d) since your hand is well bulwarked for play in notrump with good cards in all of the other suits.

With Example hand 37f) in the same auction you should not bid two notrump because of your weak holding in hearts and fitting honor card for opener's six card spade suit. Raise to three spades.

b) When opener has reversed by bidding two spades after having opened with one heart, if responder has a three card heart fit he will again have planned to show his balanced limit raise (9+ to 12-) by jumping to three hearts at his rebid. After opener's reverse responder should show his fit by jumping to four hearts since opener has shown enough in additional values that game should be bid. With a three card fit responder cannot have less than invitational values since he would have raised at his first turn.

When responder does not fit either hearts or spades and is otherwise balanced he should bid notrump at a level which expresses his values. With a minimum **Forcing Notrump** (5+ to 9-) he will bid two no-trump, while with the upper half of his range (9+ to 12-) he will jump to three notrump. Since opener's reverse has promised a good hand (16 plus points) values for game are present. Even with very minimum response values responder must bid again since opener's reverse is forcing for one round.

With a bare minimum response and a hand not suited to notrump, responder may be compelled to take a preference to hearts when holding a doubleton in support of opener's first suit.

With shortness in hearts and a good three spade holding, when responder has invitational values (9+ to 12-) he can describe his hand by raising spades with his three card support. Responder announces heart shortness, three good spades and values enough for game, and offers to play in the four-three fit.

If responder's rebid is at the three level in a minor suit, he shows a good suit and bare minimum response values.

Example 38:

a) Responder	b) Responder	c) Responder
♠ K82	♠ J32	♠ J2
♡ AJ4	♡ 8	♡ 84
◊ 97432	◊ K1083	◊ KJ932
♣ QJ	♣ QJ852	♣ KQ105
d) Responder	e) Responder	f) Responder
♠ Q8	♠ KQ5	♠ J2
♡ J4	♡ 7	♡ 7
◊ K7653	◊ A9643	◊ KQJ942
♣ J875	♣ J875	♣ 9863

With Example 38 hands the auction has begun with a one heart opening bid, a *Forcing Notrump* response, and a reverse to two spades by opener.

With Example hand 38a) responder continues by jumping to four hearts to show that he has three card heart support. Since he did not raise at his first turn his range is known to be invitational (9+ to 12-). He is accepting the invitation implicit in opener's reverse which guarantees that game values are present.

With Example hand 38b) responder continues by bidding two notrump. This shows his lack of fit for either of opener's suits and stoppers in the minors as well a minimum response values.

With Example hand 38c) responder continues by jumping to three notrump. He has good stoppers in both minors and the values to reach a game.

With Example hand 38d) responder takes a preference to three hearts. His doubleton honor in hearts and bad minor spot cards rule out a rebid of two notrump.

With Example hand 38e) responder raises to three spades. Game in the four-three spade fit looks more likely than in notrump.

With **Example hand 38f)** responder next bids three diamonds. This descriptive call suggests that a part score in diamonds will be the best place to play unless opener has game forcing values facing a minimum response that is based on nothing more than a good diamond suit.

c) If opener's rebid has been a jump shift which is forcing to game, responder will continue by finding the action which best describes his hand. Even when his response was based on a meager five or six points the auction is forcing and responder may not pass until a contract of three notrump or higher has been reached.

When responder has a maximum hand for his **Forcing Notrump** and opener makes a jump shift rebid, responder must make some move to express interest in a slam. He can show a fit for either of opener's suits below the level of game, but must not bid game in either of them.

A jump to game at that point in the auction would be application of the **principle of fast arrival.** When it has been established that game will be reached, fast arrival at a suit game contract indicates that the bidder has minimum values for his previous actions and that he has no interest in bidding further.

It should be noted that the **principle of fast arrival** applies only to contracts in suits. Jumps in notrump are always used to show additional high card values beyond what has previously been promised.

d) When opener has raised the **Forcing Notrump** to the two level showing a balanced hand of 18 or 19 points, responder has a set of systemic tools at his disposal. All of responder's rebids become transfer bids. This enables responder to control the continuation of the auction and describe many types of hands.

Responder can transfer to opener's original suit and then bid three notrump to show a three card fit with invitational values (9+ to 12-) and no ruffing values, and offer a choice of games.

Responder can transfer to opener's suit to show a balanced limit raise with three card support and then bid a new suit to show value location and suggest a slam.

Responder can transfer to his own suit and then pass when he did not have a real response and was afraid or unable to make a preemptive jump shift response.

When opener has bid spades, after the raise of the **Forcing Notrump** responder can transfer to hearts to show a five card suit, then either show a spade fit or bid three notrump, again offering a choice of contracts to opener.

After transferring to hearts responder can bid game in that suit and have the 2-6 or 3-6 heart fit played from the strong hand rather than have the strong hand as dummy.

The use of transfer bids after the raise of a **Forcing Notrump** is of inestimable value and is one of the many new tools that prompted this update of the system book.

Example 39:

a) Responder
♠ K83
♡ K105
♢ Q982
♣ Q103

b) Responder
♠ KJ4
♡ 75
♢ AQJ93
♣ 1074

c) Responder
♠ 6
♡ 642
♢ QJ9743
♣ J63

d) Responder
♠ J4
♡ KQ1073
♢ Q42
♣ 1073

e) Responder
♠ J4
♡ KQ10753
♢ Q4
♣ 1073

With Example 39 hands responder has bid one notrump (forcing) in response to an opening bid of one spade and has heard opener raise to two notrump. Responder continues as follows:

With Example hand 39a) responder bids three hearts to transfer to spades and show his three card fit with invitational (9+ to 12-) values. He then bids three notrump to indicate that he has no ruffing values. His high card values must be in the invitational range since he did not raise spades at his first turn. The exception occurs in those partnerships who have adopted *Constructive Major Raises* and may have concealed a three card spade fit with only about six points.

With Example hand 39b) responder bids three hearts to transfer to spades and show three card support with invitational values (9+ to 12-), and then bids four diamonds to suggest a slam and locate his side values.

With Example hand 39c) responder next bids three clubs to transfer to diamonds, and then passes. Responder had gambled to bid one notrump rather than pass hoping to improve the contract rather than leave opener to play one spade. Three diamonds seems to be an ideal spot.

With Example hand 39d) responder bids three diamonds to transfer to hearts, then bids three notrump to offer a choice of contracts. Opener can correct to four hearts and play from his
86

side when he holds three cards in hearts, or pass and let responder play three notrump.

With Example hand 39e) responder bids three diamonds to transfer to hearts and then raises to game. The strong hand remains concealed as opener plays the 2-6 or 3-6 heart fit in a game contract.

e) When opener's rebid has been a jump to three notrump which shows a solid six card suit and extra values, responder will usually pass. Even when responder had planned a delayed balanced limit raise holding 9+ to 12- points and three card support, slam is very unlikely and responder's only choice will be whether to pass and declare three notrump or correct and let opener play in the major suit. Since both hands are balanced the notrump game will usually be best.

f) When opener has rebid in a lower ranking suit at the two level responder's continuation will either limit his hand to the lower half of the **Forcing Notrump** range (5+ to 9-) or will invite a game by showing the upper half of that range (9+ to 12-).

When responder has the lower portion of the range he has these choices:

i) Responder can introduce his own suit at the two level. Particularly when opener's rebid has been two clubs, responder has the balance of the two level available to him. When he does introduce his own suit at the two level it will be at least five cards long.

When responder attempts to sign off at the two level in his own suit opener will usually honor that attempt and pass. There are, however, two reasons that opener might continue to bid.

Opener might have additional values that he has not yet been able to show. When his hand is in the range of a good fifteen to a bad nineteen points opener is entitled to make one more attempt to get to a game after responder attempts to sign off. Opener's next bid must be truly forward going in nature, and must not appear to simply be a correction.

The other reason that opener might continue rather than accept responder's attempt to sign off is that he sees the need for correction. When responder has introduced his new suit at the two level after having used the **Forcing Notrump** his suit will often be only five cards long. When opener has a singleton or void, he should attempt to correct to a contract that will be more playable. Since his values are minimum opener will not bypass any suit that may be more playable and may remove to his original major suit when it is only five cards long since responder may yet have a doubleton in support.

Example 40:

	a) Opener		b) Opener
♠	KQ973	♠	KQ973
♡	AJ5	♡	6
◇	62	◇	AJ5
♣	K108	♣	K1083

Both openers in Example 40 bid one spade and hear a response of one notrump (forcing). Both rebid two clubs.

With Example hand 40a) opener hears responder continue by bidding two hearts. This contract seems just right to opener and he is happy to pass.

With Example hand 40b) opener hears responder continue by bidding two hearts. Opener knows that this may be a five card suit which will not play very well and corrects to two spades to show heart shortness.

Example 41:

	a) Responder		b) Responder		c) Responder
♠	J4	♠	4	♠	4
♡	K10983	♡	K10983	♡	K10983
◇	1094	◇	10984	◇	1094
♣	A75	♣	A75	♣	A975

Responders in Example 41 have used a *Forcing Notrump* response to an opening bid of one spade and have heard opener rebid two clubs which may be a three card suit. Each responder next bids two hearts to attempt to play there.

Opener 40a) will pass and the auction will have ended in a very playable contract that could not have been reached if the *Forcing Notrump* had not been available. Without this convention responder would have bid one notrump and opener would have passed with his balanced pattern.

Opener 40b) will not pass but will bid two spades since his heart holding is not adequate facing a probable five card suit.

With Example hand 41a) responder would pass after opener's correction. The playable five-two fit might have originally been offered by responder except that hearts might have been a better place to play and responder had the opportunity to seek a contract in that strain first.

With Example hand 41b) when opener removes to two spades it is probable that his spade suit is only five cards long. If he has five spades and a singleton heart, he must have at least four clubs and probably three diamonds. If that is his shape a correction to two notrump will get the bidding side to its best spot. If opener happens to have five-five in the black suits, his auction will be the same to this point, but he will correct from two notrump to three clubs.

With Example hand 41c) responder comes to the same conclusions. Instead of correcting to two notrump he corrects to the known four-four fit in clubs.

ii) Responder might also pass opener's new suit rebid. When opener has rebid in hearts after opening in spades his heart suit will be at least four cards long. When responder has a singleton or void in spades and three or more hearts the pass will be his best second call.

When responder has two spades and three hearts his correct rebid is the "false preference" to two spades. This "false preference" will lead to the best contract whenever opener holds six spades and only four hearts. It also allows opener to continue whenever he has additional values.

If after the "false preference" opener continues to two notrump his shape will be 5-4-2-2. Responder can pass when his values are at the bottom of his minimum response range, but should continue when holding the top of his range and bid three notrump since opener has shown extra values in the range of a good fifteen to a bad nineteen points.

If opener instead continues by bidding three hearts responder will know to pass with the bottom of the minimum range, but raise to four hearts with his three card support when holding the top of this minimum range and cards that will be useful facing opening bidder's five-five pattern.

Example 42:

a) Responder	b) Responder	c) Responder
♠ Q7	♠ Q7	♠ J7
♡ 1083	♡ K83	♡ 1083
◇ K7432	◇ K7432	◇ K1084
♣ J109	♣ 1098	♣ KJ109

With Example 42 hands responder has bid a *Forcing Notrump* in response to an opening bid of one spade and has heard a rebid of two hearts from opener. All responders should take a "false preference" to two spades. Often opener will pass. If opener bids again he has extra values.

With Example hand 42a) if opener continues by bidding either two notrump or three hearts responder should pass. He wants to get no higher with these meager values.

With Example hand 42b) if opener continues by bidding three hearts responder should raise to four. If opener instead continues by bidding two notrump responder should raise to three in situations where a game bonus has great significance, but might pass at match points.

With Example 42c) if opener continues by bidding two notrump responder has enough values to raise to three. If opener instead bids three hearts showing a five-five pattern responder should probably pass since his kings outside opener's major suits will not have the value they otherwise might have.

When responder elects to pass opener's rebid in a minor suit at the two level it should be because he has a minimum response and no other contract has any appeal. Responder should have a singleton or void in opener's major suit and at least four cards in the minor that opener has rebid. Responder will also have no higher ranking five card suit when he opts to pass as his rebid.

iii) With no other expressive rebid available, responder takes a preference to opener's major suit when he holds a doubleton. When responder has the hand that produces this specific auction he might wish that he could have played one notrump.

This is the only circumstance in which the bidding side might regret the fact that they have agreed to use the **Forcing Notrump**. When responder has an otherwise balanced hand and exactly two cards in opener's major suit, one notrump might be a superior contract and system users are obliged to play in the five-two major suit fit.

However, the **Forcing Notrump** is the keystone to many auctions which improve the situation, and playing the five-two major suit fit will often produce a result as good as or better than the result that would have been attained at a contract of one notrump.

When responder holds a hand in the upper portion of the **Forcing Notrump** range (9+ to 12-) his rebid will be an invitation to game. Responder's game invitations can take several forms.

i) Responder may have the values for a limit raise of the opening major suit bid (9+ to 12-) with three card support and no side shortness. With such a hand his holding does not meet the requirement for an immediate jump limit raise since that call requires a side singleton when responder has only three card trump support.

Holding a balanced three card limit raise responder starts with a **Forcing Notrump** planning to jump to the three level in opener's major suit at his rebid. If opener rebids his suit at the two level, responder changes his plan and shows his limit raise by jumping to game in opener's major suit. Opener's announcement of the sixth card in his suit is all responder needs to hear to know that game should be bid.

Example 43:

a) Responder	b) Responder	c) Responder
♠ A54	♠ QJ6	♠ K953
♡ K63	♡ 54	♡ QJ6
◇ 965	◇ K953	◇ A1082
♣ QJ82	♣ A1082	♣ 54

With Example hand 43a) respond one notrump (forcing) to an opening bid in either major suit. If opener next bids two of a lower ranking suit jump to three of his original major suit to show your balanced limit raise with three card support. If he rebids his suit showing that his length is six cards or more, raise him to game.

With Example hand 43b) respond one notrump to partner's opening bid of one spade and continue as in 43a).

With Example hand 43c) respond one spade to partner's opening bid of one heart. Do not bypass spades to use the *Forcing Notrump* . If partner rebids one notrump you can now bid two hearts to show that you have three card heart support. Since you did not raise at your first call, partner knows that you must have a hand in the invitational range (9+ to 12-), a balanced limit raise with three card support.

If the opening bid has been one spade, make an immediate jump raise to three spades since you have four card support.

ii) When responder holds invitational values (9+ to 12-) and a good suit of his own he may be able to show that suit. After opener rebids in a new suit at the two level, if responder rebids by jumping to the three level in a new suit he shows a good suit of six cards or more (occasionally a very fine five card suit will do). He knows that opener may have no choice but to pass this invitation so he must be prepared to play the contract to which he has bid even when opener has poor trump support.

Example 44:

a) Responder	b) Responder
♠ 9	♠ 5
♡ KQJ854	♡ Q83
◊ K62	◊ AQJ954
♣ J83	♣ Q107

After the opening bid of one spade, responders in Example 44 bid one notrump (forcing).

When opener's rebid is either two clubs or two diamonds, with Example hand 44a) responder can jump to three hearts to show his good six card suit and invitational values.

With Example hand 44b) if opener's rebid is two clubs responder can jump to three diamonds to describe his good suit and invitational values. If opener rebids either two spades or two hearts, responder's best action is probably to supress his suit and bid two notrump.

ii) Responder can also invite a game by rebidding two notrump. His rebid of two notrump promises a hand in the invitational range (9+ to 12-) with stoppers in each of the suits which have not been bid. Responder will also usually have a balanced hand with two cards in opener's major suit, but on occasion he will have to make this rebid with only a singleton in opener's major.

Example 45:

a) Responder	b) Responder	c) Responder
♠ Q7	♠ KJ7	♠ 976
♡ KJ3	♡ 53	♡ J3
◊ A954	◊ QJ95	◊ KQ104
♣ 9752	♣ K1084	♣ KJ108

With Example hand 45a) you have made a *Forcing Notrump* response to a major suit opening bid. If the opening bid was one spade and opener rebids two clubs, bid two notrump to show your invitational values and stoppers in the unbid suits. If opener rebids two spades you should raise to three. If opener's rebid is either two diamonds or two hearts your choice is not clear. Your best guess is to bid two notrump and hope that partner has enough clubs to make your four to the nine a stopper. If the opening bid was one heart, you will jump to three hearts if partner's rebid is in a minor suit, or jump to four hearts if he rebids his suit.

With Example hand 45b) you again have responded one notrump (forcing) to the opening bid of one of a major suit. If opener has bid one spade and rebids in a lower ranking suit your rebid will be a jump to three spades, but if he rebids his suit you should raise him to game. If the opening bid has been one heart and opener's rebid has been in a minor suit, you have an easy rebid of two notrump. If opener rebids his heart suit your good secondary values with potential double stoppers in all other suits makes your hand appropriate to a rebid of two notrump rather than a heart raise.

With Example hand 45c) you again bid one notrump (forcing) in response to an opening bid in either major suit. If opener has bid one spade and rebids two of a minor suit you will jump to three spades to show a balanced limit raise with three card support. If opener rebids two spades you will raise him to game. If opener's rebid is two hearts the placement of your high cards justifies a rebid of two notrump even though you have three card spade support since that support is so bad and your minor suit holdings are so good.

If the opening bid has been one heart and opener rebids either minor suit at the two level your rebid should be two spades. This rebid cannot show a spade suit since you bypassed spades at your first turn to bid notrump. This rebid expresses a good hand for the auction that cannot rebid two notrump. It shows good support for the minor suit in which opener has rebid but tends to deny a spade stopper for play in notrump.

    iv) Responder may also be able to raise the suit of opener's rebid. The raise of opener's second suit promises a hand in the invitational range under discussion (9+ to 12-) but denies the ability to make another descriptive call. Responder does not have a fit for opener's major suit, he has no good suit of his own to show, he is not able to bid two notrump, and his only adequate description is a raise in the suit of opener's rebid.

Responder's raise of opener's second suit will be constructive in all situations except one. If opener's first bid was one heart and responder has available at his rebid the two spade call that cannot possibly show a suit, when instead of bidding two spades he raises the minor suit of opener's rebid, that raise is more preemptive than constructive. If responder had wanted to make a constructive raise of the minor suit which opener has rebid, he would instead use the impossible two spade call.

The two spade call in this auction always shows a fit for opener's minor suit rebid and good values within the confines of the original one notrump call. If opener continues by showing an unbalanced hand his minor suit will most probably become the trump suit at some level. If opener instead continues by bidding in notrump he shows a balanced hand and suggests that he holds a spade stopper since it is probable that responder does not have one.

Example 46:

a) Responder	b) Responder	c) Responder
♠ 1083	♠ 103	♠ 103
♡ J9	♡ J	♡ J
◊ AQ74	◊ AQ74	◊ Q754
♣ KJ103	♣ KJ9754	♣ KJ9754

With Example hand 46a) responder has bid one notrump (forcing) in response to an opening bid of one heart. If opener next bids two of either minor suit responder shows his good hand by bidding two spades. Responder will be happy if opener next bids two or three notrump since that will show a spade stopper and the values to bid to the level he has chosen.

With Example hand 46b) responder has again bid one notrump (forcing) in response to an opening bid of one heart. If opener next bids two in either minor suit responder should like his hand. He should bid two spades to indicate this fact, but should aim at a minor suit contract rather than to play in notrump. Regardless of the minor suit in which opener has made his rebid, if opener's next call is two notrump responder will continue by bidding three clubs.

With Example hand 46c) responder has bid one notrump (forcing) in response to an opening bid of one heart. If opener rebids two diamonds responder should pass, but if opener's rebid is two clubs responder should raise to three. Responder knows that the rebid could be on a two card club suit, but that does not matter here. The important thing for opener to realize is that responder's rebid was not two spades, showing a good hand for play in clubs. This raise by responder should be understood as being primarily preemptive rather than constructive since a constructive rebid was available and was not used.

The One Notrump Response By a Passed Hand

When a passed responder bids one notrump in response to a major suit opening bid, that response is only provisionally forcing. When opener has bid with a hand that he would not have opened in first or second position, he has the prerogative to pass the one notrump response. If he has opened light and does not pass but rebids in a second suit, that is because his hand is distributional and a contract in one of his suits would be far better than a contract of one notrump.

When opener does pass the response of one notrump he will often have opened with a four card major suit, and his hand will be otherwise balanced. Even when he has opened with a five card major suit and light values his pass is easy, for he knows that responder does not have a three card fit for his suit. If responder held a three card fit he would raise with minimum values or would use the **Drury** convention with values enough to invite a game.

When opener has full values (and thereby must have opened in a five card or longer major suit) he will continue as he would have if the notrump response had been truly forcing. All of his rebids are as they have been explained in the discussion of opener's rebids after a **Forcing Notrump** response to his major suit opening bid.

When responder has a balanced hand with fewer than three cards in support of opener's major suit and a maximum hand for his pass (about 11 or 12- points) he might be tempted to take vigorous action to describe his maximum pass. This would be ill advised.

Responder should not jump to two notrump to show this hand since opener in third or fourth position might have opened with as little as ten points. Responder's good passed hand may barely provide enough strength to make a contract of one notrump. Responder needs not worry about missing a game, for whenever opener has full values he will not pass a response of one notrump.

Since a response of two notrump is not needed to show a good balanced hand it has a special meaning. A jump to two notrump in response to a major suit opening bid by a passed responder shows a singleton or void in the opener's major suit and at least five cards in each minor suit, with values enough to expect to be able to make a three level contract if one of the minors is the trump suit.

Rather than attempting to first bid two diamonds (which is not a natural call if **Two Way Drury** has been agreed) and then, if given the opportunity, continue by bidding three clubs, responder sends his message of a minor two suiter with no interest in opener's major suit with one bid.

Responder	b) Responder	c) Responder
♠ K3	♠ 7	♠ 7
♡ AJ6	♡ J4	♡ J4
◊ Q9754	◊ Q974	◊ KQ973
♣ J107	♣ KQJ953	♣ KJ1043

In all Example 47 hands responder has previously passed.

With Example 47a) if the opening bid has been one spade, re-spond by bidding one notrump. If opener has full values he will not pass, so do not be concerned about missing a game. If the opening bid has been one heart, use the *Drury* convention. Bid two clubs to show that you have a limit raise for hearts.

With Example hand 47b) if opener has bid one spade, jump to three clubs. This response shows invitational values with a good six card club suit and very few spades. If the opening bid has been one heart do not rule out the possibility that hearts will be the trump suit. Although you hope not to play there, you have no option but to bid one notrump which is not forcing. If the opponents have the spade suit and do not bid you will have stolen the hand from them. If you have a second chance to bid and partner has not rebid hearts, introduce your club suit.

With Example hand 47c) if opener has bid one spade, jump to two notrump to show a hand with both minor suits and no desire to support spades.

The Two Over One Response

Here we examine the cornerstone of the system. When responder bids a new suit at the two level in response to opener's one level bid, that re-sponse has considerably more in values than in standard bidding. In the system responder's values are minimally those of an opening bid, and the response creates a forcing situation for the opening bidder that lasts until a contract of three notrump or four in some suit has been reached.

Although responder's new suit response is generally considered to be game forcing, when no fit has been established and the auction appears to be floundering, opener may pass when the auction reaches four in a minor suit. Only in this specific situation will the auction not be forcing to game after responder's original new suit response at the two level.

Responder's two level response in a minor suit will show a suit of at least four cards. There may be a rare exception when responder holds a 3-4-3-3 hand and must respond to an opening bid of one spade. Here, responder may elect to lie and bid a **Forcing Notrump**, concealing his game forcing values, or might instead elect to bid two clubs on a three card holding leaving maximum room for opener's rebid.

When responder bids two hearts after an opening bid of one spade he promises a suit at least five cards long. This is the only response with which responder promises a five card suit. After this response when opener has a three card fit and minimum values he raises to four hearts, applying the **principle of fast arrival**.

A raise to only three hearts would be for the purpose of suggesting a slam, thereby showing extra values beyond a minimum opening bid, or giving responder the chance to bid three notrump whenever his response in addition to a five card heart suit also held good minor suit values.

Example 48:

a) Responder	b) Opener	c) Opener
♠ KJ3	♠ KJ843	♠ KJ843
♡ QJ82	♡ AJ5	♡ AJ5
◇ Q86	◇ 73	◇ 73
♣ KQ5	♣ K103	♣ AQ3

Responder with Example hand 48a) has heard an opening bid of one spade from his partner. No response is completely descriptive, and responder might elect to mark time by bidding two clubs in this instance. It is rare that such a response will not be totally natural.

Opener with Example hand 48b) has bid one spade and heard a response of two hearts. Invoking the *principle of fast arrival* opener next jumps to four hearts to show three card support and minimum values for his opening bid.

Opener with Example hand 48c) again bids one spade and hears a response of two hearts. His raise to three hearts shows three card or longer support and that his opening bid is not minimum in nature.

After a two over one response opener's rebids in higher ranking suits are no longer classified as reverses. In fact when opener has bid one diamond and receives a two club response, if he rebids two of a major suit he specifically denies a hand with the shape of a reverse.

When the opening bid has been one diamond and responder has bid two clubs, whenever opener holds five or more diamonds his obligation is to repeat that suit at the two level (but with good values and a six card or longer diamond suit he may make a jump rebid in diamonds). The obligation to show a five card or longer diamond suit takes precedence over the showing of a four card major suit.

When after a one diamond opening bid and a two club response opener rebids in a major suit at the two level, he shows four cards in that major suit, denies that he holds five or more diamonds (unless he then rebids the major suit to show five), and announces that his hand is not suited to a rebid in notrump. If his hand were balanced and well suited to declaring notrump, opener would rebid two notrump with minimum rebid values even if he held one or both four card majors.

In this situation if a four-four major suit fit exists it will be shown by responder's rebid. When responder holds game forcing values with a four card major and five or more clubs, he will bid naturally and name his club suit at his first turn, planning to show his four card major suit at his rebid.

When opener has bid one diamond with a six-five hand and plans to reverse at his rebid, he understands that when he makes his rebid responder will believe that he holds fewer than five diamonds. When opener's third call is a rebid of the major suit of his rebid, responder will then understand that opener has shown six diamonds in addition to five cards in the rebid major suit.

A two over one response does not deny that responder has three card support for opener's major suit. When responder has game forcing values in the range of 12+ to 15- points he will make his two over one response with the intention of next showing his support for opener's major suit.

He will hope to clarify by next showing his fit for opener's major suit at the two level. If opener makes this impossible by rebidding either two notrump or two in his major suit, responder shows his support and his limited values facing a hand limited by its rebid by jumping to four of opener's major suit. This again illustrates the **principle of fast arrival**. Responder must remember that opener's rebid of his suit does not promise more than five cards in length.

When opener's rebid is in a suit at the two level that is lower ranking than his original major suit, responder has the opportunity to show his three card fit at the two level. Given that opportunity if responder instead jumps to game in opener's major suit his message is not one of **fast arrival**. Instead responder shows a hand with values concentrated in the two suits that he has bid. This auction promises that responder has no value better than a queen in either of the suits that he has left unbid, and that he also has no shortness value (singleton or void) in either of those suits.

When responder continues by jumping to the three level in opener's major suit he again shows a three card fit, but announces that his values are suggestive of slam. He will have a good fifteen points or more to compliment the suits that he has shown.

When opener has rebid his suit, even though that does not promise that he has more than five card length, responder has the option to make a **splinter** jump at his rebid. This will promise slam seeking values (15+ or more) and shortness in the suit of his jump rebid as well as length in his first suit and a fit of three cards for opener. If his fit for opener were more than three cards he would have made a conventional raise at his first turn rather than a two over one response.

Example 49:

a) Responder	b) Responder
♠ QJ4	♠ QJ4
♡ 83	♡ 83
◇ AQ5	◇ AK5
♣ KJ642	♣ KQJ62

With Example hand 49a) you have responded two clubs to an opening bid of one spade. If opener next bids either two diamonds or two hearts you will bid two spades to show your minimum game forcing hand with three card spade support. If opener's rebid is two spades or two notrump you will show your support for spades and indicate that your values are minimum for your two over one response by jumping to four spades in keeping with the *principle of fast arrival*. When opener limits his hand with his rebid, you show your limited hand with no slam aspirations in this fashion.

With Example hand 49b) you again respond by bidding two clubs when opener has bid one spade. If opener's rebid is either two diamonds or two hearts you show your spade fit and extra values by jumping to three spades. If opener rebids either two spades or two notrump you will show your fit for spades and your extra values by next bidding three spades.

c) Responder	d) Responder
♠ KQ4	♠ KQ4
♡ J3	♡ AJ3
◇ 953	◇ 5
♣ AKJ84	♣ KQ9742

With Example hand 49c) you respond by bidding two clubs when opener has bid one spade. If his rebid is either two diamonds or two hearts you can describe your hand very well by jumping to four spades. This jump has nothing to do with *fast arrival* since opener's hand has not been limited by his rebid. Your message when you jump to game in opener's major suit is that all of your values are in the two suits you have bid. You deny any card higher than a queen or any shortness control in either of the suits you have left unbid. If opener has instead rebid either two spades or two notrump you again will jump to four spades. This time your message will be different. Since opener's rebid has limited his hand, your jump is a *fast arrival* call even though you wish that it were not. Opener's rebid has deprived you of the opportunity to pinpoint the values in your hand.

With Example hand 49d) you again respond two clubs when opener bids one spade. If opener's rebid is either two diamonds or two hearts you can jump to three spades to show your extra values and three card spade support. If opener instead rebids two spades you can make a *splinter* jump to four diamonds. This will show your good values and shortness in diamonds while affirming three card support for spades.

When responder's rebid after a two over one response is in notrump he shows that his first suit did not warrant a rebid, he has no second suit to show, and he does not have three card support for opener's major suit. His holding in opener's major suit is expected to be a doubleton, though in some instances responder's holding in that suit will be a singleton.

If responder's rebid is two notrump it announces that his strength for the two over one response he has made is minimum. His range will be from a good twelve to a bad fifteen points.

If responder instead jumps to three notrump at his rebid, he shows greater values. His range will be from a good fifteen to about eighteen points. The **principle of fast arrival** does not apply when notrump has been bid. All bids in notrump are designed to show strength ranges, and jumps are stronger than simple rebids.

100

When responder holds a good eighteen or nineteen points he first bids two notrump at his rebid, then continues by bidding four notrump at his next turn. This auction shows that responder's rebid of two notrump which seemed to show minimum game forcing values was merely marking time so that responder could show his full strength at his next turn.

Example 50:

a) Responder	b) Responder	c) Responder
♠ Q3	♠ Q3	♠ Q3
♡ KQ5	♡ KQ5	♡ AQ5
◇ KJ832	◇ KJ832	◇ KQ832
♣ K109	♣ AJ9	♣ KQ9

With Example hand 50a) responder bids two diamonds in response to an opening bid of one spade. If opener rebids two spades or two hearts, responder continues by bidding two notrump. This shows minimum values for his game forcing two over one response and denies a fit for opener's suit or suits.

With Example hand 50b) responder bids two diamonds in response to an opening bid of one spade. If opener rebids two spades or two hearts, responder continues by jumping to three notrump to show his extra values.

With Example hand 50c) responder bids two diamonds in response to an opening bid of one spade. If opener rebids two spades or two hearts responder continues by bidding two notrump. At this point in the auction responder's values sound to be minimum. Responder corrects that impression and shows his good eighteen points by bidding four notrump at his next turn.

With other distributional hands responder may best describe what he holds by either repeating the suit in which he made his two over one response or by bidding yet another suit. If responder repeats his first suit it is at least six cards long and might make a good trump suit at a slam contract.

If responder changes suit at his rebid it is to be assumed that his first suit was of five cards or more and that his second suit is four cards long. Whatever his pattern responder has shown that his hand is best described by bids in suits rather than by suggesting a contract in notrump.

Example 51:

a) Responder	b) Responder	c) Responder
♠ AQ83	♠ AJ8	♠ A8
♡ 5	♡ 5	♡ 5
◇ KJ4	◇ KJ4	◇ KQ103
♣ AJ964	♣ AQ10963	♣ AJ8764

With Example 51a) responder hears an opening bid of one heart. He does not make the error of responding one spade but instead makes his natural bid of two clubs. If opener makes the expected rebid of two hearts responder next bids two spades to show his four card spade suit and indicate that his clubs are longer. If opener instead rebids two notrump responder bids three spades to convey that message.

With Example hand 51b) responder hears an opening bid of one heart. He responds by bidding two clubs and will rebid three clubs at his next turn. If the opening bid had instead been one spade responder would still start by bidding two clubs. If opener rebid two notrump responder would next bid three spades to show his three card support and extra values. If opener's rebid is two spades responder would next make a *splinter* jump to four hearts.

With Example hand 51c) responder bids two clubs after an opening bid in either major suit. Regardless of opener's rebid responder plans to show diamonds at his rebid. If opener's first bid was in spades and he rebids two diamonds after the two club response, responder will make a *splinter* jump to three hearts to show four card support for diamonds and heart shortness.

CHAPTER IV
REBIDS BY RESPONDER

Responder's first bid says very little about his hand. All he needs to respond is the limited values of a good five points, and some impulsive responders bid on even less than that. It is with his rebid that responder truly begins to describe the nature of his hand.

Non-Forcing Minimum Rebids: Responder's Range is 5+ to 9−

When responder's hand is in this minimum range his obligation at his rebid is to show the limit of his values and try to find a reasonable contract at a low level.

1) When responder has bid a major suit and opener has raised, that raise will nearly always show four card support. With most minimum hands responder will pass.

If the partnership has agreed to play preemptive re-raises (1-2-3 stop), when responder with minimum values holds five or more cards in his suit he should preempt by bidding his suit once more at the three level. Since opener has limited his hand and systemically shown a four card fit with his raise, when responder holds five cards in the suit he knows that the partnership holds nine cards in the suit and values limited to half the deck or less. Responder re-raises to three of the agreed suit to try to keep the opposing side out of the auction.

With a sixth card in his suit responder might even jump to game, for with a ten card fit his side has excellent offensive potential and extremely poor defense. A bid at the three level might not be sufficient to keep a good opposing pair from balancing, and they are likely to have fits and values enough to make a game if they are given a way into the auction.

Example 52:

a) Opener	b) Responder	c) Responder
♠ 842	♠ 73	♠ 7
♡ KQ63	♡ A9842	♡ A98542
◇ Q9	◇ K75	◇ K75
♣ AQ54	♣ 986	♣ 986

Opener with Example hand 52a) bids one club and raises partner's response of one heart.

Playing "1-2-3 stop" responder with Example hand 52b) should bid three hearts preemptively. The offensive potential of the two hands is 8 or 9 tricks while the defensive potential against a spade contract is from 3 to 5 tricks. If the unseen cards are so placed that we cannot make three hearts we will also be unable to beat three spades.

With Example hand 52c) responder's hand was too good to have made a preemptive jump shift response. When opener raises the one heart response, responder should probably bid four hearts preemptively regardless of the partnership's re-raise agreements. The offensive potential has been increased and the defensive potential has been decreased, both by at least a trick, by the addition of a sixth heart to responder's hand.

2) When opener's rebid is in a higher ranking suit at the one level, with minimum values (5+ to 9−) responder has four choices:

a) Responder can take a preference to one of opener's suits. With four card support for the major suit in which opener has rebid responder can pass when holding up to a bad seven points. Opener's failure to make a jump shift rebid indicates that game is highly improbable. When responder has the top of his minimum range (a good 7 to a bad 9) game is still possible since opener might have a hand just short of the values for a jump shift rebid (17 or 18 points). Responder's raise allows opener to continue to game when he has such extra values.

To take a preference to opener's first (minor) suit responder needs an unbalanced hand with at least four card support for opener's minor. When responder elects to make this rebid it will be because no other available call is as expressive of his values and distribution.

b) If responder rebids his original suit that suit should be at least six cards long. If a preemptive jump shift was available to responder at his first turn and he did not avail himself of that option, when he rebids his suit responder shows that he has good minimum values that made his hand unsuitable for a jump shift at his first turn.

c) Responder can rebid one notrump when his hand is balanced and no other rebid suggests itself. The rebid of one notrump will tend to show a stopper in the unbid suit, but may simply be the only alternative when responder is balanced and does not feel that continuation in any suit is attractive.

On occasion responder may have a weak two suited hand including the suit that is yet unbid. Although it is not his preference to rebid one notrump with a hand that is unbalanced, responder may have no choice since a rebid of his original suit would show six cards and any other rebid would distort even more. A rebid in the unbid (fourth) suit would show more values than those in the minimum range (5+ to 9−) under discussion here (see **Fourth Suit Forcing** later in this Chapter).

d) With a weak hand of four-six distribution which includes a yet unbid six card minor suit, responder can make a jump shift rebid in his concealed six card minor suit. This special rebid shows that responder has minimum response values (5+ to 9−), and that although he has responded in a four card major he also has a six card minor (if the minor suit is diamonds responder may have bypassed that suit to respond in a four card major).

When opener's rebid has been one notrump this action has complete safety since responder can count on finding at least two card support for his suit due to the fact that opener's rebid in notrump has promised a balanced hand (see **New Minor Forcing** later in this Chapter).

When opener has rebid in a higher ranking suit this special rebid is still possible but it is not without peril, for opener may have no fit for the six card suit in which opener has made his jump rebid. Unless the six card suit has good texture and will make a reasonable trump suit facing a singleton or a void, responder might again elect to rebid one notrump with his unbalanced minimum.

Example 53:

a) Responder
  ♠ J954
  ♡ K863
  ◇ J52
  ♣ 92

b) Responder
  ♠ KJ94
  ♡ K863
  ◇ J52
  ♣ 92

c) Responder
  ♠ 95
  ♡ K863
  ◇ 65
  ♣ QJ763

d) Responder
  ♠ 8
  ♡ KQJ763
  ◇ Q95
  ♣ 1087

e) Responder
  ♠ 95
  ♡ K863
  ◇ QJ76
  ♣ Q87

f) Responder
  ♠ 9
  ♡ K9862
  ◇ QJ873
  ♣ 82

g) Responder
  ♠ 5
  ♡ KJ82
  ◇ Q98632
  ♣ 86

h) Responder
  ♠ 5
  ♡ K982
  ◇ QJ10986
  ♣ 86

In all Example 53 auctions opener has first bid one club and has rebid one spade after a response of one heart.

With Example hand 53a) responder will pass since a good fit has been found and game is too remote to be probable. If responder were to raise and opener had enough in extra values to jump to game this hand would be a disappointing dummy.

With Example hand 53b) responder has enough in values to raise to two spades. If opener bids four spades with a hand that was not quite good enough for a jump shift at his rebid, this dummy should suffice at that contract.

With Example hand 53c) responder should take a preference to two clubs. This rebid will limit his values and show club length in addition to his heart suit. Although in this example responder's hand is semi-balanced it is appropriately described as unbalanced with poor holdings in the doubletons.

With Example hand 53d) responder rebids two hearts to show his six card suit. His suit does not have to be quite this good for the rebid, but responder does show values better than those for an original preemptive jump shift.

With Example hand 53e) responder rebids one notrump to limit his values and suggest that he holds something in diamonds. With a hand of this balanced pattern responder would still opt for the rebid of one notrump even if his side values were not in diamonds. Any other rebid would be a total misdescription.

With Example hand 53f) although he is not happy about it, responder again rebids one notrump. A rebid of two hearts would limit his values but would promise a sixth heart since opener may have no support for hearts at all. A rebid of two diamonds would show at least game invitational values (9+ or more) (See *Fourth Suit Forcing* later in this Chapter). One notrump with this unbalanced hand is the call that will least distort responder's values and will be the best contract unless opener can clarify the nature of his hand by bidding on. If opener passes all should be well.

With Example hand 53g) responder has a choice between the systemic call of three diamonds to show his four-six distribution and a rebid of one notrump. Since there is no guarantee that opener has any diamonds at all, the systemic jump to three diamonds is fraught with danger. Responder's suit will not do well as the trump suit if opener has a singleton or void. The prospect of a one notrump rebid again does not thrill responder, but it is the rebid most likely to succeed.

With Example hand 53h) responder has the same choices, but this time his diamond suit is good enough to play as trumps even when he has no support. The systemic jump shift rebid of three diamonds should be responder's choice.

3) When opener rebids one notrump. responder with minimum values (5+ to 9−) again has four choices.

a) With a balanced hand responder may pass. One notrump will probably be the best contract.

b) Responder may elect to repeat his first suit. In this auction since opener has limited the values of his hand and shown a balanced pattern, responder knows that he will find two or three card support for his suit in opener's hand. Responder's repeat of his suit will place the contract since it is not forcing and opener is not asked to bid again after having limited both the size and shape of his hand.

Responder promises five or more cards in his suit. If his suit is only five cards long he will feel that even if opener has only two card support the contract of two in his major suit will be better than a contract of one notrump. When he has made this decision, responder will be delighted on those occasions when opener has three card support.

c) Responder may again take a preference to opener's first suit. When he takes this action responder will have an unbalanced hand with at least four (probably five or more) card support for opener's minor suit. Responder will be sure that a contract in opener's minor suit is infinitely better than would be a contract of one notrump.

d) As has been mentioned earlier, responder may have bypassed a six card diamond suit after an opening bid of one club to respond in a four card major. Responder may also have a six card club suit when he has responded in a major suit to an opening bid of one diamond. In either case responder's values will be less than enough to force the auction to game, and the response in the four card major suit will have been a correct system action.

With minimum values (5+ to 9−) responder's rebid will be a jump to the three level in his six card minor suit. Opener will pass knowing that responder has only four cards in his major suit and six cards in the minor suit of his jump rebid. Opener will have at least two card support for the minor suit since his rebid of one notrump promised a balanced hand, and since both bidders have limited their values neither of them will have more to say in the auction.

Example 54:

a) Responder	b) Responder	c) Responder
♠ KJ94	♠ 95	♠ 8
♡ K863	♡ K863	♡ KQJ763
◇ J52	◇ 65	◇ Q95
♣ 92	♣ QJ763	♣ 1087
d) Responder	e) Responder	f) Responder
♠ 95	♠ 9	♠ 5
♡ K863	♡ K9862	♡ KJ82
◇ QJ76	◇ QJ873	◇ Q108632
♣ Q87	♣ 82	♣ 86

All Example 54 hands are repeats from Example 52. This time opener after starting with one club has rebid one notrump after the response of one heart.

With Example hand 54a) responder will pass. He will feel confident about the fulfillment of this contract, for even though opener is known to have fewer than four spades, responder has spades that are good enough that the defense will not be able to hurt the contract in that suit.

With Example hand 54b) responder again takes a preference to opener's first suit. Two clubs will usually always be a better contract than one notrump and responder will be happy to play there.

With Example hand 54c) responder again rebids his heart suit. At match points two hearts should be a fine contract. If the opening bid had been one diamond where responder has a fitting value, a jump rebid of three hearts is reasonable due to the quality of responder's heart suit. At IMP scoring that stretch would be a very reasonable action.

With Example hand 54d) responder will pass and let opener play one notrump. Responder has maximum values for his pass, but does not like the spade situation since opener can have no more than three cards in that suit. Still, no other action by responder is appropriate.

With Example hand 54e) responder will rebid two hearts. Opener is known to have either two or three cards in hearts, and responder strongly prefers to play in hearts rather than pass and have his partner declare a contract of one notrump due to his very unbalanced hand.

With Example 54f) responder has no qualms about making the systemic rebid of jumping to three diamonds. Since opener has promised a balanced hand he will have a fit for diamonds of two cards or more. Three diamonds will normally play much better than would one notrump with responder's very distributional hand.

4) When opener rebids in a lower ranking suit at the two level his first bid will most often have been in a major suit and the response will usually have been a **Forcing Notrump** (for all such auctions see Chapter III). In other cases responder may have bid one spade in response to an opening bid of one heart, or may have responded in a major suit to an opening bid of one diamond and heard a rebid of two clubs from opener. Holding minimum values (5+ to 9−) responder has these choices at his rebid:

a) Responder may show a preference for opener's second suit by passing. He may not raise as that would show a hand of greater values.

b) Responder may take a preference to opener's first suit when he holds two card support. This will often happen when the opening bid has been in a major suit. Since responder did not raise at his first turn and this rebid shows minimum values (5+ to 9−) it is clear that responder does not have three card support for opener's major, for if that had been the case responder would have raised at his first turn (see the **Forcing Notrump** in Chapter III).

If opener has rebid two clubs after having opened with one diamond responder's preference back to two diamonds can also be made with a doubleton, but responder may have a true diamond fit. Responder's first bid in a major suit does not deny the ability to raise diamonds, but responder has the obligation to try to find a playable major suit fit with his first call. When he bids a major suit in response to the one diamond opening bid he may have four cards in the major suit of his response and could have five or six card diamond support. When that is true he cannot show his diamond support with his first bid, but with limited values will be happy to return to opener's first suit when his major suit response does not find a fit.

When opener has first bid spades and has then rebid in hearts after a **Forcing Notrump** response, responder will take a "false preference" when he holds two spades and three hearts as was mentioned in Chapter III. Similar "false preferences" are in order when opener has first bid hearts and then rebids in a minor suit, or when opener has first bid diamonds and rebids in clubs.

Particularly when he has minimum opening bid values opener may have to start by bidding a four card diamond suit to prepare a rebid in a five card club suit. When opener does this his diamond suit will be good, for with a poor four card diamond suit and a good five card club suit opener would start by bidding one club rather than invite a preference back to a poor four card diamond suit (see Chapter II).

   c) If responder rebids his original (major) suit he promises that it is at least six cards long. If responder might have made a preemptive jump shift at his first turn but did not do so, when he rebids his suit to show six or more cards in length and minimum response values it is safe to assume that his hand was too good to make the preemptive jump shift. His values will be in the upper part of the minimum response range.

After opener has rebid in a new suit at the two level and responder continues by bidding the fourth suit without jumping: 1♡-P-1♠-P, 2♢-P-3♣, or 1♡-P-1♠-P, 2♣-P-2♢, or 1♢-P-1♡-P, 2♣-P-2♠, or 1♢-P-1♠-P, 2♣-P-2♡, responder has used **Fourth Suit Forcing** (which is discussed later in this Chapter) and must have a hand with better than minimum response values.

When responder jumps to the three level after opener's new suit rebid at the two level some auctions are clear and others are not. When the auction has been: 1 ◇-P-1♠-P, 2♣-P-3♡, or 1 ◇-P-1♡-P, 2♣-P-3♠ responder's rebid is clearly a splinter showing shortness in the suit to which he has jumped at his rebid and a good fit for the suit of opener's rebid and values enough to seek a slam.

If the auction has gone 1♡-P-1♠-P, 2♣-P-3◇ there is room for confusion. It is possible that this auction is also one in which responder is making a splinter raise for the suit of opener's rebid, but this auction might also be one in which responder has minimum values with four spades and six diamonds. If this auction happens at the table and there has been no prior discussion, a fiasco of monumental size may occur.

Example 55:

a) Opener	b) Opener	c) Opener
♠ J3	♠ J3	♠ 3
♡ 64	♡ 64	♡ 64
◇ KQ943	◇ AQ63	◇ KQ943
♣ AQ63	♣ KQ943	♣ AQJ63

All openers in Example 55 would bid one diamond and rebid two clubs after either a response in a major suit or of one notrump.

After a two diamond rebid by responder Opener with Example hand 55a) should pass. He should be content to play this contract even though responder might have only a doubleton diamond, for then responder will not have as many as four clubs.

Opener with Example hand 55b) should also pass. He might languish in a four-two fit when responder also had three clubs, but he must live with that situation when it occurs since his hand does not warrant another bid.

Opener with Example hand 55c) has license to continue and bid three clubs. When responder has only two diamonds and three clubs this will both improve the contract and keep the opponents from balancing when they may have a good major suit fit. Despite his minimum in values opener's shape and the placement of his high cards make this hand worth a third call.

Example 56:

a) Responder
   ♠ A652
   ♡ Q872
   ◇ J5
   ♣ 1072

b) Responder
   ♠ A62
   ♡ Q872
   ◇ J85
   ♣ 1072

c) Responder
   ♠ AQ1085
   ♡ 8
   ◇ A4
   ♣ KQ963

d) Responder
   ♠ AQ1085
   ♡ A4
   ◇ 8
   ♣ KQ963

e) Responder
   ♠ K843
   ♡ 7
   ◇ K97653
   ♣ 93

Responder with Example hand 56a) would bid one heart in response to an opening bid of one diamond and would take a preference to two diamonds if opener rebid two clubs. This "false preference" will be right more often than not. When opener has five or six diamonds and only four clubs and also when opener has enough in extra values to bid two notrump or make another forward going call the "false preference" will work well. It works poorly only in those instances where opener has only four diamonds and also has five clubs. If opener continues by bidding three clubs this responder will pass.

Responder with Example hand 56b) again takes a preference to two diamonds after opener's rebid of two clubs. Again if opener continues by next bidding three clubs responder should pass since a five-three fit has been reached and responder wants the auction to stop. If he takes a second preference to diamonds opener may bid again and the auction might get out of hand.

With Example hand 56c) when opener rebids two clubs after opening with one diamond and hearing a response of one spade, responder should show his great hand for play in clubs and the fact that he has shortness in hearts by making a *splinter* jump rebid of three hearts.

With Example hand 56d) if opener rebids two clubs after starting with one heart and hearing a response of one spade, responder can jump to three diamonds as a splinter in support of clubs only if it is clear that the partnership has agreed that this meaning applies to this call in this auction. If three diamonds is not a splinter in this auction responder must bid only two diamonds *Fourth Suit Forcing* and hope to catch up later.

With Example hand 56e) if opener rebids two clubs after starting with one heart and hearing a response of one spade, responder would like to be able to jump to three diamonds to show his weak hand with a six-four pattern. It would be advantageous to be able to describe this hand in some way, but the jump to show a six-four pattern may get the auction out of hand, and responder does not have any way to comfortably bid this hand in this auction. Not to worry since everyone else will have the same problem.

Invitational Rebids:
Responder's Range is 9+ to 12—

1) When opener has raised responder's major suit systemically showing four card support and minimum opening bid values, if responder holds a hand in the 9+ to 12— range he should make a try for game.

If the partnership has agreed to play 1-2-3 stop a re-raise of the agreed trump suit is not a game try since it is an attempt to preempt the opponents out of the auction. If the partnership has not agreed to play 1-2-3 stop a re-raise of the agreed trump suit should ask the opening bidder to bid game if he has good trumps.

If responder tries for game by bidding two notrump he suggests that his hand is balanced, his values are scattered, and his holding in the suggested trump suit is only four cards long and not very imposing. Opener is advised that if he wants to play a game contract he should bid game in the major suit only if he can provide good enough trumps to make up for responder's weakness in that department. With a maximum for his limited rebid and a mediocre holding in the suggested trump suit, opener's choice of games should be three notrump despite the known four-four fit.

With other hands which warrant a try for game responder should attempt to locate secondary honor card fits, extending the principles that were presented in Chapter II with opener's try for game after a single raise by responder.

If the partnership has agreed to use **Kokish Game Tries** as they were presented in Chapter II, they are as effective in this circumstance as they are after responder's raise of opener's major suit.

Example 57:

a) Responder	b) Responder	c) Responder
♠ 6	♠ KJ6	♠ K105
♡ J1084	♡ J843	♡ AQ63
◇ AQ106	◇ K87	◇ Q984
♣ KJ92	♣ K109	♣ 65

d) Responder	e) Responder
♠ Q105	♠ K105
♡ AQ63	♡ AQ63
◇ 95	◇ KJ83
♣ K1085	♣ 95

With Example hand 57a) responder has bid one heart after an opening bid in a minor suit and opener has raised to two hearts. If the partnership has not agreed to play 1-2-3 stop responder can bid three hearts to ask if opener has good trumps. Otherwise his best try is a call of three clubs which informs partner that cards in spades, the suit that responder has bypassed as he has made his try for game, will not be of value (other than the ace) and asks him to upgrade any honor cards he holds in clubs. Even if the opening bid has been one club this call is forcing since hearts is the agreed trump suit.

Responder 57b) who has bid one heart and been raised by the opening bidder can best describe his hand with a game try of two notrump. This shows that he has values in the other suits and weak hearts along with his game invitational (9+ to 12−) values. When responder is also balanced and has mediocre hearts a superior game of three notrump can be played.

Responder with Example hand 57c) who has bid hearts and been raised to two by opener can best try for game by bidding two spades. If opener makes a counter try of three clubs responder will sign off at three hearts, but if the counter try is three diamonds responder will accept and bid game in hearts.

Responder with Example hand 57d) should again make his game try by bidding two spades and accept if opener makes a counter try in clubs. If opener makes a counter try in diamonds instead responder should sign off by bidding three hearts.

Responder with Example hand 57e) should not make a try for game. His values are beyond the invitational range and he knows that game should be bid. If the opening bid was one club he might bid three notrump to offer a choice of games, but if the opening has been one diamond he simply jumps to four hearts.

2) When opener has rebid in a higher ranking suit at the one level responder has these rebid choices:

a) With four cards in the major suit of opener's rebid (this must be spades since with invitational values responder would have bid spades with four of them unless he also held four hearts. He would not have bid diamonds over an opening bid of one club in this range when he held a four card major) responder makes a jump rebid to three of opener's second suit to show his four card fit and invitational (9+ to 12−) values.

When responder's fit is for opener's first (minor) suit responder makes a jump preference to opener's first suit at the three level. Responder's hand will usually be unbalanced and have five card support for opener's minor suit.

Although responder's value range for a jump preference to opener's first bid minor suit at the three level is usually invitational (9+ to 12−), there is a single exception. When responder has bid one diamond in response to an opening bid of one club and his second call is a jump to three clubs in support of opener's first suit, that jump preference is forcing. Only when responder's first bid was one diamond and his rebid is a jump to three clubs is this so in the system. All other auctions in which responder makes a jump preference at his rebid are invitational and not forcing.

b) Responder can make an invitational jump to the three level in his own six card suit. This auction is more at risk than when opener has rebid one notrump since there is no guarantee that opener has a fit of any kind for responder's suit.

When responder has jump rebid a major suit it will be to try to reach a game in that major (in the auction under discussion the only major suit responder can hold is hearts). If responder has jump rebid his minor suit his hope is to reach three notrump (in the auction under discussion the only minor suit responder can hold is diamonds).

c) With a reasonable balanced hand and stoppers in the unbid suit when responder holds a hand in the invitational range he can rebid by jumping to two notrump. When he does not have a stopper in the unbid suit and is unable to make an otherwise descriptive call, responder may be able to use **Fourth Suit Forcing**, which is described later in this Chapter. Only if the partnership has agreed to play that the **Fourth Suit** is forcing to game will this not be possible. The merits of either agreement regarding the use of this tool are found in the discussion which is devoted to that topic.

Example 58:

a) Responder
♠ KJ94
♡ KQ63
♢ Q52
♣ 92

b) Responder
♠ 84
♡ KJ63
♢ Q6
♣ KQ542

c) Responder
♠ 9
♡ KQJ843
♢ K62
♣ J53

d) Responder
♠ 6
♡ J1084
♢ AQ106
♣ KJ92

e) Responder
♠ KJ6
♡ J843
♢ K87
♣ K109

f) Responder
♠ K105
♡ AQ63
♢ Q984
♣ 65

g) Responder
♠ Q105
♡ AQ63
♢ 95
♣ K1085

h) Responder
♠ 6
♡ Q84
♢ AQJ1064
♣ J106

Some Example 58 hands have been used in other auctions and are shown again here since responder's rebid problem is different than it was at the earlier presentation. In each case except 58h) opener has rebid one spade after starting with one of a minor suit and hearing a response of one heart.

With Example hand 58a) responder continues by making a jump raise of three spades. This call shows his four card spade fit and invitational (9+ to 12−) values.

With Example hand 58b) responder continues by making a jump preference of three clubs if the opening bid has been one club. If the opening bid has been one diamond responder instead jumps to two notrump with his semi-balanced hand.

With Example hand 58c) responder jump rebids his heart suit at the three level. Even though there is no guarantee that opener has any support for hearts responder's suit is virtually self sufficient.

With Example hand 58d) responder makes a jump preference to opener's first bid minor suit no matter which one it is. If opener has only three cards in clubs and that was his first bid suit his pattern will be exactly 4-3-3-3 and he will correct to the four-three heart fit.

With Example hand 58e) responder continues by jumping to two notrump to invite game.

With Example hand 57f) if opener has first bid one club responder can jump to two notrump at this point in the auction to invite game since he has a diamond stopper. If opener's first bid was one diamond responder should instead jump to three diamonds since opener is known to have at least four diamonds (opener would have raised hearts if he held only three diamonds since his shape would be 4-4-3-2).

Example hand 57g) presents some difficulties. Responder does not know whether this hand should play in clubs, in a four-three fit in either of the major suits, or in notrump if opener has a diamond stopper. The only way he can find out is to use *Fourth Suit Forcing* at this turn but if the partnership has agreed that the auction is game forcing when that particular tool is used responder cannot use it here. His best guess will be a jump to three clubs.

With Example hand 57h) responder will have bid one diamond in response to an opening bid of one club. If opener rebids in either major suit at the one level responder will next make an invitational jump rebid of three diamonds to show his good suit and invitational (9+ to 12−) values in an attempt to get to three notrump.

3) When opener has rebid in a lower ranking suit at the two level, if his first bid was in a major suit responder will either have bid one spade after an opening bid of one heart, or will have used the **Forcing Notrump**. The value range for responder under discussion here does not allow him to have bid at the two level in response to an opening major suit bid (for responder's rebids after his use of a **Forcing Notrump** response see Chapter III).

If responder has bid one spade in response to an opening bid of one heart or has responded in either major suit after an opening bid of one diamond, after opener's rebid in a lower ranking suit at the two level responder's choices are as follows:

a) Responder may make a jump preference to opener's first suit, bidding it at the three level. If he has four card or longer support for opener's second suit, he may raise that suit to the three level.

b) Responder may jump rebid his own six card suit at the three level. Again there is some risk attached unless responder's suit is very good since opener may be void in responder's jump rebid suit.

c) With a reasonably balanced hand and a stopper in the unbid suit responder's best description is an invitational rebid of two notrump. Responder may not make this two notrump rebid simply to escape from the previously bid suits. His call of two notrump confirms a hand in the invitational range of 9+ to 12−.

Example 59:

a) Responder
♠ J843
♡ KJ6
◇ K87
♣ K109

b) Responder
♠ K105
♡ AQ63
◇ Q984
♣ 65

c) Responder
♠ KQJ843
♡ 9
◇ K62
♣ J53

d) Responder
♠ KJ63
♡ 84
◇ Q6
♣ KQ542

e) Responder
♠ AQ63
♡ 95
◇ Q105
♣ K1085

With Example hand 59a) responder has heard an opening bid of one heart and has responded by bidding one spade. If opener rebids in either minor suit at the two level responder will make an invitational jump to three hearts at his rebid. This jump preference shows three card heart support, invitational values (9+ to 12−) and no side singleton or void. Holding shortness in a side suit responder would have made a direct limit jump raise at his first turn.

With Example hand 59b) responder has bid one heart in response to an opening bid of one diamond and opener has rebid two clubs. Although it would not be criminal for responder to jump to three diamonds at his rebid a call of two notrump would be more descriptive since responder's hand is balanced and does include a spade stopper.

With Example hand 59c) responder bids one spade in response to an opening bid in any of the lower ranking suits. If opener then rebids at the two level in a suit that is lower ranking than his original suit, responder continues by making an invitational jump rebid of three spades.

With Example hand 59d) responder bids one spade in response to an opening bid in either red suit. If opener rebids two clubs responder continues by making an invitational raise to three clubs to show his values (9+ to 12−) and good club support.

With Example hand 59e) responder hears an opening bid of one heart and responds by bidding one spade. If opener rebids at the two level in either minor suit responder continues by invitationally rebidding two notrump.

4) When opener has rebid one notrump he has limited both the size and shape of his hand. His message is that if weak notrumps (12+ to 15−) had been agreed by the partnership his opening bid would have been one notrump. He does not guarantee stoppers in unbid suits, just that his hand is balanced and falls in the value range expressed by his rebid.

Holding a hand with invitational values (9+ to 12−), responder continues as follows:

a) He may make a jump preference to opener's first suit. It is assumed that when responder makes a jump preference to a minor suit he will have an unbalanced hand. When the jump preference is to the club suit responder should usually have five cards in that suit since opener might have opened on a three card club suit.

(There are some auctions that will show that opener has more than three clubs. For example if the auction has been 1♣-P-1♡-P, 1NT, opener has guaranteed that he has four or more clubs since he has neither four hearts nor four spades and would have opened with one diamond if he held four diamonds and only three clubs. However if the auction has been 1♣-P-1♠-P, 1NT, opener's shape could be 3-4-3-3.)

b) Responder may make a jump rebid in his own six card suit. Since opener's rebid of one notrump guarantees a balanced hand responder is sure to find two or three card support for his suit. This makes responder's jump rebid of his suit much safer than it has been in other auctions where opener might have been shorter in responder's suit.

c) Responder may raise to two notrump. In this auction responder's invitational bid of two notrump is not a jump as it has been in some earlier discussions. Whenever responder's rebid is two notrump it promises values in the range of 9+ to 12−.

d) If opener has first bid one heart and rebid one notrump after a response of one spade, responder can continue by bidding two hearts to invite a game. Since he did not raise hearts at his first call his strength must be better than the strength of a single raise (5+ to 9−). His voluntary removal of one notrump to two hearts promises a balanced three card invitational raise (9+ to 12−), and a jump to three hearts in this auction as responder's rebid would be forcing showing a hand of a good twelve points or more.

e) Responder can use the conventional continuation known as **New Minor Forcing**. Discussion of this convention follows immediately in this Chapter. The use of **New Minor Forcing** shows that responder's values are invitational or better. Responder's values are not limited to the invitational range under discussion here although they might fall in that range. Responder might also have a much better hand with ambitions for slam.

Example 60:

a) Responder	b) Responder	c) Responder
♠ 84	♠ 9	♠ KJ94
♡ KJ63	♡ KQJ843	♡ KQ63
◇ Q6	◇ K62	◇ Q52
♣ KQ542	♣ J53	♣ 92

d) Responder	e) Responder	f) Responder
♠ J843	♠ 6	♠ Q105
♡ KJ6	♡ J1084	♡ AQ63
◇ K87	◇ AQ106	◇ 95
♣ K109	♣ KJ92	♣ K1085

With Example hand 60a) responder bids one heart after an opening bid of one club. If opener's rebid is one notrump responder continues by making an invitational jump rebid of three clubs. Responder's distribution will freqeuntly include a singleton or void in one of the unbid suits in this auction.

With Example hand 60b) responder bids one heart after an opening bid in either minor suit. If opener rebids one notrump responder continues by invitationally jumping to three hearts to show his six card suit. The suit does not need to be this good in this auction since opener is known to have a fit of two or three cards.

With Example hand 60c) responder bids one heart after an opening bid in either minor suit. If opener next rebids one notrump responder makes an invitational raise to two notrump. Since opener has denied holding four cards in either major suit the contract will be in notrump, and after hearing responder's invitational raise (9+ to 12−) opener will determine the level.

With Example hand 60d) responder bids one spade in response to an opening bid of one heart. If opener's rebid is one notrump responder next bids two hearts to show his balanced three card limit raise. Responder's values must be invitational since he shows a real three card fit for hearts and did not raise at his first turn.

2) When opener has three card support for responder's major suit and maximum values (13+ to 15−), he shows that support by bidding at the three level. When **New Minor Forcing** is agreed in its simplest form this will be a jump to the three level in responder's major suit.

When agreement has been made to use either the **Hardy Adjunct** or the **Wittes Adjunct** to **New Minor Forcing**, opener takes advantage of all bids at the three level, and selects the one which sends specific information about his hand while showing his maximum and three card support for responder's suit. The **Hardy Adjunct** allows opener to pinpoint his distribution as he conveys this general message, while the **Wittes Adjunct** instead allows opener to show the exact quality of his support for responder's major suit. Both of these adjuncts are detailed in this Chapter.

3) With a doubleton in responder's major suit and a maximum (13+ to 15−) opener rebids two notrump unless he is able to rebid a five card diamond suit.

4) With a doubleton in responder's major suit and a minimum (12 or 13−) opener rebids artificially in the unbid major suit at the two level (unless he is able to rebid a five card diamond suit). This artificial rebid in the other major suit says nothing about opener's holding in that suit, only that his holding in responder's major suit is exactly two cards. Since opener is short in responder's major suit he may also have four cards in the other major suit that he bids artificially at this time, but if so that is merely coincidental.

5) When opener's first bid has been one diamond, responder's **New Minor Forcing** call will be two clubs. As has been described above, when opener has a three card fit for opener's major suit his obligation is to show that fit as he also indicates the exact range of his values. When opener does not have a three card fit for responder's major suit his next obligation is to show whether or not he has five diamonds.

When opener does have five (or six) diamonds he next bids two diamonds to show his length. This bid in diamonds does not indicate whether opener's values are maximum or minimum for his rebid of one notrump.

6) When opener has begun with a bid of one heart and has rebid one notrump after a one spade response, if responder continues by bidding either minor suit at the two level opener has the obligation to show three card spade support when he has it. He will bid as indicated above, at the two level with minimum values (12 or 13−) or at the three level with maximum values (13+ to 15−). When opener has only a doubleton spade, he makes the call that best describes his hand.

He can still rebid two notrump when he has maximum values. With minimum values, when the **New Minor** has been a bid of two diamonds opener's only remaining alternative is to bid two hearts.

When the **New Minor** has been two clubs, opener will rebid two hearts only when in addition to a doubleton spade and minimum values he also has a good heart suit. If his heart suit is not so hot he has available an artificial call of two diamonds to convey that message.

When instead of using **New Minor Forcing** responder bids in another suit at the two level the auction is natural and non-forcing. If responder repeats his major suit he has at least five cards in that suit with minimum response values (5+ to 9−) and is signing off. If responder returns to opener's first bid minor suit at the two level that is also a signoff (both of these auctions have already been discussed in this Chapter).

When responder's rebid after opener has rebid one notrump is a jump to the three level its meaning depends upon the previous auction. If opener either jump rebids his own suit or jumps to opener's first bid minor suit, the auction is natural and invitational.

If responder has first bid one spade and his continuation after opener's rebid of one notrump is a jump to three hearts, that call is natural and forcing and promises five-five in the major suits. When responder has five spades and only four hearts he has no invitational auction available.

If responder simply rebids two hearts the auction is not forcing, and he may have either four or five cards in the heart suit. If responder instead first uses **New Minor Forcing** and then rebids three hearts he shows five spades and four hearts and the auction is forcing.

Responder's Weak Six-Four

When responder to an opening bid of one club holds a weak hand with a four card major and a longer diamond suit he will bypass the diamond suit to respond by bidding his four card major. Responder will only bid his longer diamond suit when his values are great enough to force the auction to game (12+ or more).

When responder's values were maximum to have bypassed the longer diamond suit (9+ to 12−), at his rebid responder will ignore his diamond length and raise to two notrump. The length in diamonds will most often furnish a source of tricks for play in notrump, and diamonds need not become the trump suit. The bidding side will have sufficient high card strength to make a notrump contract at the level that has been reached.

When responder's values are just minimum for his response (5+ to 9−), if his diamond suit is only five cards long responder will pass and one notrump will become the contract. If responder's diamond suit is six cards long the best contract will be in diamonds.

Responder cannot bid two diamonds and get to play there since a bid of two diamonds is **New Minor Forcing**. That bid would be totally artificial and ask for information about opener's hand.

In order to get to play a part score in diamonds responder continues with a jump to three diamonds. This jump identifies his hand as having minimum values (5+ to 9−) and a six-four pattern. Opener is required to pass this rebid from responder.

When the opening bid has been one diamond and responder has a similar hand with a four card major and a six card club suit, he does not bypass his longer suit but does bid as has been indicated above. If his values are great enough to force to game (12+ or more) responder will bid a five or six card club suit at his first turn rather than bid unnaturally in his four card major suit. With less than game forcing values, responder bids his major suit rather than his longer club suit, staying at the one level.

If opener rebids one notrump responder's actions are as mentioned above when the discussion focused on diamonds. A jump rebid of three clubs by responder will show that he has minimum response values (5+ to 9−) and a six card club suit in addition to the four card major expressed at his first call. Again responder would not be able to only bid two clubs at his rebid since that call would be New Minor Forcing .

Responder's Continuations After New Minor Forcing

When responder has used **New Minor Forcing** holding only game invitational values (9+ to 12−), if opener's next call shows a maximum responder will know which game to play. If a five-three major suit fit has been disclosed responder will bid game in the major, but if opener has shown a maximum with only two card support for responder's major suit, responder bids game in notrump.

If instead opener shows only minimum values responder must sign off below the level of game when his values are only invitational (9+ to 12−). When opener has shown a minimum with a three card fit by bidding responder's major suit at the two level, responder will pass.

When opener has shown a doubleton in responder's major suit and a minimum, responder can sign off by bidding two notrump. Responder can also elect to play in a five-two major suit fit. When his suit is spades and opener has artificially bid two hearts to show a minimum with a doubleton, responder can sign off by bidding two spades. When opener has made a natural bid of two diamonds responder can sign off at two of his major suit no matter which major that is, or he can sign off at two notrump.

When opener has maximum values and has bid two diamonds, he will not honor responder's attempt to sign off, since game values are known to exist. Opener will belatedly accept responder's game invitation and bid three notrump.

When responder's continuation is beyond the level of two notrump his call is natural and the auction is forcing to game. If responder bids either minor suit at the three level his bid is a slam try. Opener may cooperate in a slam quest by cue bidding, or may retreat from responder's slam suggestion by bidding three notrump.

Example 61:

a) Responder
♠ A63
♡ KJ1076
♢ Q93
♣ 54

b) Responder
♠ A63
♡ KJ1076
♢ K8
♣ Q93

c) Responder
♠ AQ985
♡ AK83
♢ 52
♣ 96

d) Responder
♠ A6
♡ KQ95
♢ K86
♣ AJ76

e) Responder
♠ AQ985
♡ AK853
♢ 2
♣ 96

f) Responder
♠ A6
♡ KQ95
♢ K6
♣ AJ876

g) Responder
♠ 7
♡ KQ953
♢ AJ876
♣ A6

With Example hand 61a) responder has heard a one notrump rebid from opener after a one club opening bid and his one heart response. Responder now bids two diamonds *New Minor Forcing* to find out how many hearts and how many points opener holds. If opener shows three card heart support hearts will be played, but if he shows only two hearts the contract will be in notrump. If opener shows only 12 or a bad 13 points responder will stop in a part score, but if opener shows 13+ to 15−, responder will bid a game.

With Example 61b) responder has the values to play a game regardless of whether opener's hand is maximum or minimum. The game to be played will depend on the number of hearts opener shows in response to *New Minor Forcing*.

With Example hand 61c) responder bids one spade in response to a minor suit opening bid. If opener rebids one notrump responder first uses *New Minor Forcing* and then bids three hearts. This auction shows five spades and four hearts and is forcing.

With Example hand 61d) responder bids one heart after an opening bid of one club and opener rebids one notrump. Although he has only four hearts and is not interested in the number of hearts in opener's hand, responder wants to invite a slam in clubs. Since a jump to three clubs would only be invitational and opener could pass, responder uses *New Minor Forcing* by bidding two diamonds. No matter what opener's next bid happens to be, responder next bids three clubs to invite a club slam (if the agreement to play either the *Hardy Adjunct* or the *Wittes Adjunct* causes opener to jump to the three level in a higher ranking suit, responder can either bid three notrump and abandon the slam search, or make the natural slam try of four clubs).

With Example hand 61e) responder bids one spade after an opening bid in either minor suit. If opener rebids one notrump responder next jumps to three hearts which shows five-five in the major suits and is forcing.

With Example hand 61f) responder bids as he did in 61d). If opener's first bid minor suit was diamonds, after a *New Minor Forcing* call of two clubs responder next bids naturally in clubs to make his slam try. If opener's first bid suit was clubs, after a *New Minor Forcing* call of two diamonds responder will make his slam try as he shows support for opener's first bid suit.

With Example hand 61g) responder has heard an opening bid of one club and has responded one heart. After opener's rebid of one notrump responder bids two diamonds *New Minor Forcing*. If opener shows support for hearts responder will seek a heart slam, but if opener bids to show only a doubleton heart, responder continues by introducing diamonds naturally, making a slam try in that suit.

Example 62:

a) Opener
  ♠ K94
  ♡ Q63
  ♢ A42
  ♣ A1063

b) Opener
  ♠ K2
  ♡ Q86
  ♢ AQ4
  ♣ K9865

c) Opener
  ♠ K109
  ♡ Q4
  ♢ A963
  ♣ AJ85

d) Opener
  ♠ Q109
  ♡ J4
  ♢ A96
  ♣ AJ853

e) Opener
  ♠ Q109
  ♡ J4
  ♢ AQ853
  ♣ A96

With Example hand 62a) opener starts with one club and rebids one notrump after a major suit response. If responder next bids two diamonds, *New Minor Forcing*, opener returns to two of opener's major to show three card support and minimum values. His thirteen points are scattered and his shape is bad.

With Example hand 62b) opener starts with one club and rebids one notrump after a major suit response. If responder continues by bidding two diamonds, *New Minor Forcing*, responder will next bid two notrump to show a doubleton and maximum values if responder's major was spades, but will jump to the three level to show a maximum with a three card fit if responder's major suit was hearts.

If the *Hardy Adjunct* is in use opener will bid three diamonds to pinpoint a doubleton spade, while if the *Wittes Adjunct* is in use opener will bid three diamonds to show that he holds the queen of hearts.

With Example hand 62c) opener's major suit situation is reversed. He once again starts by bidding in a minor suit (the choice of suits is dictated by partnership preference — see Chapter I) and rebids one notrump after a major suit response. If responder then uses *New Minor Forcing*, when responder's major suit is hearts opener shows his doubleton heart and maximum values by bidding two notrump. When responder's major suit is spades opener will bid at the three level to show that he has maximum values and three card spade support. If no adjunct has been agreed by the partnership that call will be a jump to three spades. If the *Hardy Adjunct* has been agreed opener will bid in the minor suit that was not the suit of his opening bid to pinpoint that he has a doubleton heart. If the *Wittes Adjunct* has been agreed opener will bid three hearts to show that he has one of the top two heart honors.

With Example hand 62d) opener bids one club and rebids one no-trump after a response in either major suit. If responder continues by bidding two diamonds, *New Minor Forcing* opener, next bids two spades. If responder's major is spades opener has shown a three card fit with a minimum. If responder's major is hearts opener has shown a doubleton heart and a minimum hand with his artificial two spade bid.

With Example hand 62e) opener starts with one diamond and rebids one notrump after a major suit response. If responder next bids two clubs, *New Minor Forcing*, if responder's major suit is spades opener can bid at the three level to show his maximum for spades with three card support. If the *Hardy Adjunct* has been agreed opener bids three clubs to pinpoint a doubleton heart. If the *Wittes Adjunct* has been agreed opener bids three diamonds to show the spade queen. If responder's major suit is hearts, opener does not bid two notrump but instead bids two diamonds to show his five card suit.

The Hardy Adjunct

The function of the **Hardy Adjunct** to **New Minor Forcing** is to allow opener to show his distribution when he bids at the three level in response to responder's **New Minor** to show maximum values and a three card fit for responder's major suit. With no adjunct available, opener would always jump to responder's major suit at the three level and no additional information would be conveyed.

The **Hardy Adjunct** utilizes all five bids that can be made at the three level to show different hand patterns. When opener jumps to the three level in responder's major suit he promises that his hand has 4-3-3-3 distribution and includes the ace, king, or queen in responder's suit. When opener has 4-3-3-3 distribution and does not also hold a top honor in responder's major suit, he instead jumps to three notrump.

If opener bids at the three level in any other suit, he marks the suit that he has neither bid nor implied (he implies three cards in responder's suit) as being a doubleton (since he has rebid one notrump he can have no suit shorter than two cards). He has opened the bidding in a first suit, bid a second suit in response to **New Minor Forcing**, and implied a three card holding in a third suit (responder's major). The remaining suit is announced as being a doubleton.

For example, if opener has first bid one club and then rebids one notrump after a response of one heart, when responder bids two diamonds, **New Minor Forcing**, if opener next bids three spades he marks the suit he has omitted, diamonds, as a doubleton. Since opener is now known to hold three spades (his rebid was one notrump rather than one spade), three hearts, and two diamonds his distribution is 3-3-2-5.

If opener instead bids three diamonds after responder's **New Minor Forcing** call of two diamonds, he marks himself with a doubleton spade. His distribution will be either 2-3-3-5 or 2-3-4-4 (some partnerships open with one club and some with one diamond when holding a balanced pattern with four-four in the minor suits).

If opener's third bid in the same auction were to be three clubs, he would mark doubletons in two suits. His pattern would be 2-3-2-6 with good doubletons which prompted a rebid of one notrump rather than in a broken six card club suit.

Example 63:

a) Opener
♠ KJ4
♡ 1063
◇ AJ6
♣ KQ92

b) Opener
♠ K64
♡ Q103
◇ AJ6
♣ KJ92

c) Opener
♠ K6
♡ Q103
◇ AJ62
♣ KJ92

d) Opener
♠ K64
♡ Q103
◇ A6
♣ KQ1063

e) Opener
♠ KJ
♡ Q103
◇ A6
♣ K96432

Using the *Hardy Adjunct* in Example 63 opener has bid one club and rebid one notrump after a response of one heart. Responder continues by bidding two diamonds, *New Minor Forcing*.

With Example hand 63a) opener next jumps to three notrump to show his 3-3-3-4 pattern with maximum values and deny a top honor in hearts.

With Example hand 63b) opener jumps to three hearts. Again he identifies a 3-3-3-4 pattern, but promises that he has one of the top three heart honors.

With Example hand 63c) opener next bids three diamonds (if he has instead opened with one diamond the *New Minor* will have been two clubs and opener next bids three clubs) to mark the doubleton spade in his hand along with three card heart support and maximum values.

With Example hand 63d) opener continues by bidding three spades to indicate that he has a doubleton diamond, and marks his 3-3-2-5 pattern.

With Example hand 63e) opener continues by bidding three clubs. This indicates that he has doubletons in both of the suits he has not bid, and marks a pattern of 2-3-2-6.

The Wittes Adjunct

Conceived by World Champion Jon Wittes of Los Alamitos, California, another adjunct is available that enables opener to show trump quality when he bids at the three level to show a maximum and a three card fit for responder's major suit after responder has used **New Minor Forcing**.

Regardless of which major suit responder has shown, opener's rebids at the three level are as follows: Three clubs shows a holding of three small or jack third in responder's major suit, three diamonds shows queen third, three hearts shows ace or king third, three spades shows two of the top three honors, and three notrump shows three small or jack third with a strong desire to play three notrump.

At the time of its conception the **Wittes Adjunct** was extremely useful since any tool that conveys information regarding trump quality is vital when the bidding side is contemplating a slam. This vital information could allow a close slam to be bid, or keep the bidding side out of a slam which is unlikely to make due to poor trump quality.

More recently, nearly all serious tournament players have adopted another tool which conveys information about trump quality as it shows controls. This tool is **Roman Key Card Blackwood (RKC)**. Since **RKC** will furnish the needed information regarding trump quality in most slam going auctions, the **Wittes Adjunct** now is no longer as vital a tool as it once was.

Game Going Rebids: Responder's Range is 12+

When responder has values enough for game facing an opening bid and knows which game to play but has no interest in slam, he may bid the game directly. When this is the case responder's value range will be 12+ to 15−.

1) When opener's rebid is in a major suit for which responder has four card support, responder knows that game in opener's suit should be bid. He jumps to four in opener's major suit to show four card support and limit his values, but only when his hand is balanced. When his hand is unbalanced and the other factors mentioned apply, responder should **splinter** with a hand in this range to allow opener the opportunity to evaluate fits.

2) When responder has a good six card (or longer) major suit in which he has made his first call, if opener rebids one notrump responder has an easy jump rebid to game in his suit since opener is known to have a two or three card fit.

Even if opener has not rebid so as to show a fit for his suit, responder can jump to game when his suit is of good enough quality to be the trump suit without support from opener. With a suit of lesser quality responder must create a forcing auction and then rebid his suit to see if opener has any kind of support.

3) When opener has either rebid one notrump or raised responder's suit, responder knows to bid game in the indicated denomination. Responder can raise one notrump to three when his own major suit is only four cards long or can use **New Minor Forcing** when his suit is five cards long and opener's rebid has been one notrump.

Regardless of his suit length, when opener has raised showing four card support and a limited hand responder can jump to game in his supported major suit. If he has a side singleton or void responder again should **splinter** rather than jump to game to allow opener to reevaluate the placement of his high cards.

4) When opener has rebid in a higher ranking suit at the one level responder has the option to jump to three notrump. This will show that responder has a hand in the range under discussion, is reasonably balanced, and has the unbid suit under control. In this auction opener's hand is not yet limited, and when he hears that responder has values enough to jump to game he may be able to move on toward a slam.

Example 64:

a) Responder	b) Responder	c) Responder
♠ KQ86	♠ K6	♠ K95
♡ KJ86	♡ KJ10963	♡ AQ76
◊ A54	◊ AQ4	◊ KJ10
♣ 72	♣ 83	♣ J95

With Example hand 64a) responder has bid one heart after an opening bid of one club. If opener's rebid is one spade, one notrump, or two hearts responder should jump to game in the denomination of opener's rebid.

With Example hand 64b) if opener's rebid is either a heart raise or a call of one notrump responder jumps to four hearts. He knows that opener has an adequate fit for hearts. If opener's rebid is one spade or two clubs responder must make a forcing bid and should

132

bid two diamonds. **This allows opener to show three card heart support if he has it.** If opener does not show heart support at that turn responder can then bid three hearts which is forcing to ask opener to raise if he has a doubleton or a singleton honor in hearts (if opener's rebid was one spade the two diamond call is *Fourth Suit Forcing* which is detailed later in this Chapter).

With Example hand 64c) if opener makes any non-jump rebid responder can express his hand by bidding three notrump.

5) Although jump preferences are generally invitational showing a hand in the range of 9+ to 12−, there is one jump preference in the system which is forcing. System users should make careful note of this one exception to the general rule.

Responder will sometimes be dealt a hand with a good diamond suit as well as reasonably good clubs. When responder holds this hand and opener bids one club, rather than make an **Inverted Minor Raise** which would emphasize clubs when the primary feature of the hand is diamonds, responder bids one diamond.

At the time of the one diamond response opener knows that if responder holds a second suit, either minor or major, he is likely to have a good hand. If his second suit is a four card major responder has opening bid values and will indicate that fact when he bids the major suit as his rebid.

If responder's second suit is clubs, he can show his fit for opener's first suit and minimum values (5+ to 9−) by taking a club preference at the cheapest level as his rebid. When responder holds clubs and diamonds and invitational values (9+ to 12−) he will conceal one of those suits and show the longer one. He may respond one diamond and then raise a one notrump rebid to two, or he may start with an **Inverted** raise of two clubs and limit his values in the subsequent auction.

When responder does elect to first bid one diamond and then jump to three clubs as his rebid his values are 12+ or more and the auction is forcing. Using this rebid as forcing rather than invitational is of great help when a minor suit slam is to be sought. When responder only has values enough to invite a game, that game is more likely to be in notrump even though responder's hand is distributional.

Example 65:

a) Responder	b) Responder	c) Responder
♠ K5	♠ K5	♠ K5
♡ 3	♡ 3	♡ —
◇ AQJ63	◇ J10542	◇ AKQ1075
♣ J10542	♣ AQJ63	♣ QJ954

With Example hand 65a) when opener bids one club responder will bid one diamond. If opener rebids one notrump responder will have to show his values by raising to two notrump. His hand is not good enough to make the forcing jump rebid of three clubs. Responder will be able to show his club fit in other auctions, but in this case since opener's values are limited the only prospective game is three notrump.

With Example hand 65b) responder best describes by making an *Inverted Raise* in clubs. He will limit his hand at his second turn. Again if game is reached it is likely to be in notrump, but if opener wants to play in clubs responder will give him a good dummy with good trumps.

With Example hand 65c) responder must be able to first show his diamond suit in response to one club, then make a forcing call in clubs to show his good fit. Fortunately his jump to three clubs at his rebid will be forcing.

Slam Try Rebids: Responder Announces Fits and Seeks or Shows Controls

When opener's rebid suddenly makes responder's hand grow in value and he wishes to sound the alarm for slam, he may do so by making a **splinter** bid or an **Asking Bid**.

An unusual jump at any time that does not otherwise carry systemic meaning is a **splinter** bid. A **splinter** announces values enough to reach game (with a few exceptions), shortness in the suit of the **splinter** jump (either a singleton or a void), and good support for the suit last bid by partner.

Although when a suit has been bid for the first time a **splinter** jump in support generally shows four card or longer support, if that suit has been bid and rebid, strongly suggesting that the suit is six cards or longer, when the facing hand meets all other criteria it may **splinter** when holding only three card support.

A rare splinter that does not necessarily force to game is the jump reverse by opener in support of responder's suit (see Chapter III). Another is the **mini-splinter** which we suggest be used after an opposing takeout double of a major suit opening bid (see Chapter VII). Most **splinters**, however, force the bidding side to game.

When game is forced, the value of the **splinter** is the information that it furnishes which may lead to a slam on what would seem to be marginal values. When perfect fits exist, slam can sometimes be made when the bidding side has less than half of the 40 points in high cards that is available. It follows that when it was possible for either opener or responder to have made a **splinter** bid and instead the bidder jumped to game in one of the suits known to be a possible trump suit, the inference conveyed is that the bidder did not have a short side suit in which to **splinter**.

In any auction where an unusual jump would be a **splinter**, with a single exception, a jump one level higher is an **Asking Bid**. **Asking Bids** are a tool which serve a special purpose. When it becomes apparent that a slam might be reached but there is one specific suit in which losers exist, it is possible to focus on that suit and get information which will solve the problem.

After an **Asking Bid** has been used, the response to it will indicate whether the necessary control in the suit exists in partner's hand. If that control has been found slam can be bid, and if that control has been denied a slam which would not have been fulfilled can be avoided.

The single exception to the general rule that a jump in a new suit to a level one higher than would be necessary to **splinter** is an **Asking Bid** is the double jump reverse by opener. When opener makes a jump reverse, that bid shows a **splinter** which will always be a singleton. The double jump reverse also shows shortness but promises that the shortness is a void. This is possible due to the fact that both jump reverses and double jump reverses by opener cause the auction to remain below the level of game.

Complete information about **Asking Bids**, when they apply and what the responses to them indicate, appears in Chapter VIII.

Example 66:

a) Responder	b) Responder	c) Responder
♠ 6	♠ KJ104	♠ AK62
♡ AKJ83	♡ AKJ83	♡ KQ843
◊ A54	◊ 6	◊ J75
♣ KJ104	♣ A54	♣ 4

With Example hand 66a) responder bids one heart after a one club opening bid. When opener rebids two clubs responder shows good club support, shortness in spades and interest in slam by making a *splinter bid*, jumping to three spades.

With Example hand 66b) responder to an opening bid of one club bids one heart and hears a rebid of one spade. Responder shows his spade support and slam interest by making a *splinter* jump of four diamonds. He cannot jump to three diamonds since that bid in this auction would show a different hand. Responder would show a weak hand with six diamonds and four hearts if his rebid were a jump to only three diamonds.

With Example hand 66c) responder bids one heart after an opening bid of one diamond. If opener continues with a rebid of one spade responder makes a *splinter* jump rebid of four clubs.

Example 67:

a) Responder	b) Responder	c) Responder
♠ 64	♠ AK104	♠ 62
♡ AKJ83	♡ AKQJ3	♡ AKJ63
◊ A5	◊ 62	◊ AK5
♣ AJ104	♣ A3	♣ A42

With Example hand 67a) responder bids one heart in response to an opening bid of one club. Opener rebids two clubs and responder knows that slam depends upon a control in spades. Since a jump to three spades would be a *splinter* responder continues by jumping to four spades, an *Asking Bid*.

With Example hand 67b) responder again bids one heart in response to an opening bid of one club (yes, we do play preemptive jump shift responses). When opener rebids one spade responder needs to know about controls in diamonds. He continues by making an *Asking Bid* by jumping to five diamonds. A jump to three diamonds would have shown a weak six-four and a jump to four diamonds would have been a splinter.

With Example hand 67c) responder bids one heart after an opening bid in either minor suit and hears opener raise to two hearts. Again responder needs to know about specific controls and makes his *Asking Bid* by jumping to four spades. A jump to three spades would have been a *splinter*.

Responder's Rebids After Opener Has Reversed

When opener has reversed (see Chapter II) he has described a hand that has specific shape and value minimums. Opener will have bid two suits and promised that the first suit is longer, and he will also have promised that his value range is at least an ace better than a minimum opening bid. His range will be 16+ points, and his maximum will be any hand that he felt was not quite an opening bid of two clubs (artificial and forcing).

Opener's decision in some cases will have been to open at the one level and hope that the auction does not die so that he will have a chance at his rebid to reverse to show the two suits he holds as he makes a forcing rebid. He may have done this rather than open with two clubs (artificial and forcing) since it is often very difficult to describe a two suited hand when the first natural bid is at a high level.

When responder hears opener's reverse he is aware that it shows a good hand and is forcing for one round, but it is not clear whether the two hands have game going values between them unless responder has at least what normally would be invitational values (9+ or more). When responder's values are only those of a minimum response (5+ to 9−) and opener's reverse is minimum, game will be out of reach.

Responder needs the capacity to show his value range at his rebid so that opener will be able to assess the situation accurately. When opener's reverse values are enough to force game he has no problems, and even if responder is able to describe a minimum response (5+ to 9+) opener can push to game. When opener's values are good enough to reverse but not good enough to force to game, he needs the information about responder's minimum to keep from getting too high.

The complex which follows was suggested by the late Monroe Ingberman, an expert recognized as an outstanding bidding theorist. We feel that incorporation of the ideas it presents will enable the bidding side to have a cogent exchange of information that will allow the best contract to be reached in most instances.

1) When responder rebids his original major suit he shows minimum values (5+ to 9−) and says that his suit is at least five cards long. When opener hears such a rebid and his values are not adequate to force to game, if he holds three card support for responder's major suit he can pass and the contract should be quite adequate.

2) In the auction: 1♣-P-1♠-P, 2♦-P, if responder bids two hearts he promises a five card spade suit and four or more hearts. This rebid is not forcing but will rarely be passed by opener. Opener would be tempted to pass only with a 0-3-4-6 hand with three good hearts and minimum reverse values. With any other hand a two heart contract would not be inviting (opener cannot have four hearts since he would reverse into hearts rather than diamonds if he did).

3) The auction: 1♣-P-1♡-P, 2♦-P-2♠ is quite different. Here two spades should be treated as **Fourth Suit Forcing**. Since opener is known not to have four cards in spades a natural spade bid by responder at this point would be futile. Responder will have at least invitational values (9+ points — actually this constitutes game going values after opener's reverse) without a three card fit for clubs or a four card fit for diamonds.

Responder will also feel that if notrump should be played, it should be played from opener's side of the table. As with all **Fourth Suit Forcing** auctions responder will often be interested in hearing belatedly about a three card fit for his first suit. However the nature of the **Fourth Suit** bid in this situation is primarily to convey values.

4) When after opener has reversed responder rebids two notrump he indicates minimum values for his response. Responder asks opener to next bid three clubs unless his reverse values are game forcing. If opener's values are good enough to force to game facing a minimum (5+ to 9−) response he will not bid three clubs, but will make any other expressive call.

Responder's intention may be to pass three clubs either because that is opener's first suit and he holds three card support, or because he was unable to respond in his own six card (or longer) club suit due to his poor values.

Responder's relay to three clubs does not always indicate that his desire is to play in clubs. He may use this route to show a fit for one of opener's suits as he also indicates minimum response values. He does this by next returning to either of opener's suits, having limited his values by using this auction.

When opener bids three clubs as responder's two notrump bid asks him to do he indicates that his reverse values are not of game forcing proportions. The only other rebid opener can make with a less than game forcing reverse is to return to diamonds when that was his first suit. If he has an excellent six card diamond suit and club shortness he does not want to give responder the opportunity to pass and allow three clubs to become the contract rather than three diamonds.

If responder instead of rebidding two notrump or two of his original suit continues by supporting either of opener's suits at the three level the auction is game forcing. Responder will have shown at least three card support for opener's first suit or four card support for opener's second suit and values enough (9+ or more) for game even when opener's values are minimum for his reverse. If responder's values are great enough to suggest slam, that will be shown as the auction continues.

If responder's rebid is three notrump he shows game going values for this auction (9+ to 12−) without interest in bidding further, denies the ability to support either of opener's suits, and shows that the suits that opener does not hold are well controlled for notrump play.

If responder uses the **Fourth Suit** other than as has been mentioned above that call is ambiguous and forcing. Responder will have values enough to reach a game without the ability to support either of opener's suits and needs to find out more about opener's reverse in order to continue intelligently with the auction.

Example 68:

a) Opener
♠ A6
♡ AQ105
◊ AQJ1073
♣ 5

With Example hand 68a) opener first bids one diamond and after a response of one spade reverses by rebidding two hearts. If responder next bids two notrump to show minimum response values and ask opener to bid three clubs opener should not comply, but should bid three diamonds since he does not want to play in clubs if responder should want to pass that rebid. His good diamond suit should be the trump suit, and this call does not show more than minimum values for his reverse.

b) Opener
♠ AQ6
♡ AQ105
◇ AQJ76
♣ 5

c) Opener
♠ AJ
♡ AQ105
◇ AJ1098
♣ 104

With Example hand 68b) opener again reverses to two hearts after his opening bid of one diamond and a one spade response. If responder tries to sign off by next bidding two notrump opener will bid three spades. This rebid shows game forcing values and a three card spade fit. Responder has the option of playing game in the four-three spade fit or bidding three notrump. He will opt for three notrump only with bad spades and good clubs since opener has indicated a singleton or void in clubs.

With Example hand 68c) opener again reverses to two hearts after his opening bid of one diamond and a one spade response. This time if responder bids two notrump artificially, opener complies and bids three clubs. He is content to play three clubs if responder passes.

Example 69:

a) Responder
♠ K10953
♡ K6
◇ 542
♣ 876

b) Responder
♠ K10953
♡ K964
◇ 52
♣ 86

c) Responder
♠ K1093
♡ K96
◇ K54
♣ Q72

d) Responder
♠ K1093
♡ 84
◇ 4
♣ QJ9872

With Example hand 69a) responder has bid one spade in response to a minor suit opening bid and hears opener reverse. Responder next bids two spades to show his five card suit and minimum values. If opener has a minimum reverse with two or three spades he can pass and the contract will be as playable as any. If opener's next call is two notrump or three of his original suit the auction is no longer forcing and responder may pass.

With Example hand 69b) responder bids one spade after an opening bid of one club. If opener next reverses by bidding two
diamonds responder will bid two hearts which is non-forcing. If
opener's reverse is to two hearts responder must not pass since the
reverse is forcing, and must also not raise hearts as that would
show game forcing (9+ or more) values. Responder next bids two
notrump to ask opener to bid three clubs. If opener does bid three
clubs his values are not enough to force a game, and when responder corrects to three hearts that will end the auction. If
opener does not rebid three clubs his alternate call will show game
forcing values. Responder will then show his heart fit at his
next call.

With Example hand 69c) responder bids one spade in response to
a minor suit opening bid. If opener continues by reversing at the
two level responder has the values (9+ or more) and three card fit
for opener's first suit to take a preference directly there. A five-
three (or longer) fit will have been established and the auction will
be known to be forcing to game.

With Example hand 69d) responder has bid one spade in response
to an opening bid of one diamond. If opener next reverses to two
hearts responder bids two notrump to attempt to escape to three
clubs. If opener bids three clubs as requested responder will pass.
If opener instead bids three spades responder will know that
opener has a three card spade fit and game forcing values. Responder should bid three notrump since his clubs are adequate
and there is no guarantee that opener's spades are good enough to
play game in the four-three fit.

Compare the hands for opener in Example 68 with the hands for
responder in Example 69 to see the contracts that would be
reached on each pair of hands.

Responder's Rebids After Opener's Jump Rebid of Two Notrump

When opener's rebid is a jump to two notrump his message is that his
hand is balanced and that its range falls between the ranges of opening
bids of one notrump and two notrump (about a good 18 points to a bad
20 points). Opener with this rebid also denies four card support for the
major suit that has been bid by responder although he may have four
cards in the other major suit.

If opener with his balanced hand also had four card support for responder's major suit he would make a jump raise in that suit, usually to the four level but possibly to the three level with only 18 points. Opener's hand must be balanced since if it were not his rebid in support of responder's major suit would be a **splinter**.

Regardless of which major suit responder has bid, when opener holds four of the other major suit he makes his size and shape definition with a jump rebid of two notrump rather than showing four cards in the unbid major suit at that time. If responder has bid one spade opener would have to reverse to show four hearts and his hand will usually not meet the shape requirements for a reverse. If responder has instead bid one heart it would be easy for opener to rebid one or two spades but the size and shape definition takes preference over this possible choice. When opener does make a jump shift rebid of two spades after a one heart response, or if he jump shifts in either major suit after a response of one diamond, he promises an unbalanced hand.

When responder hears opener's description of a balanced hand of 18+ to 20— he knows that game should be reached unless he has stretched to make his response. When responder has a balanced hand that did not really have the expected values for a response he will pass and hope that opener will make exactly eight tricks in notrump.

When responder's first call was prompted by a shapely hand with less than expected values he will want to sign off and play in one of his suits at the three level. Although in standard bidding a bid by responder at the three level in this auction would be forcing, the system employs a convention that allows responder to stop in the suit of his choice at the three level. This convention is the **Wolff Signoff**, a creation of many time World Champion Bobby Wolff of Dallas, Texas.

Regardless of what the opening bid has been, responder's continuation of three clubs is artificial and asks opener to do one of two things. Opener is asked to show three card support for responder's suit if he has it, otherwise to artificially bid three diamonds. If opener bids at the three level in responder's suit responder can then pass to end the auction. If opener instead bids three diamonds responder can pass or sign off in either major suit at the three level, or sign off at four clubs.

If responder uses the artificial bid of three clubs and then continues by bidding three notrump, that call is a mild slam try showing clubs. If clubs were not bid originally by opener, responder will have a five card club suit when he makes this slam try.

When responder does not have a value problem other auctions are possible. When his hand is balanced responder bids to the level that shows his values. Three notrump signs off at game; four notrump invites a small slam; six notrump places the contract as does seven notrump; and five notrump invites seven while forcing the auction to six notrump.

When responder's major suit is six cards or longer he can rebid it at the four level to sign off at game, but can bid it at the three level to show its length and invite a slam. Opener rejects the slam try by raising to four of responder's suit or bidding three notrump based on his holdings, but accepts the slam try by cue bidding his nearest ace or using **RKC Blackwood**. Without values enough for game responder uses the **Wolff Signoff** to get to play in his six card suit at the three level.

When responder has the need to check back for a major suit fit in opener's hand he uses an artificial bid of three diamonds. Responder will either have a five card major for which he wants to find a three card fit, or he will have four-four in the majors and will be looking for a four card fit in spades in opener's hand, or he will have five spades and four hearts and will seek a fit for either after having responded with one spade.

When responder's major suits are four spades and five hearts his first bid will have been one heart, and rather than check back with the artificial bid of three diamonds he will make a natural reverse in spades to show that his hearts are longer than his spades. If responder instead continues by bidding three hearts after having responded one spade, he shows five-five in the major suits.

When responder uses the artificial three diamond checkback opener's first obligation is to show hearts. If responder has bid one heart opener will show three card support for hearts. If responder has bid spades at the one level opener will only show hearts when he holds four of them. If opener does show support for hearts as has been explained and responder corrects to three notrump he shows that he wanted to hear about spades, not hearts.

If responder has bid hearts first, when he corrects he will have four-four in the majors. If opener has shown three card heart support and also had four spades he will correct to the contract of four spades. If responder has bid spades at his first turn and opener shows four hearts, when responder corrects to three notrump he shows that he was looking for a three card fit for his five card spade suit.

Of course when opener shows hearts as requested and that is what responder wanted to hear he will continue to game in hearts or make some slam try, depending on his values.

When responder has used the artificial checkback of three diamonds and opener does not have a heart holding to show, his next obligation is to show support for spades. If responder's first bid was in hearts opener will show spades at this turn only when he holds four of them, catering to the possibility that the checkback was made because responder's holding is four-four in the major suits. If responder's first bid was in spades opener will show three card support for spades since responder will be known to hold five cards in that suit.

Example 70:

a) Responder
♠ J54
♡ Q109853
◇ J6
♣ 43

b) Responder
♠ K954
♡ 5
◇ J107652
♣ 97

c) Responder
♠ Q9742
♡ Q10964
◇ 85
♣ 7

d) Responder
♠ J5
♡ A963
◇ 42
♣ KQ942

With Example hand 70a) responder would have made a preemptive jump shift in response to an opening bid of one club. If this pair has not elected to play preemptive jump shifts responder would have bid one heart rather than pass the opening bid of one club. After opener's jump rebid of two notrump responder employs the *Wolff Signoff* by bidding three clubs. If opener next bids three hearts to show a three card fit responder can pass. If opener instead next bids three diamonds to show only a doubleton heart, responder bids three hearts and opener must pass.

With Example hand 70b) responder systemically bids one spade in response to one club, stretching to try to play in one of his suits. If opener next jumps to two notrump responder bids three clubs, the *Wolff Signoff*. If opener shows a three card spade fit responder passes and plays the four-three fit. If opener instead bids three diamonds to deny holding three spades, responder passes and opener finds lots of trumps in his dummy at his three diamond contract.

With Example hand 70c) responder again stretches to bid one spade in response to an opening bid of one club. If opener makes a jump rebid of two notrump responder uses the *Wolff Signoff* by bidding three clubs. If opener bids three spades to show three card support responder passes, but if opener bids three diamonds to show a doubleton spade responder corrects to three hearts and opener must pass.

With Example hand 70d) responder bids one heart in response to an opening bid in either minor suit. If opener next bids two no-trump responder bids three clubs, ostensibly because he wishes to sign off below the game level. When opener next bids three hearts or three diamonds responder continues by bidding three notrump to indicate interest in a club slam.

Example 71:

a) Responder	b) Responder	c) Responder
♠ Q93	♠ K93	♠ KJ1062
♡ A109642	♡ A109642	♡ 4
◇ 84	◇ 4	◇ Q62
♣ 64	♣ A64	♣ J943

With Example hand 71a) responder has bid one heart in response to a minor suit opening bid (note that his hand is too good for a preemptive jump shift). If opener next jumps to two notrump responder places the contract by bidding four hearts. This shows his six card suit and values enough only to play game.

With Example hand 71b) responder bids one heart in response to a minor suit opening bid and hears a jump rebid of two notrump from opener. Responder next bids three hearts which is a slam try showing a six card suit. Opener will cue bid if he is interested in slam, but otherwise will raise to game holding honor doubleton or three small hearts, or will bid three notrump with a small doubleton heart.

With Example hand 71c) responder has bid one spade in response to a minor suit opening bid and heard a two notrump rebid from opener. Responder now checks back for a three card spade fit by artificially bidding three diamonds. If opener next bids three hearts to show a four card heart suit responder will bid three notrump to show that he was not interested in hearts but was looking for a three card spade fit. Opener will then pass with a doubleton spade or correct to four spades if he holds three of them. If the three diamond checkback elicits a three spade call responder signs off at four spades, but if opener bids three notrump to deny holding either four hearts or three spades, responder passes.

d) Responder
♠ KJ83
♡ QJ95
♢ 62
♣ J104

With Example hand 71d) responder has bid one heart in response to an opening minor suit bid and heard a rebid of two notrump from opener. Responder next checks back by bidding three diamonds since although opener does not have four hearts he may hold four spades. If opener next bids three hearts to show three card support responder continues by bidding three notrump to show that his interest was not in three card heart support but rather in finding a four-four spade fit. If opener has four spades he will then correct to four spades. If opener instead replies to the three diamond inquiry by bidding three spades he denies holding three hearts but shows a four card spade suit. Responder ends the auction by raising to four spades.

Fourth Suit Forcing

We have noted that when responder's rebid is a jump to a suit that has previously been bid, with a single exception he has shown a hand with invitational values. Responder's range is a good nine points to a bad twelve points.

Since jumps are not forcing responder must have at his disposal some means by which he can create a forcing auction. A time honored principle in bridge bidding is that, with a few notable exceptions, A NEW SUIT BY AN UNPASSED RESPONDER IS FORCING.

Let us note the exceptions:

1) If opener has rebid one notrump a new suit by responder is not forcing unless it is a reverse or a jump. In the system we alter this by using **New Minor Forcing** which causes some jumps to be weak, although reverses are still natural and forcing. Systemically after a rebid of one notrump by opener if responder bids a minor suit that has not yet been bid his call is artificial and forcing, seeking further information about opener's hand, but in standard bidding such a rebid would be natural and not forcing.

2) If there has been a takeout double of the opening bid responder's new suit is forcing only if it is at the one level. After the takeout double if responder bids a new suit at the two level his call is natural and non-forcing. Responder promises a void or singleton in opener's suit and at least a five card suit of his own.

Since he is short in his partner's suit and the takeout doubler is also assumed to be short in that suit, the doubler's partner may well have a hand with which to pass for penalties. Responder wants opener to be assured that in this case he will find at least a doubleton in support in responder's hand when he passes after the takeout double.

3) After there has been an overcall of one notrump (natural) by the opponent next to bid after the opening bid, if responder elects to bid in a new suit his call is natural and not forcing. Responder will have a hand that is valuable offensively but not defensively. With a good defensive hand responder would double the notrump overcall for penalties. If responder feels that the overcall of one notrump may have been psychic or if he has other reasons to wish to make a forcing call responder can make a cue bid of two notrump.

Having noted the exceptions let us see how we apply the basic principle when responder needs to be able to create a forcing auction.

When opener has bid and rebid in two different suits and responder has bid yet a third suit we come to the point in the auction where responder needs to make a forcing bid when his values are such that game should be reached (normally when he holds 12+ points or the equivalent in combined high card and distributional values). Since a rebid or a jump rebid in any previously bid suit at this point is only invitational, responder forces by bidding in the only remaining suit, no matter what his holding in that suit happens to be.

Responder's values for the use of **Fourth Suit Forcing** will nearly always be game forcing as described above. On rare occasions he will need to fish for information when his values are only invitational (9+ to 12−). When this is the case responder must be prepared to close the auction below the level of game if he learns that opener's values are minimum by use of his **Fourth Suit** probe. Therefore, if the use of **Fourth Suit Forcing** elicits that opener's values are minimum and responder next bids at the level of two notrump or lower, the auction is no longer forcing to game.

When it has been agreed that **Fourth Suit Forcing** can be used by responder with invitational values (9+ to 12−), it follows that a responder who has previously passed still has use of this tool.

Note should be made that while this approach solves many bidding problems, in order to insure that there is no confusion in such auctions, many experts play that all **Fourth Suit** auctions are forcing to game.

When responder at his rebid has used **Fourth Suit Forcing** opener should further describe his hand based on a list of priorities. Opener's further bids are as follows:

1) Opener's first priority will be to show three card support for responder's first bid suit, especially since that suit will nearly always be a major suit. As he bids to show three card support opener also has the obligation to show the range of his values by bidding responder's suit as cheaply as possible when his values are minimum (12 or 13 points), but by jumping in support of responder's suit when his values are greater. If opener fails to jump to show his good values, when responder's values are invitational he will pass and a game that should be bid will be missed.

2) When opener does not have three card support for responder's suit his second priority is to bid notrump to show that he has a stopper in the **Fourth Suit**. Again he must show his values as he shows his stopper by bidding notrump at the cheapest level when his values are minimum (12 or 13) but by jumping (usually this will be to game) when his values are greater. Again if opener fails to jump when his values warrant that action, when his values are invitational responder will pass and a game that should be bid will be missed.

3) Except in one particular auction if opener raises the **Fourth Suit** he promises four card support for that suit. The only exception is in the auction which has gone: 1 ◊ -P-1 ♡-P, 2♣-P-2♠. Opener has denied holding four spades since his rebid was two clubs rather than one spade. In this **Fourth Suit** auction if opener raises spades he will be showing pattern. He will have a 3-1-5-4 or 3-1-4-5 pattern with three small spades, since if he held a spade honor he would bid notrump rather than raise spades.

4) When the rebids by opener that have first priority are not available opener makes the bid that most naturally describes his hand. If his first suit was six cards long or a very good five cards, opener is happy to rebid that suit. If his first suit was five cards long and not a particularly good suit, the rebid of that suit still may be his only option.

5) On rare occasions opener will have a hand that is impossible to describe. He will not be able to show three card support for responder's first suit, he will be unable to bid notrump for lack of a stopper in the **Fourth Suit**, he will not be able to raise the **Fourth Suit** due to lack of appropriate length in that suit, and he will not have enough length in his first suit to rebid that suit. When opener has this dilemma his solution is to make the rebid that is least plausible.

If opener rebids his second suit that should show that he has five cards in the second suit, ergo he has six cards in his first suit. Since the five-six hand is extremely rare, when responder who has used **Fourth Suit Forcing** hears opener rebid his second suit he should continue under the assumption that opener's hand was the problem hand which could not be described. On those rare occasions when opener actually does have a five-six hand, he will bid his five card suit once again at his next turn.

There is one systemic situation in which responder should clarify what would otherwise be an ambiguous auction for opener. When opener has bid one club and has rebid one heart after a response of one diamond, responder's continuation of one spade is **Fourth Suit Forcing** and guaranteed to be artificial. Responder will not hold four or more spades in this auction.

If responder holds four spades in this auction he must also have five or more diamonds and game forcing values. If responder did not have such a hand he would not have bid in this fashion, but would have bypassed diamonds to bid one spade at his first turn.

To clarify that he has the hand with four spades, five or more diamonds and game forcing values, responder's second bid is a systemic jump to two spades. This jump identifies a specific hand type for opener and allows him to continue knowing that responder truly does have a four card spade suit.

Example 72:

a) Opener
♠ KJ63
♡ J54
◇ 92
♣ AK86

b) Opener
♠ AK64
♡ Q93
◇ 62
♣ AJ42

c) Opener
♠ AQ43
♡ 62
◇ K85
♣ K1096

d) Opener
♠ KJ54
♡ 3
◇ KQ103
♣ A984

e) Opener
♠ KJ54
♡ A982
◇ 3
♣ KQ103

f) Opener
♠ AQ43
♡ 62
◇ 5
♣ AK8432

g) Opener
♠ K954
♡ 86
◇ J3
♣ AKJ83

h) Opener
♠ AQ65
♡ Q7
◇ 762
♣ AJ83

i) Opener
♠ KQ93
♡ Q2
◇ J94
♣ KQJ4

With Example hand 72a) opener has started with one club and rebid one spade after a response of one heart. If responder continues with two diamonds *Fourth Suit Forcing* opener next bids two hearts to show three card support and minimum values.

With Example hand 72b) opener again bids one club and rebids one spade after a response of one heart. If responder next bids two diamonds *Fourth Suit Forcing* opener shows his three card heart fit and maximum values by jumping to three hearts.

With Example hand 72c) in the same auction after the *Fourth Suit Forcing* call opener next bids two notrump to deny holding three hearts but to show minimum values and a diamond stopper.

With Example hand 72d) Opener starts by bidding one diamond and rebids one spade after a one heart response. If responder continues by bidding two clubs *Fourth Suit Forcing* opener raises to three clubs to show four cards in the *Fourth Suit* while denying the capacity to show a heart fit. When opener shows four clubs it will be assumed that he is likely to have a club honor, but showing the 4-1-4-4 pattern is more important than the club stopper which is implied by the club raise.

With Example hand 72e) opener starts with one club and rebids one heart after a one diamond response. If responder continues by bidding one spade *Fourth Suit Forcing* opener raises to show a four card spade holding. Systemically responder is known not to hold a spade suit, but opener must describe his spade length anyway.

150

With Example hand 72f) opener starts with one club and rebids one spade after a red suit response. If responder then bids the unbid red suit opener will rebid naturally in his six card club suit.

The auction will be the same with Example hand 72g) but this time opener will be rebidding in a five card suit. Happily, on this occasion it is a good suit, but that will not always be so.

With Example hand 72h) opener again starts with one club and rebids one spade after a one heart response. If responder next bids two diamonds *Fourth Suit Forcing* opener has no descriptive call available to him. He cannot show three card support for hearts, he does not have a stopper in diamonds, his first suit is only four cards long, and he cannot raise the *Fourth Suit*. To solve his problem opener tells the most outlandish lie available that will not get his side in trouble by rebidding his second suit. This rebid either shows five spades and six clubs or a hand of this nature. When opener makes no move to bid spades again responder will know which hand opener has.

With Example hand 72i) in the same auction opener might make the same choice when required to describe his hand after responder's *Fourth Suit Forcing* rebid, but it would not be outlandish to consider his diamond holding to be almost a stopper and bid three notrump. It would be most unlucky if responder's diamonds were so anemic that the defenders could scuttle this game contract with the diamond suit.

After using the **Fourth Suit Forcing** with one exception if responder returns to a previously bid suit at the three level or higher the auction is forcing to game. The premise is that responder is able to show support or rebid a suit in any of three ways. He can bid or rebid that suit as cheaply as possible to show minimum (5+ to 9−) values. He can bid or rebid that suit by jumping to show invitational (9+ to 12−) values. When he goes out of his way to use **Fourth Suit Forcing** and then show support at the three level or higher for a previously bid suit responder does so to make the auction forcing since his values are greater (12+ or more) and game should be reached.

The one exception is a repeat of the **Fourth Suit** by responder. This is responder's only way to show a very shapely hand and when this auction occurs it is highly invitational but not forcing.

Example 73:

Responder
♠ 6
♡ AJ1085
♢ KJ9763
♣ 5

With Example hand 73 responder has bid one heart in response to an opening bid of one club and opener has rebid one spade. It would be bizarre for responder to continue by bidding in notrump with a hand that is this distributional. Responder bids two diamonds, *Fourth Suit Forcing* knowing that a better hand is expected but hopes that he will hear a heart preference. If he does not responder can show his shapely hand and invitational values by repeating the *Fourth Suit.*

The following Examples summarize responder's choices with hands in the minimum (5+ to 9−), invitational (9+ to 12−), and game forcing ranges, and illustrate responder's use of **Fourth Suit Forcing.**

Example 74: Responder returns to opener's first suit

a) Responder	b) Responder	c) Responder
♠ 85	♠ K5	♠ K5
♡ QJ64	♡ QJ64	♡ AQJ6
♢ 93	♢ 93	♢ 93
♣ KJ653	♣ KJ653	♣ KJ653

With the hands in Example 74 responder bids one heart in response to an opening bid of one club.

With Example hand 74a) responder takes a preference to two clubs to show his minimum (5+ to 9−) hand.

With Example hand 74b) responder takes a jump preference to three clubs to show his invitational (9+ to 12−) values.

With Example hand 74c) responder bids two diamonds at his second turn which is *Fourth Suit Forcing* if opener's rebid has been one spade or *New Minor Forcing* if opener has rebid one notrump. In either case responder's third bid will be three clubs to show his support with game forcing (12+ or more) values.

Example 75: Responder supports opener's second suit

a) Responder	b) Responder	c) Responder
♠ K642	♠ KJ64	♠ KJ64
♡ QJ64	♡ KJ104	♡ KQ104
◇ 93	◇ 93	◇ 93
♣ 653	♣ 653	♣ Q53

d) Responder	e) Responder	f) Responder
♠ KJ64	♠ KJ64	♠ KJ64
♡ AQ1064	♡ AQ1064	♡ AQ104
◇ 93	◇ 9	◇ 93
♣ Q5	♣ AQ3	♣ AQ3

With Example 75 hands responder has heard a one club opening bid and a rebid of one spade after his one heart response.

With Example hand 75a) responder will pass. He does not expect that values for game exist in the combined hands since opener did not make a jump shift rebid.

With Example hand 75b) responder will raise to two spades. Even though opener did not jump shift at his rebid he may hold sufficient extra values to be able to bid and make game in spades.

With Example hand 75c) responder makes an invitational jump raise to three spades to show his 9+ to 12− values.

With Example hand 75d) responder raises to four spades. This limits his values as he places the contract.

With Example hand 75e) responder makes a *splinter* jump rebid of four diamonds to show his good values with four card spade support and diamond shortness.

With Example hand 75f) responder first uses *Fourth Suit Forcing* and then raises spades. Since he had the option to jump to four spades but did not, this auction shows values beyond what is usually necessary for game and invites a slam while denying the ability to *splinter*.

Example 76: Responder rebids his own suit

a) Responder	b) Responder	c) Responder
♠ 8	♠ 9	♠ 9
♡ KQJ763	♡ KQJ763	♡ KQJ763
◊ J95	◊ K62	◊ AQ3
♣ 1087	♣ J83	♣ J83

All responders in Example 76 begin by bidding one heart after an opening bid in either minor and continue in such fashion as to show a six card suit while also stating their values.

With Example hand 76a) responder rebids two hearts after any minimum rebid by opener to show his minimum (5+ to 9−) values.

With Example hand 76b) responder's rebid is a jump to three hearts to show his invitational (9+ to 12−) values.

With Example hand 76c) if opener has rebid one notrump or raised hearts responder can jump to game in hearts since a fit of some sort has been shown. If opener's rebid is one spade responder uses *Fourth Suit Forcing* by bidding two diamonds. When responder next bids three hearts to show a six card suit opener will support with any doubleton or a singleton high honor.

CHAPTER V
RESPONSES TO OPENING
NOTRUMP BIDS

The systemic responses to opening bids in notrump are complex but complete. They include **Stayman, Jacoby Transfers, Texas Transfers, Minor Suit Stayman, Walsh Relays** and other relay sequences, **Smolen Transfers** after **Stayman**, and **Lebensohl** after interference when the opening bid has been one notrump. In addition included are **Puppet Stayman** and special minor suit slam try auctions in response to opening bids of two notrump, or after a two club opening bid and a two notrump rebid.

This complex of responses allows for description of all types of hands the responder might hold, and simply requires that he employ the correct systemic device to match the hand he was dealt.

The presentation which follows assumes the following notrump ranges:

An opening bid of one notrump shows a good fifteen points to a bad eighteen. A good fifteen will be fifteen that is not 4-3-3-3 in distribution, and will have some good spot cards for which high card points are not assigned. A point should always be added for a good five card (or six card) suit. The one notrump opener may hold a five card major if he also has three cards in the other major and no weak doubleton, or if his five card major suit is so weak that he evaluates it as being only a four card suit.

An opening bid of two notrump shows a good twenty points to twenty two points. The hand may again contain a five card major suit as systemic devices can uncover and identify the five card length quite readily. A very good twenty two points should be evaluated as twenty three.

With twenty three or twenty four points opener first bids two clubs, then rebids two notrump. With twenty five to twenty seven opener rebids three notrump after opening with two clubs, and with twenty eight to thirty points his rebid is a jump to four notrump.

Stayman Auctions

When responder uses **Stayman** after opener's notrump bid he will have at least one four card major except when he holds a specific hand. If responder wishes to invite game in notrump he will have a balanced hand with a good seven to a bad nine points. He will be unable to raise one notrump directly to two for that auction is one of the relay sequences that show a different specific hand type. In order to invite game in notrump, responder uses **Stayman**, then bids two notrump.

If the notrump opener bids either two diamonds or two spades in response to **Stayman**, when responder continues by bidding two notrump it will not be known whether or not he holds a four card major suit. When opener bids two hearts in response to **Stayman** responder will be known not to have a four card major suit when he continues by bidding two notrump. If he held four card support for hearts he would pass or raise hearts, and if he held a four card spade suit with invitational values (7+ to 9−) his continuation would be two spades.

This is possible since in response to **Stayman** opener will bid hearts when he holds four cards in each major. When he bids two hearts a four-four fit in spades might still exist and responder must seek that fit if he holds four spades with his invitational values. Also, since the system incorporates **Jacoby Transfers** responder will not have a five card spade suit when he continues by bidding two spades in this auction.

If responder held five spades and four hearts he would use **Stayman**, but once opener showed a four card heart suit responder would play in that known fit rather than bid spades. And if responder held five spades without four hearts he would not have used **Stayman**, but would have transferred to his five card spade suit.

If responder intends to pass any rebid made by opener, his use of **Stayman** can be done with no values at all. The classic hand pattern for responder to have for this action is 4-4-5-0 distribution. If opener shows a four card major in response to **Stayman** the major suit contract will play far better than one notrump. If instead opener bids two diamonds to deny a four card major suit responder can pass knowing that a diamond fit is likely. If opener's shape happens to be 3-3-2-5 responder's good gamble will not pay the dividends it deserves.

Responder takes a greater risk if he takes this course with hands of other distributional patterns, but he may well improve the contract when his pattern is 4-4-4-1, or even 4-3 (3-4)-5-1.

When opener bids two diamonds in response to **Stayman** and responder continues by bidding either two hearts or two spades, the nature of the auction will be determined by prior partnership agreement. One such agreement is that responder has used **Stayman** with a weak hand that is five-four in the major suits, hoping to be able to pass a major suit response. When opener denies a four card major by bidding two diamonds responder signs off in his five card suit.

Another possible agreement is that when responder continues by bidding a major suit after the two diamond response to **Stayman** he is using a version of the **Smolen** convention. There are two versions of **Smolen** both of which are detailed later in this Chapter.

When opener bids two diamonds in response to **Stayman** and responder next jumps to three notrump, his values will be in the range of a good nine to a bad fifteen points. Responder will be known to hold a four card major suit since he would not use **Stayman** without a four card major unless his values were only invitational (7+ to 9−).

If responder jumps in notrump to a higher level his call will either invite a slam or place the contract in a slam. A jump to four notrump invites a small slam in notrump just as it would if **Stayman** had not been used, and a jump to five notrump invites opener to a grand slam while forcing the contract to at least a small slam.

When opener bids two diamonds in response to **Stayman** and responder continues by bidding three of either minor suit, he shows a hand that has at least five cards in the minor suit he is bidding at this turn as well as a four card major suit, and interest in playing a slam. It is not known at this point in the auction which major suit responder holds.

The auction is similar if opener has shown a four card major in response to **Stayman**. When responder continues by bidding three of a minor suit after opener has bid hearts, if opener also holds four cards in spades he must next bid three spades to show that major suit as well.

Otherwise opener should show that he has interest in a slam in responder's minor suit by cue bidding an ace, but deny interest in a slam by bidding three notrump. Note that opener cannot cue bid the ace of spades if he has first shown a four card heart suit, for instead of showing the spade ace and interest in a slam in responder's minor suit a bid of two spades by opener at that point would show a four card spade suit.

When opener has shown a four card major suit in response to **Stayman**, if responder has a four card fit for that major suit he will pass or raise the major suit to an appropriate level. If his values are invitational (7+ to 9−) he will raise to the three level, but with nine plus points and not enough in values to consider a slam responder raises the major suit to game.

When **Stayman** has divulged a four-four fit and responder has visions of slam, he can continue in one of these ways:

1) He can jump to four clubs which is **Roman Key Card (RKC) Gerber**. This jump by responder establishes the major suit which was bid in response to **Stayman** as the trump suit, and responder asks opener how many key cards he holds. Key cards consist of the four aces and the king of the agreed trump suit (Complete details on RKC appear in Chapter VIII).

2) When responder has shortness in some side suit as well as a fit for the major suit shown in response to **Stayman** in addition to his slam try values, responder announces a hand of that nature by bidding artificially in the unbid major at the three level. When opener hears this description and has no desire to play a slam he signs off at game in the agreed major suit. Although it is known that dummy will include shortness in some side suit opener has no need for that information and does not seek it, so the opening lead must be made before the defense knows which is dummy's short suit.

If opener's hand does seem suited to playing a slam in the major suit fit which has been discovered and he wishes to know the location of responder's short suit he asks where that shortness is by making the cheapest call available at that point in the auction.

When the agreed major suit is hearts, responder will have announced his hand type by bidding three spades, and opener's continuation of three notrump asks for the location of responder's shortness. Responder will then bid four clubs or four diamonds to show his shortness in the suit he bids, or will bid four hearts to show that shortness is in spades.

When the agreed major suit is spades responder will have bid three hearts to announce his hand type, and opener will ask for information about responder's shortness by next bidding three spades. When responder's shortness is a singleton he next bids four clubs, diamonds or hearts to show the location of that singleton.

With spades as the agreed suit an extra step is available in the continuation auction, and responder uses that step to announce that his shortness is a void. The extra step that responder uses to show that he has a void is a bid of three notrump after opener's inquiry of three spades.

When responder shows a void by bidding three notrump opener bids four clubs to ask the void's location. Responder bids either four diamonds or four hearts to show the void in that suit, or shows a club void by bidding four spades.

3) When responder does not have side suit shortness and his hand is not suited to taking control with **RKC Gerber**, he can announce his slam interest and his fit for the suit opener has bid in response to **Stayman** by making an artificial jump to four diamonds. Four diamonds is an otherwise idle bid, the only such bid below the level of game in a major suit.

Use of this jump to four diamonds to send a message telling about responder's specific hand type allows opener to make the decision as to whether or not to pursue a slam. Opener can sign off at game in the agreed suit, or can bid four notrump which is **RKC Blackwood** in the agreed major suit (see Chapter VIII).

Example 77:

a) Responder	b) Responder
♠ J874	♠ J874
♡ 9853	♡ Q95
◇ J7532	◇ 108652
♣ —	♣ 9

With all Example 77 hands responder should bid two clubs in response to an opening bid of one notrump either as *Stayman* or to start a relay to an invitational call of two notrump.

With Example hand 77a) responder will pass opener's next bid no matter what it is. If opener bids a major suit he will play a major suit two level part score which will certainly be more palatable than one notrump would have been. If opener instead bids two diamonds it is likely that a good diamond fit has been found.

With Example hand 77b) responder takes the same course of action although he knows that a four-three contract in hearts may be reached. If that occurs, two hearts should be as good as one notrump would have been.

c) Responder
♠ Q954
♡ KQ3
◇ J1062
♣ 86

d) Responder
♠ Q9
♡ KQ3
◇ J1062
♣ 10865

e) Responder
♠ KJ86
♡ A5
◇ K1095
♣ 963

f) Responder
♠ KQ94
♡ 6
◇ AQJ963
♣ K2

g) Responder
♠ A92
♡ KQ103
◇ K4
♣ KJ86

h) Responder
♠ KQ103
♡ 954
◇ A6
♣ AQ83

i) Responder
♠ AQ83
♡ KJ986
◇ 5
♣ K65

With Example hand 77c) responder will next bid two notrump if opener bids two diamonds to indicate no four card major. If opener bids two spades responder will raise to three spades to invite a game. If opener bids two hearts he does not deny also holding a four card spade suit so responder makes the invitational call of two spades which promises a four card spade suit. If he does not have a spade fit opener can correct to two or three notrump depending on his values since he knows that responder's values are invitational. If he does hold four spades opener can pass or bid to the level indicated by his values.

With Example 77d) responder's two club bid was not truly *Stayman* since he had no interest in playing in a major suit. His two clubs was a relay to allow him to make an invitational call of two notrump at his second turn. It is because the system includes this alternate use for a two club response to one notrump that the two club call must be alerted.

With Example hand 77e) if opener shows a four card spade suit in response to *Stayman* responder bids game in spades. If opener bids either two diamonds or two hearts instead, responder will next bid three notrump. This auction promises that responder does have a four card major suit, but not one bid by opener.

With Example hand 77f) if opener's response to *Stayman* is either two diamonds or two hearts responder next bids three diamonds to show his long diamond suit and slam interest in addition to a four card major. If opener instead bids two spades, responder can bid three hearts to show a four card spade fit and some side short-

160

ness, or he can show his diamond suit depending upon whether he believes that showing a good side suit first or announcing a *splinter* and a fit is of greater importance.

With Example hand 77g) if opener bids either two diamonds or two spades in response to *Stayman* responder continues by making an invitational jump to four notrump. If opener has shown a four card heart suit responder instead jumps to four diamonds which invites a slam as it shows a balanced hand with a four card heart fit.

With Example hand 76h) responder's auction is similar except that it is a four card spade suit in opener's that will cause responder to jump to four diamonds at his rebid. He will make the invitational jump to four notrump if instead opener's rebid is two diamonds or two hearts.

With Example hand 76i) if opener's rebid has been two diamonds responder will next make a *Smolen Transfer* (detailed later in this chapter) but if opener shows four cards in either major responder will next bid the other at the three level to show a four card fit and shortness in some side suit.

Smolen Transfers

Smolen Transfers are the creation of expert Mike Smolen of Marina del Rey, California. They apply after **Stayman** has been used and opener has bid two diamonds to deny possession of a four card major. The **Stayman** bidder will have four cards in one major and five or more cards in the other major. The function of the convention is to arrange for the opening notrump bidder to become declarer if responder's longer major suit is to become the trump suit.

Since the concept was introduced two varieties of the convention have emerged. One variety requires responder to have game forcing values (this will be referred to as **Forcing Smolen**) while the other variety can be used when responder's values are invitational or better (this will be referred to as **Invitational Smolen**).

When **Forcing Smolen** has been agreed, after opener's two diamond response to **Stayman** responder continues by jumping to the three level in his four card major. This jump shows four cards in the suit in which responder has jumped, and since opener has denied a four card fit it will not become the trump suit. However the other major suit is identified by this jump as being five cards or longer.

When opener holds only two cards in responder's known longer major suit he assumes it to be a five card suit and next bids three notrump. If responder's longer major suit is exactly five cards in length he knows that opener has only two card support, so he passes and three notrump becomes the contract.

When opener has shown a doubleton in responder's longer major suit, if that suit is six or seven cards long responder next transfers to that suit by bidding the suit that ranks immediately below it. When responder's longer major suit is hearts his transfer bid is four diamonds. When responder's longer suit is spades his transfer bid is four hearts.

When **Forcing Smolen** has been agreed, if opener bids two diamonds in response to **Stayman** and responder has poor values he can continue by bidding his five card major suit at the two level which asks opener to pass. If responder instead has invitational values his choice is to conceal his distribution and next bid two notrump which is in line with his values, or to overbid and continue by making a jump to the three level in his shorter major suit.

Those who opt to use **Invitational Smolen** continue after a two diamond response to **Stayman** by bidding their four card major suit at the two level. This again shows that responder has five cards or more in the unbid major and that his values are game invitational or better.

When opener has a doubleton in responder's known five card or longer major suit he continues by bidding two notrump with minimum values, but must accept responder's invitation and jump to three notrump when his values are maximum. When opener has three cards in responder's known five card or longer suit he bids that suit to play the five-three (or better) fit, but again must show his values. He bids that suit at the minimum level to show minimum values, but jumps to game in that suit if his values are maximum.

If opener shows minimum values responder will pass when his own values are invitational, but with better values he will continue to game.

Again if opener has shown a doubleton in responder's known longer major suit, when responder has more than five cards in his suit he can transfer by bidding the suit that ranks just below that longer suit.

Using either form of **Smolen,** after opener has bid two diamonds in response to **Stayman,** when responder's suit is six cards or longer he has a choice to transfer immediately to his longer suit at the four level rather than bid in his four card suit. If he elects to make this transfer immediately after opener's two diamond call, responder announces that his values are sufficient for game but that he has no interest in slam.

Since this immediate transfer is available to deny interest in slam, when responder utilizes the auction that causes him to first bid his shorter major and then transfer to his six card or longer suit there is an inference that responder has at least mild interest in slam. If opener's hand is very slam oriented instead of transferring as requested he can make a cue bid to show his slam interest, or jump to four notrump which becomes **RKC Blackwood** in the agreed trump suit.

When **Invitational Smolen** is agreed and responder has a weak hand with five-four in the majors he does not have the luxury of using **Stayman** to explore for fits in both major suits. He simply transfers to the longer or better major at the two level and then passes.

However, **Invitational Smolen** allows jumps to the three level to have a different meaning after **Stayman** and a two diamond rebid by opener. In that auction if responder jumps to three hearts he shows five-five in the majors and invitational values. Opener may decline by passing or correcting to three spades, or may accept the invitation by bidding four of either major.

If responder instead jumps to three spades in the same auction he shows five-five in the majors with game forcing values. Opener continues by chosing the trump suit and bidding it at the four level.

Example 78:

a) Responder
♠ AQ85
♡ KJ963
◇ 84
♣ 62

b) Responder
♠ AQ85
♡ J10963
◇ 84
♣ 62

c) Responder
♠ AQ8542
♡ AK96
◇ 84
♣ 6

d) Responder
♠ AQ8542
♡ QJ96
◇ 84
♣ 6

e) Responder
♠ AQ854
♡ KJ963
◇ 84
♣ 6

f) Responder
♠ A9854
♡ QJ963
◇ 84
♣ 6

g) Responder
♠ KQ842
♡ 96532
◇ 84
♣ 6

All Example 78 responders have heard an opening bid of one notrump.

With Example hand 78a) responder uses *Stayman* by bidding two clubs. If opener shows a four card major suit responder raises to game. If opener bids two diamonds, when *Invitational Smolen* is agreed responder next bids two spades to show his four card major and indicate longer hearts. If opener rejects the invitation by bidding either two notrump or three hearts responder continues to game in that denomination with his game going values. If *Forcing Smolen* has been agreed responder shows his hand with a jump to three spades and passes when opener determines the contract.

With Example hand 78b) responder again uses *Stayman* and raises a major suit response to the three level. If opener rebids two diamonds, when *Invitational Smolen* has been agreed responder can continue by bidding two spades and will pass opener's next action whatever it may be. If *Forcing Smolen* has been agreed responder can next sign off in two hearts which is an underbid, bid three spades and force to game which is an overbid, or bid two notrump which is his value bid but does not show his five card heart suit.

With Example hand 78c) responder again uses *Stayman* and if opener shows a four card major suit bids the other major at the three level to show a four card fit and shortness in some side suit. If opener bids two diamonds responder next bids two hearts to show his longer spade suit if *Invitational Smolen* is in use or jumps to three hearts if *Forcing Smolen* has been agreed. If opener then shows a doubleton spade and responder transfers to spades he has made a mild slam try.

With Example hand 78d) if *Stayman* finds no four card major in opener's hand responder can next jump to four hearts to transfer to spades and deny slam interest.

With Example hand 78e) if *Invitational Smolen* is agreed responder can use *Stayman* and after a two diamond response jump to three spades to show a game forcing hand with five-five in the majors. If *Forcing Smolen* is agreed the partnership should also have the agreement that a direct jump to three of a major suit in response to one notrump shows a five-five hand with hearts being invitational and spades forcing. Responder in this instance will not use *Stayman* but will jump directly to three spades.

With Example hand 78f) responder will show an invitational hand with five-five in the majors by bidding three hearts directly or after *Stayman* depending on the type of *Smolen* that has been agreed.

With Example hand 78g) if *Forcing Smolen* is agreed responder can first use *Stayman* to find a four card major in opener's hand, and sign off in spades if he does not find one. If *Invitational Smolen* is agreed responder does not have the luxury of trying for both suits and must transfer to spades and pass.

Jacoby Transfer Auctions

Perhaps the most popular of the many contributions of the late, great Oswald Jacoby to bridge theory is the concept of transfer bids in response to notrump opening bids. The use of transfers does two positive things for the bidding side. The transfer causes the strong balanced hand to become declarer when responder's long suit becomes the trump suit, and the use of transfers gives responder great latitude in invitational and forcing situations.

In response to an opening bid of one notrump, responder's call of two hearts is a transfer to spades. It promises that responder has five or more spades but says nothing about the rest of his hand. Responder may then pass or bid on as his hand indicates.

If opener has four card spade support and a good hand, when he hears the transfer bid he can show his good hand for play in spades by jumping to three spades instead of bidding just two spades. If responder had intended to pass after making his transfer bid but has values that are almost invitational, he will be able to bid a·game that would not have been bid if opener had not shown his good hand for spades.

On occasion responder's hand will be very weak and three spades will fail by a trick. If this is true the opponents may have been preempted out of an auction where they might have balanced and found their own makable contract.

When opener has a good hand for play in spades but only three card support, he describes that hand by bidding at the three level in his better minor suit. The distinction between three and four card support for spades can be of great importance to responder who may not only have to decide at what level to play, but also what to do if the opponents compete.

When opener has made this descriptive call to show three card support for spades, responder will continue by bidding three hearts which is a repeat of the transfer bid. This again causes opener to become declarer at the final spade contract, whatever the level. Responder then passes or continues as his hand suggests.

Example 79:

	a) Opener		b) Opener
♠	KQ87	♠	AK7
♡	A5	♡	A943
◇	AJ98	◇	86
♣	K65	♣	KQJ4

With the hands of Example 79 opener has started with one no-trump and heard responder bid two hearts which is a transfer to spades.

With Example hand 79a) opener jumps to three spades to show his maximum with four card support. If responder's hand was not quite good enough to have made a game invitation, opener's descriptive jump will allow responder to bid a game which will most likely make. If responder has nothing but five spades to the jack three spades will have little play unless responder is short in diamonds, but the opponents are favorites to be able to make four hearts and will not be able to get into the auction.

With Example hand 79b) opener bids three clubs to show a ha.. that is good for play in spades with a three card fit and a concentration of values in clubs. This leaves room for responder to repeat his transfer by bidding three hearts.

When responder to the opening bid of one notrump bids two diamonds he may have one of two types of hand. Opener should assume that responder has hearts for most often the two diamond bid will be intended as a transfer to that suit. If responder continues by passing or bidding anything other than two spades, he confirms that he has hearts.

If responder does continue by bidding two spades his message is that rather than hearts, he has a long suit that he wants to describe. Responder uses this auction to make a slam try in a long minor suit, or to describe any totally solid suit.

Responder's bid of two spades asks opener to mark time by bidding two notrump after which responder's next bid will describe his long suit.

Responder continues by bidding three clubs to make a slam try with a broken club suit, or three diamonds to similarly show a broken diamond suit with slam interest.

If responder instead continues by bidding three hearts he shows a nearly solid club suit, missing only one of the top three honor cards. Alternately a rebid of three spades will show a nearly solid diamond suit.

When responder's rebid after the relay is three notrump he shows a completely solid suit with seven winners in his hand. Although he does not tell which suit he has, the notrump opening bidder should be able to tell. Responder's solid suit will be the one in which opener has no honor cards. A rebid in notrump at each successive higher level shows the same hand type but indicates one additional winner for each additional level.

This sequence is called the **Walsh Relay**. Its creator is Richard Walsh, formerly a tournament star from Los Angeles, who has given up bridge and now resides in Switzerland.

Example 80:

a) Responder	b) Responder	c) Responder
♠ AQ3	♠ KQ3	♠ AQ3
♡ 5	♡ 5	♡ 2
◇ K97	◇ AJ10876	◇ 954
♣ KJ10964	♣ A97	♣ AQJ1085

d) Responder	e) Responder
♠ Q92	♠ AKQJ63
♡ A63	♡ 5
◇ AKJ1074	◇ A104
♣ 5	♣ 732

After an opening bid of one notrump each of the responders in Example 80 needs to describe a one suiter with interest in slam. All responders begin by bidding two diamonds which opener will believe to be a transfer to hearts. After opener bids two hearts as requested each responder then bids two spades to cancel the heart transfer and ask opener to bid two notrump. After opener bids two notrump continuation sequences are as follows:

With Example hand 80a) responder bids three clubs to show a broken club suit.

With Example hand 80b) responder bids three diamonds to show a broken diamond suit.

With Example hand 80c) responder bids three hearts which artificially shows a club suit that is nearly solid, missing one of the top three honors.

With Example hand 80d) responder bids three spades which artificially shows a diamond suit that is nearly solid, missing one of the top three honors.

With Example hand 80e) responder bids three notrump which shows that he has some solid suit and a hand with seven winners. The one notrump opener will be able to determine the identity of the solid suit since he will not see any spade honors in his own hand.

When opener hears responder bid two diamonds and his opening notrump bid includes good support for hearts, he must continue carefully since rather than a hand with hearts responder might have the hand for a **Walsh Relay**. Opener's rebid to show good support for hearts must not get in the way if the relay sequence was intended.

To show a hand that has good support for hearts, opener bids two spades. When opener bids two spades to show good heart support and responder does have hearts, he bids two notrump to re-transfer to hearts. If responder instead makes any call at the three level he describes a hand as he would have after the **Walsh Relay** had been completed to send a message about a long suit and slam interest.

Example 81:

a) Opener	b) Responder
♠ KJ5	♠ A4
♡ AQ97	♡ J86532
◇ A4	◇ 962
♣ K1097	♣ 83

With Example hand 81a) opener bids one notrump. Responder with Example 81b) transfers to hearts and opener bids two spades to show his excellent hand for hearts. Responder bids two notrump to show that he truly has hearts and opener duly bids three hearts. Although responder's original plan was to transfer and then pass, knowledge that opener's hand is good for hearts allows him to continue to game. The game would have not been reached if opener had not been able to show his good hand for the auction.

After responder has made a transfer bid to either major suit and opener has bid that suit as requested, with any weak hand responder will pass and let opener play in the major suit at the two level.

When responder's hand is otherwise balanced and he has the values to bid on, he will bid notrump at the appropriate level. When opener hears responder's rebid in notrump he will understand that responder's suit is exactly five cards long. When he holds only two card support for the suit of responder's transfer bid opener will elect to play in notrump, but when he has three or four card support opener will correct from notrump to responder's major suit at the appropriate level.

When responder has rebid two notrump opener must accept or reject the invitation to game that has been tendered. He should pass with a doubleton in responder's major suit and minimum values but carry on to three notrump if his values are maximum. With a better fit for responder's major suit and minimum values opener corrects to that suit at the three level, but if his values are maximum he must jump to game as he makes his correction.

When responder has values enough for game and holds a second suit of four cards or more, after transferring he will describe his hand and offer a choice of contracts by bidding his second suit. Since this auction is forcing to game opener needs only indicate the denomination in which he wishes to play when he makes his next bid.

Opener can return to responder's major suit to show three or four card support. He can return to three notrump to show a doubleton in responder's major suit and no real interest in responder's second suit. Since he has been warned that responder has at least nine cards in the two suits he has bid, opener needs to have the two remaining suits well under control if three notrump is to be the best contract.

If responder's second suit is attractive to opener and he wants to show his fit for that suit and indicate interest in slam, opener will cue bid an ace at this point in the auction. With only game going values responder will sign off at three notrump, but if his values also suggest slam he will also cue bid to alert opener to that fact.

When responder transfers to a major suit and then raises he promises at least six cards in the suit. A raise to the three level invites opener to bid game. If responder raises the suit of his transfer bid to game he has made a mild slam try. If responder had wanted to get to game in his suit without suggesting slam, instead of transferring at the two level he would have used a **Texas Transfer** (described later in this Chapter). When responder has transferred at the two level and jumped to game in his suit, opener may pass, cue bid, or bid four notrump which is **RKC Blackwood** in the agreed major suit.

When opener bids two notrump in response to either **Stayman** or a **Jacoby Transfer** bid he shows an unexpected hand for his one notrump opening bid. The focus of his hand will be a good six or seven card minor suit and his distribution will be either 6-3-2-2 or 7-2-2-2. Opener should take this action only when he feels that it is important to play in notrump or his minor suit rather than in a major suit which responder might suggest. Responder may escape to opener's minor suit by bidding three clubs and opener will pass or correct to diamonds.

In this auction, when responder has values and wants to play in game, he is warned of the nature of opener's hand. He should insist on playing in a major suit only when he feels that it will be superior to a game in notrump, and when two small cards in opener's hand will be adequate support for the major suit that he feels should be the trump suit.

Example 82:

a) Responder
♠ Q8543
♡ J106432
♢ 84
♣ —

b) Responder
♠ 1082
♡ KQ943
♢ Q5
♣ J96

c) Responder
♠ A82
♡ KQ943
♢ Q5
♣ J96

d) Responder
♠ 42
♡ KQ9843
♢ Q86
♣ 95

e) Responder
♠ 43
♡ KJ985
♢ AJ102
♣ 95

f) Responder
♠ 4
♡ KQ9843
♢ KJ6
♣ 954

With Example hand 82a) in response to an opening bid of one no-trump you wish to escape to a major suit at the two level. Most likely you will transfer to hearts and then pass. If you have agreed to play *Forcing Smolen* you might first use *Stayman* since it is possible that opener has four spades. If his response is two diamonds you can still sign off at two hearts.

With Example hand 82b) in response to one notrump you should first transfer to two hearts and then bid two notrump. This invites game and gives opener the choice of denomination.

With Example hand 82c) in response to one notrump you should transfer to hearts and then bid three notrump. Opener will pass if he has only two hearts, but with three or more will correct and play four hearts.

With Example hand 82d) in response to one notrump you should transfer to hearts and then raise to three. This will show partner that you have six or more hearts and leave him to choose the level but not the denomination.

With Example hand 82e) in response to one notrump you should transfer to hearts and then bid three diamonds. This auction does not cancel hearts and say that you really had diamonds all the time. It says that in addition to the five card heart suit shown by your transfer bid you also hold four or more diamonds and values enough to play game.

With Example hand 82f) do not transfer to two hearts and then jump to four hearts since that would be a mild slam try. This hand calls for a *Texas Transfer* (see the next section in this Chapter).

g) Responder	h) Opener	i) Opener
♠ 4	♠ K6	♠ A7
♡ KQ9843	♡ K8	♡ K6
◇ KJ6	◇ Q105	◇ AKQ965
♣ A95	♣ AK9865	♣ 876

With Example hand 82g) your hand is good enough to transfer to two hearts and then jump to four. Your values are now adequate for a slam invitation.

With Example 82h) or 82i) if you have elected to open with one no-trump (there is no reason for any other opening bid with Example hand 82h) and responder uses either *Stayman* or a *Jacoby Transfer* make the unusual bid of two notrump. This will alert responder to the fact that your hand is most suitable for play in notrump or in your minor suit.

The Texas Transfer

Oswald Jacoby created the **Texas Transfer** as a companion to his transfers at the immediate level. When responder to an opening no-trump bid transfers by jumping to the four level instead of at the two level he shows a different kind of responding hand. He will always have a six card or longer suit, and his values will either be adequate for game with no extras or so good that responder will next drive toward a slam. With values only to suggest a slam responder transfers at the two level and then raises to game to describe to opener the nature of his hand.

Texas Transfers have great value in competitive situations after there has been an opening bid of one notrump. When the competition has been at the two level or with a bid of three clubs responder is still able to make his **Texas Transfer** jump to the four level without resultant confusion.

If the competitive bid has been at a level higher than three clubs there is a problem with the use of **Texas Transfers** since a cue bid of the suit bid by opponents becomes **Stayman**. If an opponent has bid three diamonds after partner's opening bid of one notrump, responder's bid of four diamonds is **Stayman** and responder must make a natural bid of four hearts when he holds hearts or four spades when he holds spades.

When opener has a concentration of high cards facing responder's shortness he will rebid three notrump to show values that are wasted for play at a slam, but will provide adequate stoppers for play at game in notrump.

When opener does not have wasted values facing responder's shortness he also does not have adequate stoppers to play in notrump. If opener has shown a four card minor suit at his rebid the trump suit will have been established and opener's continuation will be a cue bid of a first round control. If opener has denied holding a four card minor suit in response to **Minor Suit Stayman** he will introduce a three card minor suit holding, trying to find a five-three minor suit fit in which to play.

When opener bids three of a minor suit in response to **Minor Suit Stayman** if responder continues to four of the same minor he intends his bid as **RKC** in the agreed minor suit. By keeping the ace asking bid at this low level the bidding side will be able to stop short of slam when enough controls are not present.

Example 84:

a) Responder	b) Responder	c) Responder
♠ 1063	♠ 5	♠ 102
♡ 9	♡ 86	♡ K4
◇ Q108762	◇ K8532	◇ KQ105
♣ J43	♣ J10654	♣ AQ963

With Example hand 84a) responder to an opening bid of one notrump would rather play in a diamond contract even at the three level than have opener play one notrump. Responder bids two spades, *Minor Suit Stayman*. If opener bids three diamonds to show four cards in that suit, responder will pass, but if opener bids either two notrump or three clubs, responder corrects to three diamonds and opener must pass.

With Example hand 84b) responder to an opening bid of one notrump knows that a minor suit partial will be a better contract than one notrump. He uses *Minor Suit Stayman* by bidding two spades and will pass if opener shows that he has a four card minor suit fit. If opener bids two notrump to deny holding a four card minor responder continues by bidding three clubs to offer opener a choice of trump suits. Opener will pass or correct to three diamonds depending upon his minor suit holdings.

With Example hand 84c) after using *Minor Suit Stayman* in response to an opening bid of one notrump responder next bids three notrump. This rebid shows two-two in the major suits along with five-four in the minors and mild interest in slam.

d) Responder
♠ K2
♡ K4
◇ KQ105
♣ AJ963

e) Responder
♠ A5
♡ 6
◇ KQ642
♣ AJ985

f) Responder
♠ 9
♡ A63
◇ KQ95
♣ AJ1086

g) Responder
♠ 7
♡ 5
◇ AQ984
♣ KQJ763

With Example hand 84d) the auction is similar, but responder has the values to jump to four notrump at his rebid to strongly urge a slam while showing his distribution.

With Example hand 84e) after using *Minor Suit Stayman* responder next bids three hearts to show shortness there. If opener shows heart values by bidding three notrump responder will pass, but if opener continues by showing a control or seeking a minor suit fit responder has a good hand for slam since he knows that all of opener's values will be working.

With Example hand 84f) responder again shows his major suit shortness after having used *Minor Suit Stayman*. This time if opener has not shown a minor suit fit and also has not bid three notrump, unless opener can show that he has three card club support this hand should be careful not to get too high.

With Example hand 84g) if opener bids two notrump responder will show his spade shortness. If opener rebids three notrump responder will then also show his heart shortness and pass if opener bids four notrump since opener will have most of his values in the major suits.

If opener does show a four card minor suit responder continues by bidding four of that same minor suit which is *RKC* seeking key cards in opener's hand for slam. Since responder has shown length in both minor suits there will be six key cards to be shown, the four aces and both minor suit kings. Regardless of which minor suit has been agreed if opener can show three key cards a small slam should be easy, and if opener shows four key cards a grand slam can be bid.

Two Notrump Transfer Auctions

When responder bids two notrump after an opening bid of one notrump, his bid is conventional. Instead of being an invitational raise in notrump, responder's bid is a relay which requires opener to bid three clubs. Responder will have one of two types of hand:

1) Responder may have a club bust. He will know that a part score in clubs will fare better than a contract of one notrump even if clubs must be played at the three level. Responder will have at least six clubs and very little in high cards.

2) Responder may have a good three suited hand with interest in slam. His distribution will be 5-4-4-0 or 4-4-4-1. When he does have a five card suit that suit will be a minor suit rather than a major. With a 5-4-4-0 pattern that included a five card major responder would instead use **Stayman** followed by a **Smolen Transfer** if necessary if one of the four card suits were the other major. If the two four card suits were both minor suits responder would transfer to his five card major and then bid clubs. Five card major suits are excluded from the convention being discussed because a five-three major suit fit is too important to lose.

When responder has bid two notrump and opener has bid three clubs as required, responder shows his good three suited hand by bidding his short suit at his next turn. Opener then knows that responder is interested in slam in one of the three remaining suits.

If responder's short suit is clubs he has a choice of ways to send the message of the location of his shortness. If responder has only mild interest in slam he bids three notrump to show club shortness. When his slam interest is strong responder instead bids four clubs to show his shortness in clubs.

Opener is again asked to evaluate the placement of his high cards. When he holds a concentration of values facing responder's announced shortness opener knows to sign off and play a game contract in notrump. He will be able to sign off at three notrump unless responder has bid four clubs. If opener signs off at four notrump over four clubs he does so knowing that responder has excellent values.

When opener is interested in playing a slam in one of the suits that responder has shown, he must select the trump suit. If the suit he selects is a major suit and he bids that suit at the four level he shows interest only in playing a game contract in the major. Opener can bid a major suit at the three level and let a slam probe ensue if that is possible, jump to five of the major invitationally, or simply bid a slam in the major suit as he has been invited to do.

If the suit that opener selects is a minor suit and he bids that suit below the level of game the auction is forcing. Since responder's auction has invited a slam the bidding will not stop at a part score but will at least reach the game level.

Example 85:

a) Responder	b) Responder	c) Responder
♠ 854	♠ KJ104	♠ AK94
♡ J3	♡ 7	♡ KQ63
◇ 96	◇ AJ83	◇ AJ942
♣ K98543	♣ AQ104	♣ —

d) Responder
♠ KJ64
♡ KQ63
◇ AJ94
♣ 7

With Example hand 85a) responder to an opening bid of one no-trump wants to play a part score in clubs. To arrange this he responds by bidding two notrump which is not an invitation in notrump. It is a relay which requires opener to bid three clubs. This having been accomplished, responder passes.

With Example hand 85b) after the relay to three clubs, responder continues by bidding three hearts. This announces shortness in hearts and a three suited hand with interest in slam. If opener next bids three notrump responder should pass, for opener will have good heart values which will be stoppers for notrump, but wasted for play in a suit contract.

With Example hand 85c) after the relay to three clubs responder next bids four clubs to show club shortness and a strong desire to play in a slam. If opener does not have wasted club values it is reasonable to believe that a grand slam might be reached in one of responder's suits. If opener tries to sign off at four notrump responder's values are so great that he should insist on reaching a slam either in diamonds or in notrump. A jump to six diamonds should offer that choice since it is known that responder cannot have more than five cards in diamonds.

With Example hand 85d) responder again has shortness in clubs to show after making the relay to three clubs. This time his interest is only mild and he describes his hand with club shortness by bidding three notrump over three clubs.

Jump Responses in Suits

1) Responder's jump to three of a minor suit facing a one notrump opening bid invites opener to bid three notrump. It promises that responder has six or seven cards in his minor suit headed by the ace-queen or king-queen with little or nothing else in values. If responder's suit is headed by the ace-king it is too good for this action.

If opener has a top honor card in responder's minor suit and a reasonable stopper in each of the other suits, responder's suit should produce enough tricks for the notrump game to be made. When he has a hand of this nature opener should accept the invitation and bid three notrump.

Even with maximum values, opener should reject the game invitation when he does not have a fitting honor card for responder's minor suit. The fitting honor card is necessary since without it the source of tricks that is needed will probably be inadequate. Opener should reject the invitation and pass. The contract of three of responder's minor suit will be the best place to play.

When responder's suit is as good as six headed by the ace-king there is too much chance that three notrump will be made even when opener's holding in the minor suit is two small cards. Opener will be able to duck one round of the suit and then the suit should run. Instead of jumping to three of his minor suit when his holding includes the ace and king, responder should raise notrump by first using **Stayman** and then rebidding two notrump.

Example 86:

a) Responder	b) Opener	c) Opener
♠ 963	♠ AK4	♠ AK4
♡ 4	♡ QJ6	♡ KQJ6
◇ AQ9862	◇ K3	◇ 73
♣ 987	♣ K653	♣ KJ65

With Example hand 86a) responder would bid three diamonds in response to an opening bid of one notrump.

With Example hand 86b) when opener hears the invitational jump to three diamonds he knows that six or seven diamond tricks are available in notrump due to his fitting king in that suit. He also has reasonable stoppers in all of the other suits, and should bid three notrump.

With Example hand 86c) opener has a very good hand for his one notrump bid but should not bid three notrump. He lacks the fitting honor card for diamonds that will cause the suit to become a source of tricks.

2) Responder's jump to three of a major suit can be used to show any of several types of hands. Most commonly, one of the following three agreements is used in System partnerships.

a) The jump to three of a major suit can be used to show a broken six or seven card suit with interest in slam. Opener is warned that if slam is to be played he needs to hold at least one fitting honor card in responder's major suit. Otherwise there will be trump losers which does not augur well for the making of twelve tricks.

When a jump to three of a major is used in one of the other ways described here, it is possible to show this sort of hand by using a **Walsh Relay**, then jumping to four clubs to show a broken heart suit or four diamonds to show a broken spade suit. After the **Walsh Relay** if responder jumps to four hearts or four spades he shows a nearly solid suit, missing one of the top three honors.

b) When the partnership has agreed to play **Forcing Smolen**, that convention can be complimented by the use of a direct jump to three hearts to show a hand with five-five in the majors and invitational values, and a jump to three spades to show five-five in the majors with game forcing values.

When these jumps are agreed and responder jumps to three hearts, with minimum values opener can pass or correct to three spades, declining the game invitation. With maximum values opener can bid game in either of the major suits, selecting the suit of the best fit to be the trump suit.

When responder's jump has been to three spades opener selects the trump suit by bidding either four hearts or four spades with no concern about values. If opener has the rare hand with doubletons in both major suits, when he bids three notrump responder will know to pass since no five-three major suit fit exists.

c) Yet another use for a jump to three of a major suit by responder is to show shortness in the major suit bid, at least five-four distribution in the minor suits, and values enough to make a game but not enough to suggest a slam (with values enough to suggest a slam responder would instead use **Minor Suit Stayman**).

Opener knows that with a concentration of values facing responder's announced shortness three notrump will be an adequate contract, but if his values in that suit are not good enough to stop the suit for play in notrump (a double stopper is necessary), a suit contract should be reached.

With a good four card holding in the unbid major suit, opener can offer that as a possible trump suit, since responder could have a three card fit for that major and the best game contract could be in the four-three fit.

When responder notes that opener could not bid three notrump after being told of a short major suit, responder cooperates in the search for a playable trump suit. If the other major has been suggested by opener, responder agrees if he holds three cards in that major but otherwise offers a five card minor suit. If opener has suggested a minor suit contract responder will have ample support since his first call promised a minimum of four cards in each minor suit.

3) Responder's jump to four of a red suit is a **Texas Transfer** (detailed earlier in this Chapter).

4) Responder's jump to four clubs is **Gerber**, asking for the number of aces in opener's hand. It is possible to agree upon an **RKC** variation in which opener continues by bidding four diamonds to show zero or three aces, four hearts to show one or four aces, four spades to show exactly two aces but to deny interest in slam, and four notrump to again show two aces but show a hand that is interested in slam.

5) A response of four spades to an opening bid of one notrump appears to be a call for which a meaning can be assigned. We suggest that this idle bid be utilized to invite a slam in notrump, but to also show the number of controls in responder's hand.

Counting an ace as two controls and a king as one control, there is a total of twelve controls in the deck. If slam is to be bid in notrump the bidding side should have ten or more of those controls. They might bid a slam missing one ace or two kings, but if three kings or an ace and a king are missing the slam is very risky and should not be bid.

When responder makes a jump raise from one notrump to four notrump to invite a notrump slam, he shows the values expected for the invitation he makes, but limits the number of controls in his hand to a maximum of five. When opener is rich in controls he can bid the slam, but if he has doubt, he next shows the number of controls in his hand so responder can judge to either bid six notrump or sign off at five notrump.

If opener continues by bidding five clubs he shows five controls (the minimum needed if responder has his maximum), five diamonds will show six controls, five hearts will show seven controls, etc. Responder will know exactly how many controls the bidding side has and whether to bid five notrump or six.

Of course opener can pass four notrump if he has a minimum and should not accept the slam invitation.

Responder utilizes the otherwise idle jump to four spades to again invite a small slam in notrump, but the four spade bid promises that responder has six or more controls. If opener has minimum values and should reject the slam try he bids four notrump and responder will pass. If opener has the values to accept it will be rare that his side does not have sufficient controls to bid and make six notrump.

Example 87:

a) Responder	b) Responder	c) Responder
♠ A8	♠ A9854	♠ AQ854
♡ KJ109542	♡ QJ963	♡ KJ963
◇ 6	◇ 84	◇ 84
♣ K32	♣ 6	♣ 6

With Example hand 87a) responder to an opening bid of one no-trump would like to make a slam try to show his broken heart suit. If an immediate jump to three hearts is agreed to show this kind of hand, that is the course responder will take. If a jump to three hearts is used to show another kind of hand, the partnership might agree to use a *Walsh Relay* followed by a jump to four clubs to show this hand.

With Example 87b) if *Invitational Smolen* has been agreed this hand will be shown by the use of *Stayman* followed by a jump to three hearts to invite game with five-five in the major suits. If *Forcing Smolen* has been agreed that auction is not available for this hand, and it can be agreed that a direct jump to three hearts in response to the one notrump opening bid is used for this description.

With Example hand 87c) the situation is similar to that in 87b) except that responder's jump will be to three spades to show a game forcing hand with five-five in the majors.

Example 88:

a) Opener	b) Opener	c) Opener
♠ AJ52	♠ AQJ6	♠ AJ5
♡ AQJ6	♡ A653	♡ A653
◇ J105	◇ J105	◇ K109
♣ K7	♣ K7	♣ K73

d) Responder
♠ K83
♡ 5
♢ AQ74
♣ Q10865

e) Responder
♠ K3
♡ 5
♢ AQ742
♣ Q10865

Example 88 illustrates the use of a jump to three of a major suit in response to an opening bid of one notrump to show shortness in the suit of the jump, at least five-four distribution in the minor suits, and values enough to make game but no interest in slam.

With Example hand 88a) opener who has bid one notrump hears responder jump to three hearts. With good values in hearts opener next bids three notrump to end the auction.

With Example hand 88b) in the same auction opener's hearts are not strong enough to play three notrump and he is not eager to play in a minor suit. Opener bids three spades to offer to play in a four-three spade fit if responder has three card support.

With Example hand 88c) opener cannot offer to play game either in notrump or the unbid major suit, so he runs to four clubs. He expects that if responder has only four clubs and five diamonds he will correct to diamonds on the way to a minor suit game so that the best trump suit will eventually be reached.

Both responder 88d) and 88e) have jumped to three hearts in response to an opening bid of one notrump. If either hears a rebid of three notrump from opener, a pass is in order.

With Example hand 88d) if responder hears opener continue by bidding three spades, he will raise to four spades and game will be played in the four-three fit. If he hears opener continue by bidding four clubs instead, he will raise to five clubs, but if he held only four clubs and five diamonds, he would offer to play in diamonds on the way.

With Example hand 88e) if responder hears opener continue to three spades he will bid four clubs to deny a three card spade holding. When opener has three card club support he will raise, but with a doubleton club and three diamonds he will bid four diamonds.

Example 89:

a) Opener	b) Opener
♠ KQ7	♠ AQ7
♡ A105	♡ A83
◇ A987	◇ KQJ107
♣ K65	♣ 105

With Example hand 89a) opener has bid one notrump and hears a response of four clubs. The agreement is that *RKC Gerber* will be used. Opener bids four spades to show two aces but no particular interest in slam.

With Example hand 89b) in the same auction opener bids four notrump to show two aces and indicate that he likes the idea of a slam. His good five card diamond suit will be a source of tricks, and that factor makes him like his hand.

Example 90:

a) Opener	b) Responder	c) Responder
♠ KQ7	♠ J6	♠ J6
♡ AJ5	♡ K107	♡ KQ10
◇ A9632	◇ KQ5	◇ QJ5
♣ Q8	♣ AK943	♣ AK943

Opener in Example 90a) bids one notrump and hears responder raise to four notrump to invite a notrump slam and show five or fewer controls. Opener has the values to accept the slam invitation, but checks for controls on the way. He bids five clubs to show exactly five controls in his hand.

Responder with Example hand 90b) adds his own five controls to the five shown by opener and bids six notrump.

Responder with Example hand 90c) has only four controls. Since he knows that three controls are missing he signs off by bidding five notrump.

Lebensohl

The **Lebensohl** convention is reputedly the creation of expert Ken Lebensold of New York City, but received its name from an article which appeared in **The Bridge World** magazine. The author of the article attempted to give credit to the assumed originator, having first been exposed to the idea when playing against Lebensold. However the author of the article did not remember the correct spelling of the name, and the spelling deviation which was the title of the article stuck with the convention from that presentation forward.

The function of the **Lebensohl** convention is to define the meaning of auctions that ensue when an opponent has interfered after the opening bid of one notrump. Responder's actions are as follows:

1) An immediate jump to three notrump shows adequate values to play that contract, but denies that responder has a stopper in the suit of the overcall.

2) A cue bid of the suit of the overcall is **Stayman**, asking opener to show a four card major suit, but this auction also denies that responder has a stopper in the suit of the overcall. Responder's values must be adequate for game when he makes this cue bid.

3) A suit bid at the two level after the overcall is natural and non-forcing. Responder will have limited values and at least five cards in his suit.

4) A new suit at the three level again shows five or more cards in length and is forcing. By agreement, a partnership may choose to play that the bid is forcing only if it is in a major suit, since with a good hand and a minor suit responder would be content in most cases to jump to three notrump. If this agreement is in effect, a minor suit bid at the three level is invitational as if responder has jumped to three of that minor suit when there has been no interference (see discussions of that auction earlier in this Chapter).

The cornerstone of the convention which allows the agreements stated above to work is the use of a bid of two notrump by responder after the interference as a relay bid. When responder bids two notrump after the interference he requires opener to bid three clubs. When opener bids three clubs as required, responder's continuations are as follows:

1) A bid of three notrump shows that responder has a stopper in the suit of the overcall as well as values enough to bid this game. If responder had not held a stopper he would have bid three notrump directly as stated in 1) above.

2) A cue bid of the suit of the overcall is **Stayman**, asking opener to bid a four card major suit, but this auction promises that responder has a stopper in the suit of the overcall. Without a stopper responder would have made an immediate cue bid as stated in 2) above. Again responder's values must be sufficient to produce a game.

3) A new suit bid after the relay is natural and non-forcing if responder could not bid that suit at the two level. If responder could have bid that suit at the two level and instead used the **Lebensohl** relay, the auction is invitational. Responder promises a suit of five cards or more but wants opener to make the choice between game and part score.

4) If the overcall has been two clubs and that call was natural, if responder relays to three clubs and then continues by bidding three diamonds, that call is **Stayman** promising a club stopper. Responder could have bid two diamonds naturally after the two club overcall if he wanted to play there, and could have jumped to three diamonds to invite.

If the overcall of two clubs is artificial and shows a one suited hand with the suit to be shown at the overcaller's next turn (this is part of the convention known as **Hamilton** or **Cappelletti** which is very popular), responder does not use **Lebensohl**. In this auction responder uses a double as **Stayman** and all other system bids apply as though there had not been interference.

Since two notrump cannot be bid naturally, a double of the overcall can be used to show a reasonably balanced hand that has the values of a raise to two notrump. The double should show at least two cards in the overcaller's suit. Since it is not a penalty double (although opener is free to convert it) an alert is required.

Example 91:

a) **Responder**
♠ K108
♡ 754
◇ AQ75
♣ J63

b) **Responder**
♠ K1086
♡ 75
◇ AQ75
♣ J63

c) **Responder**
♠ K10875
♡ 75
◇ Q75
♣ J63

d) **Responder**
♠ J8
♡ 75
◇ J63
♣ KQ9765

e) **Responder**
♠ K10985
♡ 75
◇ AQ7
♣ J63

f) **Responder**
♠ K10985
♡ 75
◇ A75
♣ J63

g) **Responder**
♠ K108
♡ A75
◇ Q754
♣ J63

h) **Responder**
♠ K1085
♡ A7
◇ Q754
♣ J63

i) **Responder**
♠ Q8
♡ 75
◇ Q109763
♣ J63

j) **Responder**
♠ K108
♡ 754
◇ A875
♣ J63

With all Example 91 hands you have heard partner open with one notrump and your right hand opponent has bid two hearts.

With Example hand 91a) bid three notrump. You have the values to play a notrump game and your call tells opener that you do not have a heart stopper.

With Example hand 91b) bid three hearts. This call is *Stayman* looking for a four-four fit in spades and showing values enough for game, but denying a heart stopper.

With Example hand 91c) bid two spades. This call is natural and non-forcing.

With Example hand 91d) bid three clubs unless you have agreed that a minor suit bid at the three level is forcing. Your three club bid shows a good suit and invites three notrump. If opener has hearts stopped and a high honor in clubs he will bid three no-trump. If your agreement is that three clubs is forcing you can only bid two notrump and pass when opener bids three clubs. You will not be able to invite if that is your agreement.

With Example hand 91e) jump to three spades. This call is natural and forcing, asking opener to bid game in spades if he has three card support. It says nothing about stoppers in hearts.

With Example hand 91f) bid two notrump and continue to three spades after opener bids three clubs. This shows a five card suit and invitational values.

With Example hand 91g) bid two notrump to relay to three clubs, then bid three notrump. With this auction you show the values to play three notrump and promise a stopper in hearts.

With Example hand 91h) bid two notrump and after opener has bid three clubs continue by bidding three hearts. This call is *Stayman* promising four spades in this auction, and also showing a heart stopper and the values to play game.

With Example hand 91i) bid two notrump and after opener has bid three clubs correct to three diamonds. This auction is a signoff.

With Example hand 91j) double the overcall. This is not a classic penalty double, but instead shows opener that you have the values of a raise to two notrump. Opener may pass and convert the double for penalties or may remove to a suit of his own.

Responses to Two Notrump

When opener has bid two notrump to show a balanced hand with a good twenty to a bad twenty two points, or has opened with two clubs and rebid two notrump to show a balanced hand of twenty three or twenty four points, much of the system is still available.

Responder is still able to make transfer bids at either the three or four level, and the distinction between **Jacoby** and **Texas** transfer auctions still applies.

Responder's raise to three notrump can be natural, or it can again be used as a transfer to four clubs. If it is a transfer to four clubs responder may use the auction to escape when he holds long clubs and a very weak hand. The continuation sequences after the relay to four clubs can be as before, or a correction to four diamonds can be used as an escape with long diamonds and a very poor hand.

Caution is advised if your partnership agrees to use the raise of two notrump to three as a relay to four clubs rather than as a natural call. It is very easy for one partner or the other to forget and a muddled auction will follow. Remember that if you do have this agreement, when you wish to raise two notrump to three you must use **Stayman**.

Stayman can be used as it is used in response to one notrump, and if opener bids three diamonds in response to **Stayman** it is possible to utilize responder's continuations to three of a major suit as **Smolen Transfers**. Responder can continue by bidding in his four card major when he has a longer holding in the other major so that opener will be declarer when the longer major becomes the trump suit.

Puppet Stayman

Frequently opener's twenty point plus hand has 5-3-3-2 distribution. When the five card suit is a minor suit opener has no problem concealing his five card suit in a notrump auction. When the five card suit is a major suit, the ability to find the five-three major fit is important enough to pose a problem.

One solution is to have opener start by bidding his five card major, or by bidding two clubs and naming his five card major at his rebid. These solutions emphasize the major suit too strongly and do not identify the hand type as balanced. Another solution is to use **Puppet Stayman** in these auctions.

When **Puppet Stayman** has been agreed, responder's **Stayman** call of three clubs asks opener to bid a major suit if it is five cards long. If opener does not have a five card major but does have one or both four card majors, he indicates that fact by artificially bidding three diamonds. If he has neither a five nor a four card major, opener rebids three notrump.

If opener bids three diamonds to show that he does have a four card major, responder continues as follows:

1) If responder has no four card major but has used **Puppet Stayman** because he could not make a direct raise in notrump, or because he was interested in playing a five-three major suit fit, he bids three notrump which ends the auction.

2) When responder holds one four card major he bids the major that he does not hold. When opener hears that responder has a four card major that fits with his own, opener still becomes declarer since he will be the one to actually bid the major suit in which the four-four fit is known to exist.

3) When responder holds both majors and hears opener bid three diamonds to promise that he has a four card major, responder bids four diamonds. Opener will know from the four diamond bid that responder has a fit for his four card major suit and can bid game in that suit.

4) A logical extension of this idea is to play that when responder bids four diamonds he promises four-four in the majors but denies interest in slam. When he does have interest in slam responder instead bids four clubs to show four cards in each of the major suits. When opener also has slam interest, his continuation of four diamonds becomes an **RKC** ask embracing both of the major suits (there are six key cards including both major suit kings). In Chapter VIII the use of **RKC** when two suits are of importance is discussed.

Example 92:

> a) Opener
> ♠ KJ6
> ♡ AQ
> ♢ KJ765
> ♣ AQJ

With Example hand 92a) open with two notrump. If responder bids three clubs, *Puppet Stayman,* bid three notrump to indicate that you have neither a five nor a four card major suit.

b) Opener	c) Opener	d) Opener
♠ KQJ6	♠ AQ985	♠ A53
♡ AQ9	♡ AJ7	♡ AKJ75
◇ KJ76	◇ AJ	◇ A109
♣ AJ	♣ AQ6	♣ KJ

With Example hand 92b) Open two notrump and if responder bids three clubs bid three diamonds to indicate that you do have a four card major suit. If responder next bids three spades he shows four hearts and denies holding four spades. You will sign off at three notrump. If responder instead bids three hearts he promises four spades, and you will bid spades and play them from your side. If instead responder's next call is four diamonds you know that he has four cards in each major and will bid four spades.

With Example hand 92c) open two clubs and rebid two notrump. If responder next bids three clubs bid three spades to show your five card suit.

With Example hand 92d) open two notrump. If responder bids three clubs you will bid three hearts to show your five card suit.

Example 93:

a) Responder	b) Responder	c) Responder
♠ 10943	♠ 10943	♠ J106
♡ K84	♡ K842	♡ 853
◇ Q2	◇ Q2	◇ K832
♣ 8765	♣ 876	♣ J94

d) Responder	e) Responder
♠ J1094	♠ KJ106
♡ Q62	♡ Q1098
◇ 5	◇ KQ4
♣ 86432	♣ 87

With Example hand 93a) when opener has bid two notrump or rebid two notrump after opening with two clubs, bid three clubs, *Puppet Stayman*. If opener rebids three notrump to deny a four or five card major you will pass. If he bids a major to show a five card suit you will raise him to four. If he bids two diamonds to show a four card major you will next bid three hearts to show a four card spade suit. Visualize this hand facing 92a) or 92b).

With Example hand 93b) bid three clubs after opener's strong bid of two notrump and pass if he rebids three notrump to deny a four or five card major. If he shows a five card major raise him to four. If he bids three diamonds to announce that he has a four card major, you should bid four diamonds so that opener will declare in the known four-four fit.

With Example hand 93c) bid three clubs to look for the five-three fit. If opener happens to hold 92c) four spades will play much better than three notrump. If opener does not have a five card major you will bid three notrump.

With Example hand 93d) again seek a major suit fit by bidding three clubs. If opener holds 92d) four hearts is a good contract while three notrump will not fare well.

With Example hand 93e) use *Puppet Stayman* and if opener bids three diamonds to show a four card major, continue by bidding four clubs to show both majors and interest in slam. If opener continues by bidding four diamonds that will be *RKC* with six key cards being identified.

Three Spades as a Minor Suit Slam Try

When opener has bid or rebid two notrump to show a balanced hand of twenty or more points, responder will often be able to visualize a slam in a minor suit. He may have either a single suited hand or a hand that contains length in both minor suits. Rather than use either **Minor Suit Stayman** or **Walsh Relays**, responder has the option of using a bid of three spades to announce interest in a minor suit slam.

When opener hears responder bid three spades he is required to bid three notrump and listen to responder's continuation.

If responder continues by bidding either minor suit his message is that he is interested in slam in the minor suit that he has not bid. In this instance responder will have a hand that is primarily one suited. Opener can show interest in playing a slam in the unbid minor suit by making a cue bid at this time or by asking for controls (opener's cheapest call should be **RKC** in responder's known minor suit) and if slam is reached in the minor suit it will often be possible to have the strong hand declare.

If responder instead continues by bidding in a major suit at the four level he shows a singleton or void in the suit that he has bid, and shows a minor two suiter rather than a one suiter. Opener is then able to evaluate his holding facing responder's announced shortness and bid notrump to show that he has wasted values for suit play which are good stoppers in notrump, or to make a move toward slam by cue bidding or asking for key cards.

Example 94:

	a) Responder		b) Responder
♠	Q92	♠	A5
♡	A5	♡	7
◇	KJ8764	◇	KJ876
♣	98	♣	Q10983

With Example hand 94a) when opener has shown a big balanced hand with an opening bid of two notrump or a two notrump rebid after an opening bid of two clubs, responder can bid three spades to relay to three notrump. Responder then bids four clubs to show slam interest and a one suited hand in diamonds.

With Example hand 94b) in the same auction, after his relay of three spades and opener's forced call of three notrump, responder next bids four hearts to show shortness in that suit and five-five in the minor suits with interest in slam.

CHAPTER VI
OPENING BIDS
AND REBIDS AT HIGHER LEVELS

The opening bid of two clubs is strong, artificial and forcing. It is the only strong two bid in the system. When opener has a balanced hand his values will be too great for an opening bid of two notrump. He will have a minimum of twenty three high card points. When opener's hand is unbalanced, with one exception his hand will be one that can take nine or more tricks when his suit is named as the trump suit.

The single exception is a hand with a totally solid major suit that is worth eight or eight and one half tricks. This adjunct to the **Namyats** convention is detailed later in this Chapter.

Not all hands of great strength should be opened with a bid of two clubs. One must be aware of the problem of describing a hand that is two suited, or a hand with a magnificent minor suit, and realize that if two clubs is the opening bid, that very opening bid will often preempt the side which has much to tell and make the exchange of information very difficult. Although it takes great restraint to decline to open two clubs when one has a very good hand, it will often be a better idea to open with a one bid and have more bidding space available.

Opening with a strong two bid gives a psychological lift to the one who makes that bid. Those who are able to open with a very strong bid often experience a feeling of power which is exhilarating, and the experience becomes an end unto itself. Opening with a plebian one level bid is so common that there is no thrill.

Nevertheless, when one has a hand that will take several bids to describe it is better to conserve bidding space so that end may be accomplished. When you open with a bid of two clubs it should be because no other opening bid can possibly do the job for you, and it is essential that you show your strong hand at once.

The strong balanced hand presents no problem. When opener can count the twenty three points or more that he must describe and he knows that his rebid in notrump will tell the story of his hand, it is comfortable to open with a bid of two clubs to show this great strength. With unbalanced hands the admonition presented above should cause the bidder to take heed.

Responder to the opening bid of two clubs needs to understand that it is very important that he allow opener the latitude to describe the nature of his two club bid. Unless responder has the capacity to send a message that describes his hand quite completely with one bid, it is more important that responder mark time and allow the opening two club bidder the opportunity to describe the nature of his strong hand. As responder, do not get in opener's way without purpose.

When responder to the opening bid of two clubs has a poor hand he may describe that fact in one of two ways. The traditional approach is for responder to bid two diamonds at his first turn. The two diamond bid is completely artificial, saying nothing about the diamond suit.

The two diamond response is a waiting bid that allows opener complete freedom to describe his excellent hand. In addition to being completely artificial and allowing opener full latitude to describe his strong hand, this response sends no message at all about responder's values. After opener has rebid to describe his good hand, responder's next call is used to indicate his value range. When responder's rebid is at the three level in the lowest ranking denomination, he artificially shows a negative response to the strong opening bid.

If responder's second call is not the cheapest available bid at the three level, he shows that he holds a positive response in values, and his bid is natural. The values for a positive response are minimally an ace, a king, or two queens. When responder has as little as this, game is expected to be makable facing any hand that truly merits a two club opening bid.

A modern alternative to this use of a waiting bid followed by a natural positive or artificial negative at responder's second turn is the use of an immediate response of two hearts as an artificial negative complimented by two diamonds as an artificial positive and waiting response.

When two hearts is agreed to be an artificial negative response to the opening bid of two clubs, a replacement bid of two notrump shows that responder has positive values with a heart suit. Alternately it is possible to use a response of two spades to show hearts and two notrump to show spades in order to have the strong hand become declarer more often.

The only time it makes sense for responder to disrupt opener's conveyance of the nature of his strong hand after the strong and artificial opening bid of two clubs is when responder has a very good suit of his own and no other feature in his hand to describe. In this case responder uses his first bid to tell opener about that good suit and lets opener proceed with that information to the contract that he deems to be most suitable. Responder will have a five card or longer suit headed by at least two of the top three honors when he intrudes on opener's bidding space in this fashion. When opener has a fit that includes a top honor card, he is instantly aware of a source of tricks.

If the partnership's agreement is to use two diamonds as a waiting bid and make a "second negative" by bidding as cheaply as possible at the three level, when responder has values and a reasonable club suit it is necessary for the partnership agreement to allow him to show that suit at his first turn even when it does not contain two of the top three honors. This is because a second bid of three clubs by responder after a waiting two diamond response would not show clubs, but would be an artificial negative.

Other than to show a good suit, responder has no need to get in the way of opener's rebid. Responder should be patient, even when holding good values, for as the auction progresses he will be able to express those values and he needs to hear about the strong two bid before he will know how to proceed.

When after opening two clubs opener rebids in notrump, he will have expressed his value range and shown a balanced hand. A rebid in notrump is not forcing and can become the contract when responder has no values and elects to pass. With other hands responder has available the full gamut of responses to opening notrump bids and can use **Stayman, Jacoby** and **Texas** transfers, and whatever else the partnership has agreed to use in such an auction.

When opener rebids in a suit after having opened with two clubs, that rebid is forcing even if responder has been able to express negative values with his first call. The auction continues to be forcing unless opener repeats his major suit at the three level, or repeats his minor suit at the four level. Only when opener repeats his suit below the level of game is responder permitted to pass.

If opener's rebid after two clubs is a jump to a suit, he shows that his suit is at least six cards long and that it is totally solid. Opener stipulates with his jump that his suit needs no support and will be the trump suit no matter how few cards responder may hold in that suit. This jump also starts an **Asking Bid** sequence, details of which are found in Chapter VIII.

When responder has made a waiting bid of two diamonds with negative values and opener rebids in a major suit for which responder has support, a different negative continuation is available. Responder's immediate jump to game in opener's major suit shows a hand with three card or longer support for that suit, but denies that responder has any control card that would be useful for play at a slam. Responder denies holding an ace or a king, and does not have a side void or singleton in this auction. Responder also denies holding as much in values as two queens, although he might hold one queen and any number of jacks.

When responder has the positive values of an ace, a king, or two queens or more and has a fit for opener's major suit, he shows that fit and conserves bidding space by raising only to the three level when his hand is balanced. When his hand is unbalanced, responder shows his fit for opener's suit and positive values by making a **splinter** bid, jumping to the suit in which he has shortness.

If responder instead bids a new suit he tends to deny support for opener's suit. Responder's suit will be assumed to be five cards or longer when he introduces it.

Example 95:

a) Responder	b) Responder	c) Responder
♠AQ1087	♠KJ865	♠A87
♡653	♡653	♡AK6
◇98	◇A8	◇987
♣542	♣542	♣6542
d) Responder	e) Responder	f) Responder
♠K3	♠862	♠J62
♡853	♡6543	♡6543
◇J4	◇J5	◇5
♣KJ9864	♣Q963	♣K9632

With Example 95 hands responder has heard an opening bid of two clubs by partner.

With Example hand 95a) responder bids two spades. If the partnership has agreed to use two hearts as an immediate artificial negative, they may also play that two spades shows hearts and responder will bid two notrump with this hand to show spades. Regardless of the means, responder will show that he has a good spade suit, and if opener has a holding as good as three to the king he will know that the spade suit will furnish at least five tricks.

With Example hand 95b) responder does not show his spade suit at once, but instead marks time by bidding two diamonds. If opener's rebid is in hearts or clubs responder will make a single raise to show his three card fit, but otherwise responder will be able to show his spade suit at his second bid.

With Example hand 95c) responder again marks time by bidding two diamonds. Responder will show a fit for any suit in which opener may rebid, but would raise a rebid of two notrump to slam.

With Example hand 95d) responder's first bid depends upon the methods that have been agreed. If after a waiting response of two diamonds responder's second bid of three clubs is an artificial "second negative" responder must be able to show his good club suit at his first turn. If two diamonds is waiting and positive since the agreement is that two hearts is an immediate negative, responder will be able to show his club suit at his second turn.

With Example hand 95e) responder has negative values. If two hearts is an immediate negative responder should make that call. If responder cannot show a negative response until his rebid he will first bid two diamonds. If opener's rebid is in either major at the two level, responder should jump to four in opener's suit to show his negative hand with a fit for opener's major suit while denying any control that might be useful for slam.

With Example hand 95f) responder will make a waiting bid of two diamonds at his first turn. If opener's rebid is two spades responder should raise to three spades to show his fit and indicate some reasonable values. If opener's rebid is two hearts responder should instead jump to four diamonds, a *splinter* in support of hearts because of his fourth trump.

Weak Two Bids

Opening two bids in the major suits are weak two bids and usually show a value range of five to eleven high card points. The extremes of the range may vary slightly, but if the range has a spread of more than seven points or, if the bottom of the range is less than five high card points, in ACBL events the partnership will not be allowed to use any systemic responses.

The suit length shown is usually six cards although the modern tendency is to allow a weak two bid with a good five card suit. The suit will tend to be seven cards long only when the bidder's side is vulnerable and the opponents are not.

The shape of a weak two bid should be a subject of discipline. When the weak two bid is based on a two suited hand or a hand of wild distribution, finding the correct contract will be virtually impossible. Hand patterns for a weak two bid in first or second seat should be limited to these: 6-3-2-2, 6-3-3-1, 6-4-2-1, 5-3-3-2, 5-4-2-2, and more rarely 5-4-3-1, 7-2-2-2, 7-3-2-1.

The first two patterns are most typical. With the third pattern shown opener should not have four cards in an unbid major suit, but may have a four card minor suit. The hands that open weak two bids on five card suits should have suits of good quality and a side four card suit should be poor. Seven card weak two bids should be made only when vulnerable against not vulnerable when it appears that an opening three bid would be too dangerous.

The quality of the suit will vary according to partnership agreement. The classic weak two bid shows a hand with a good suit and not much in side values. Some partnerships require that the suit quality be as good as two of the top three honors. Since the suit will be known to be good, response and rebid mechanisms will focus on the determination of maximum or minimum values in the weak two bidder's hand, and the placement of his side values when his hand qualifies as maximum.

When the partnership has agreed to use this classic style for weak two bids a response of two notrump is used to ask whether the weak two bid is maximum or minimum. With minimum values the weak two bidder repeats his suit at the three level. With maximum values the weak two bidder indicates that fact by bidding in a side suit where he holds a feature of some kind.

Determination of what constitutes a "feature" will vary from one partnership to another. Some require that to be shown as a feature the side asset must be an ace or a king. Others extend the definition to include queens, and some even show shortness as a feature. If you agree to play this style of weak two bid your partnership should define exactly what a feature should be.

A second philosophy regarding weak two bids allows for weaker suits and more scattered values in the weak two bidder's hand. When this philosophy prevails it is important that the partnership have available to it tools by which to determine suit quality.

Users of this approach adopt the **Ogust** convention, devised by the late Harold Ogust who once headed the Goren organization and played on the very successful Goren teams. When **Ogust** is agreed, a response of two notrump asks opener to rebid in steps as follows:

1) Opener's rebid of three clubs shows a bad hand with a bad suit. The suit should be headed by at least the queen in order to provide lead value if the weak two bidder's partner becomes the opening leader. If vulnerable the weak two bidder should have good enough texture in the suit to avoid being punished when his suit is stacked and the opponents decide to defend.

2) Opener's rebid of three diamonds shows a bad hand with a good suit. This weak two bidder will have made the same call as those of the other philosophy.

3) Opener's rebid of three hearts shows a good hand with a bad suit. In this case opener will have values which would also be useful on defense. Responder should decide to play with opener's suit as trumps only when he can furnish an honor card or support of three cards or more so that there will not be too many trump losers.

(The Encyclopedia of Bridge and several convention books show steps two and three above interchanged, but both make mention of the fact that many partnerships play as has been presented here. The reason for the change from the original is to allow hands with better values to bid more than hands with lesser values.)

4) Opener's rebid of three spades shows a good hand with a good suit. Since responder has a good enough hand to ask, the only decision is which game to play, and that will be responder's decision to make.

5) Opener's rebid of three notrump shows a completely solid suit. Responder can pass and play three notrump if all suits are stopped since the weak two bidder will furnish six tricks. Responder can also assess slam potential since with a solid suit the weak two bidder will not have outside values.

Example 96:

a) Opener	b) Opener
♠64	♠KQJ1084
♡KJ8653	♡96
◇Q9	◇63
♣642	♣842

With Example hand 96a) opener cannot make a weak two bid if a good suit is promised. If the partnership has agreed to use the *Ogust* convention opener can bid two hearts and in response to two notrump can bid three clubs to show a bad hand with a bad suit.

With Example hand 96b) two spades is an easy opening bid. If two notrump asks for a feature this hand will rebid three spades to show its minimum. Its good suit is expected. *Ogust* bidders will rebid three diamonds after a two notrump response to show a bad hand with a good suit.

c) Opener	d) Opener	e) Opener
♠KJ8653	♠K5	♠62
♡A64	♡AQJ963	♡953
◊Q95	◊9642	◊AKQJ64
♣3	♣3	♣52

With Example hand 96c) opener again will not be able to make a weak two bid if he promises a good suit. Users of *Ogust* will bid two spades and in response to two notrump will bid three hearts to show a good hand with a bad suit.

With Example hand 96d) opener has a full value weak two bid. In fact in some styles this would be considered an opening one bid. Weak two bidders with this hand will rebid three spades to show a feature there with a maximim weak two bid. The fact that opener's suit is bypassed should not be of consequence since if responder's values are great enough to ask, opener's values are adequate for game. It may be important for responder to know about the king of spades in order to bid a slam. *Ogust* bidders will also rebid three spades to show a good hand with a good suit.

With Example hand 96e) there are again those who would eschew a weak two bid and open with one diamond. Since there is no feature to show those who espouse classical weak two bids might take this course. Those who use *Ogust* however will be able to show a solid suit by rebidding three notrump in response to responder's inquiry of two notrump.

Although two notrump is always used as a probe to find out more about the weak two bidder's hand, bids in new suits are subject to partnership agreement. Opinions vary as to whether new suits should be forcing or not. Some play that all new suits are forcing, some play that all new suits are not forcing, and some play that responder's call in a major suit is forcing but if he bids in a minor suit that is not forcing.

If a new major suit is forcing and responder bids it at the two level (two diamonds may also be a weak two bid) responder will be seeking information about the weak two bidder's holding in that suit. Responder may have some length in the major suit he has bid and be seeking a fit so that it may become the trump suit. Alternately, responder may be seeking an adequate holding in the weak two bidder's hand in a suit that needs to be stopped to allow a game in notrump to succeed.

When responder has bid a major suit at the two level, opener is asked to describe his holding in that suit as follows:

200

1) If opener has three cards headed by ace, king or queen, he raises the major suit in which responder has bid at the two level.

2) If opener has any lesser three card holding, or a doubleton in responder's major that includes the ace, king or queen, he rebids two notrump.

3) With any lesser holding, opener makes the same rebid he would have made if responder had bid two notrump instead of two of the major suit.

a) If two notrump would have asked the weak two bidder to rebid his suit with a minimum but show the location of a feature with a maximum, that is the action he takes when his support for responder's major suit is not adequate to either raise or bid two notrump. Opener cannot, however, show a feature in responder's major suit unless he holds the required three cards headed by a high honor.

b) If two notrump would have asked for an **Ogust** rebid, opener should make the call that shows the quality of his hand and suit when his support for responder's major suit is not adequate to either raise or bid two notrump. One **Ogust** step must be deleted. When opener has any good hand, he shows that hand by bidding in the major suit not shown by responder. He cannot express the quality of his suit since one major suit is eliminated from the **Ogust** steps.

Example 97:

a) Opener	b) Opener	c) Opener
♠K83	♠K8	♠83
♡5	♡543	♡AQ10973
◇AJ10862	◇AJ10862	◇J106
♣543	♣53	♣75

With Example hand 97a) opener has bid two diamonds. If responder bids two spades responder should raise to show three card support with a high honor. If responder bids two hearts it costs opener nothing to continue by bidding two spades. He is known to have three spades at most, and he might as well show his honor card since he can do so cheaply.

With Example hand 97b) opener has bid two diamonds. If responder bids two in either major suit opener rebids two notrump since that rebid promises either a doubleton high honor or three small cards.

With Example hand 97c) opener has bid two hearts. If responder bids two spades opener's rebid will be three hearts to show a minimum with no side feature, or three diamonds to show a bad hand with a good suit.

Although weak two bids in first and second seat are structured in one way or another, weak two bids in third position have greater latitude. Particularly when not vulnerable, if partner has passed and your own values are meager it is probable that your opponents can make a game. Your job in this situation is to make the auction difficult for your opponents and a bit of imagination is in order. An unorthodox weak two bid might be just the tool that will achieve the desired result, causing the other side to miscalculate and reach the wrong contract, whether they elect to enter the auction or stay out of it.

Fourth seat weak two bids present yet another tactical situation. Here you have the option to pass and end the auction, or to make an opening bid of some kind. When the strength of the hand seems to be pretty evenly distributed you may want to keep your opponents out of the auction by opening with a weak two bid with a hand that might otherwise have been opened with a one bid.

Fourth seat weak two bids should be made with reasonably good hands rather than the lesser hands which would qualify in first or second position. The range for a fourth seat weak two bid should be about ten to thirteen points in high cards, and should show one of the classic hand patterns described earlier.

Response patterns facing a weak two bid in either third or fourth position should be of a different variety than facing a weak two bid in first or second seat. Since responder is a passed hand a new suit should not be forcing.

Reaching a game when a weak two bid faces a passed responder will be correct only if the two hands fit well together. Since that is true, particularly facing a fourth seat weak two bid which is known to be maximum, the use of two notrump to ask opener to show shortness will probably serve better than the uses recommended facing a first or second seat weak two bid.

When responder has not yet passed an available systemic tool is the use of a jump shift response as an **Asking Bid**. Complete description of the use of the **Asking Bid** in this context appears in Chapter VIII.

When after partner's weak two bid an opponent makes a takeout double the **McCabe Adjunct** is a useful tool. Responder can redouble to show a good hand or can raise to further the preemptive action.

When responder has raised after the double the weak two opener will often be the opening leader, and should usually lead his suit. The reason for this is that responder has the capacity to indicate a lead in another suit after the double by bidding the suit that he wants to have led.

Such a lead directing call by responder also says that he has a fit of some kind for the suit of the weak two bid. Opener is asked to return to his suit rather than let responder play in the suit he has bid in order to suggest a lead.

If responder truly wishes to escape and play in another suit after the takeout double, that suit will almost always be lower ranking than the suit of the weak two bid. In order to get to that suit, responder bids two notrump which asks opener to bid three clubs and pass if responder corrects to another suit.

Example 98:

a) Responder	b) Responder	c) Responder
♠83	♠83	♠A3
♡K74	♡1074	♡5
◇QJ2	◇KQ10	◇KQ10864
♣Q10962	♣J10962	♣J1083

With Example 98 hands responder has heard an opening weak two heart bid from his partner and a takeout double by the opponent next to speak.

With Example hand 98a) responder should raise to three hearts. This action both extends the preempt and indicates that opener should lead a heart if he becomes the opening leader.

With Example hand 98b) responder should bid three diamonds. This call is really a raise in hearts while indicating that a diamond lead will be good if opener becomes the opening leader. Opener will not pass but will bid three hearts if there is a pass after the three diamond bid.

With Example hand 98c) responder bids two notrump after the takeout double. This conventional call requires opener to bid three clubs and pass if responder corrects to another suit. Responder will correct to diamonds indicating a desire to play there.

Opening Two Diamond Bids

There is a common feeling (not shared by this writer) that the opening bid of two diamonds does not have much preemptive effect. For this reason many different uses for the two diamond opening bid have been developed and are in use today.

If your agreement is that two diamonds is a weak two bid, the previous discourse will have touched upon all the points that also pertain to responses and rebids after the weak two opening bid in diamonds. This agreement is as good as any, and superior to many.

Although it enjoys great popularity, there is no need in the system for an opening two diamond bid to be used as **Flannery**. When the opener has four spades and five hearts he can open with one heart and if responder bids one spade he can raise. If responder makes a two over one response in a minor suit at the two level, opener can bid two spades to show his shape. Systemically, since the two over one response promises that the bidding side has values enough to bid to game, the two spade rebid is not a reverse in the true sense. It expresses opener's shape, but does not show more than minimum opening bid values.

If responder's bid has been a **Forcing Notrump**, when opener has minimum values (12+ to 15-) he does not have the luxury of bidding spades to show his shape. Since responder's values are limited, if opener does rebid two spades he must have a hand with the values to reverse (a good sixteen or more). With minimum values opener will need to rebid in a minor suit at the two level.

When opener has a three or four card minor suit to bid, the auction will be normal since opener is expected to rebid in a three card minor suit often after a **Forcing Notrump** response. The only possible problem hand that opener can hold is the exact pattern 4-5-2-2.

If opener has the problem hand that has been identified he continues by bidding two clubs on his doubleton. When responder has minimum values and must attempt to sign off at some playable contract he will often have a doubleton heart, and will prefer back to opener's first bid major suit. If responder has fewer than two hearts as well as three or fewer spades he must hold a five card or longer minor suit. When responder's minor suit is clubs he will pass and the two-five or two-six will be the best available fit. When responder's long minor suit is diamonds he will continue by bidding two diamonds and opener will pass. Again the best fit will have been found.

When **Flannery** bidders face the same problem, that is when opener is 4-5-2-2 and responder is 3-1-5-4 or 3-1-4-5, they play in two spades from the three card side. System users who do not play **Flannery** should reach the same contract when the three-four fit is of good quality.

When responder has a 3-1-5-4 or 3-1-4-5 hand with reasonable spades and minimum response values, he should cater to the possibility that opener has four spades and respond by bidding one spade. He does this with the intention of playing in spades if opener raises, but his one spade response also has the advantage of allowing opener to rebid one notrump and play that contract when he has fewer than four spades.

Flannery is a convention that does have merit for those who open four card majors. They do not have a solution to the dilemma that can be presented when opener has a hand with four spades and five hearts and no systemic tools to solve the attendant bidding problems.

Roman Two Diamonds is another useful convention if its users agree upon a value range that makes the tool valuable. The original **Roman Two Diamonds** was created to solve the problems of missing games when opener had a strong three suited hand and his opening bid was passed by responder. Often responder had very little in values but a good fit for one of opener's major suits was enough to produce a game. Using two diamonds as an opening bid to show a strong hand with three suits has been shown to have great merit.

When the opening bid range for a three suited **Roman** type opening two diamond bid is less than an ordinary opening bid, the result can be similar. When responder has a good fit a game can often be reached and made that would not be bid if opener had passed. The range of ten to thirteen points can create action, and even when the convention does not get the bidding side to a thin game, the action it creates often makes the auction one that opponents cannot cope with.

The range that makes least sense for a **Roman Two Diamond** bid is one that seems to have widespread use. When opener's value range is eleven to fifteen points he has a hand that can be opened with a one bid and not be concerned about missing a game if responder should pass. When responder does bid, opener will nearly always be able to bid to show his pattern. The use of two diamonds to show pattern in this range gets the job done with one bid, but since the job is easily accomplished by normal bidding, those who play **Roman** in this range essentially give up what a two diamond bid might well accomplish for them that cannot be accomplished otherwise.

An even more frightening complex occurs when a pair agrees to play that two diamonds is **Roman**, using a range that achieves nothing for them, and then also plays that two hearts is **Flannery** . **Flannery** creates enough problems when the opening bid is two diamonds. When the opening **Flannery** bid is two hearts the situation worsens, for a weak two bid in hearts is no longer available. Loss of this valuable tool for no systemic gain is a very high price to pay.

Other uses for an opening two diamond bid are possible, but the discussion here has focused on those most widely in use. The recommendation here is that an opening bid of two diamonds be weak, or **Roman** in a range that has effectiveness, or that it be some other special tool.

Opening Three Bids

Opening bids of three of a suit in the system are reasonably standard. Except in clubs (also in diamonds if a conventional use is assigned to the opening bid of two diamonds) an opening three bid will usually show a seven card suit. Since opening two level preempts are not available in clubs (and sometimes in diamonds), common practice is to preempt at the three level when the need to preempt seems apparent and opener's suit is only six cards long.

The rule of two and three which was the guideline for preemptive bidding for many years has given way to the rule of two, three and four. Winning tactics in today's tournament arena have caused bidders to know of the need to preempt more often and with hands that have less trick taking potential than in previous years. The most successful pair in National Championships in recent history (at the time of this writing) is noted for its outlandish preemptive style. Marty Bergen and Larry Cohen have been consistent winners using a style that allows preempts that would scare most readers of this book half way to death (or more).

The rule of two, three and four is a reasonable rule for preemption which should not cause disaster situations in any auction. This rule stipulates that the preemptive bidder have enough winners to be within two tricks of his bid if vulnerable against non vulnerable opponents. The preemptive bidder will have enough winners to be within three tricks of his bid if the vulnerability is equal (either both vulnerable or both not vulnerable). The preemptive bidder will have enough winners to be within four tricks of his bid when his side is not vulnerable and the opponents are. If you use this guide for your preemptive opening bids you should be on reasonable ground.

A suit bid in response to an opening bid at the three level is natural and forcing. The preemptive opening bidder should raise responder's suit when it is possible to do so. The raise should show three card support, but a doubleton high honor and shortness in another side suit make the raise attractive as well.

A jump shift response to an opening three bid is an **Asking Bid**. Details will be found in Chapter VIII.

An important concept regarding opening three bids is that of offensive and defensive strength. The measure of offensive strength is provided by the rule of two, three and four, but just as important is that the opening preemptive bidder not have too much defensive strength.

The reason for preemption is good offense and poor defense. If the hand that opens preemptively has defensive strength he defeats the purpose of his preempt. Expecting that the opening bidder has little defense, the partner of the preemptive bidder may sacrifice against a game contract reached by the opponents after the preemptive opening. This can be a real problem when the preemptive bidder holds defensive values, for the sacrifice will be a "phantom". The game bid by the opponents would not have been made.

The absolute maximum in defensive strength for a preemptive three level opening bidder is one and one half tricks. Even that may be too much. The reason to preempt is that the hand dealt to you has great offense but little to offer on defense. Do not count points to determine the strength that you have. Look to the tricks that can be won if your suit is named the trump suit, and look to the tricks you can win if any other suit becomes trumps. Preempt only when your offensive potential meets the measure that has been presented, but do not preempt if your defensive strength precludes the need for that action.

Bidding theorist Marty Bergen has suggested that when an opening preemptive bid has been made and the partner of the preemptive bidder has visions of slam, the space taken by **Blackwood** is often too great. By virtue of trying to determine if adequate controls for slam exist, the bidding side that uses **Blackwood** often finds itself one level too high after the slam exploration.

Bergen suggests that facing a preemptive opening bid the **Gerber** convention be used. Since opener's suit will be the trump suit whether or not slam is reached, the use of **Gerber** should also include the **Roman Key Card** modification. Responder's bid of four clubs facing an opening preemptive bid at the three level is **RKC Gerber**, seeking controls with opener's suit agreed as trumps.

Example 99:

a) Opener
♠96
♡84
◇932
♣AQJ1087

Example hand 99a) has an excellent club suit with five offensive winners. It can be opened three clubs if not vulnerable vs. vulnerable since it conforms to the rule of four, but not two or three. At match points a tactical gamble can be made at other vulnerabilities since the frequency with which a penalty will be extracted will be low.

b) Opener
  ♠KQJ9853
  ♡63
  ◇ A82
  ♣6

c) Opener
  ♠AK87543
  ♡854
  ◇ A2
  ♣9

Example hand 99b) has seven winners if spades are trumps. If vulnerable vs. not you should apply the rule of two and open with three spades. At other vulnerabilities this hand is too good for an opening three spade bid and should be opened with four spades. Note that the maximum defensive expectancy is that the ace of diamonds will cash but defensive spade tricks are not likely.

Example hand 99c) has too much defensive value for an opening preemptive bid. It should be opened with one spade.

Opening Four Bids

Opening bids at the four level are systemically correlated. An opening bid of four hearts or four spades shows that based upon the rule of two, three and four, opener is within the number of tricks called for by the vulnerability. Opener's maximum, however, is seven and one half tricks.

When opener has a major suit that is nearly solid or completely solid (the choice between these is to be established by prior partnership agreement) and his hand is worth eight or eight and one half tricks, he uses the **Namyats** convention.

Namyats, which is Stayman spelled backwards came about when Sam Stayman suggested that opening four club and four diamond bids be used to show weak preempts in hearts and spades, respectively, and that the opening bids of four hearts and four spades show better hands. Some theorists thought that this was a good idea, but felt that Sam had it backwards. The opening bids of four hearts and four spades should be those which required greater preemptive action. Those who thought that Sam had it backwards determined the name of the convention by spelling Stayman backwards, and **Namyats** was quickly adopted as the name by which the convention is recognized.

A **Namyats** opening bid of four clubs shows hearts, and four diamonds shows spades. The hand is worth exactly eight or eight and one half tricks. Partnership agreement determines what the suit quality will be. Some partnerships establish that the suit must be completely solid. Others permit the suit to be missing one honor, either the king or queen but not the ace.

When the suit quality agreement is that the suit is missing one honor and opener is dealt a solid suit with eight or eight and one half winners he describes that hand by starting with an opening bid of two clubs. After responder's expected bid of two diamonds (or even the artificial negative of two hearts) opener continues by jumping to his major suit at the four level. This four level jump rebid promises that opener has the hand described above, with a solid suit and eight or eight and one half tricks. When responder cannot furnish enough additional strength for opener to make his contract the opponents will have been able to make at least a game, and often a slam.

Responder to the **Namyats** opening bid of four clubs or four diamonds has a choice of continuations. He can sign off by bidding four of the suit indicated by the opening bid or he can bid the "relay" suit which ranks between the suit bid and the suit shown by opener. When responder bids the "relay" suit he requires opener to bid the suit shown by his first call and become declarer rather than dummy.

If responder instead makes a call in a suit beyond the anchor suit as his first response, that call is an **Asking Bid** (see Chapter VIII).

Example 100:

a) Opener	b) Opener	c) Opener
♠AQJ10853	♠A93	♠AKJ10953
♡6	♡AKQJ653	♡8
◊KQJ	◊5	◊A1052
♣95	♣84	♣7

With Example hand 100a) you can open with four diamonds *Namyats* unless your agreement requires a solid suit. In that case you should open with one spade and rebid four spades. Your hand is much too good for an original opening bid of four spades.

With Example hand 100b) you can open with four clubs *Namyats* unless your agreement is that that bid shows a suit missing either the king or queen. When that agreement prevails you should open with two clubs, then jump to four hearts to show a completely solid suit with eight or eight and one half tricks.

With Example hand 100c) open with four diamonds if your agreement is that a *Namyats* bid shows a suit with one missing honor. If your agreement requires a solid suit, bid one spade and plan to rebid four spades. Your hand is too good for an opening bid of four spades.

Opening Three Notrump Bids

Since opening bids of four clubs and four diamonds are used artificially, the opening bid of three notrump is used to show hands which qualify for a standard opening bid of four in a minor suit. These are typically hands with a broken eight card minor suit.

Example 101:

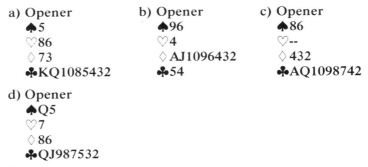

a) Opener
- ♠ 5
- ♡ 86
- ◇ 73
- ♣ KQ1085432

b) Opener
- ♠ 96
- ♡ 4
- ◇ AJ1096432
- ♣ 54

c) Opener
- ♠ 86
- ♡ --
- ◇ 432
- ♣ AQ1098742

d) Opener
- ♠ Q5
- ♡ 7
- ◇ 86
- ♣ QJ987532

All hands in Example 101 might be opened with a four level pre-emptive bid in the eight card minor suit if the *Namyats* convention had not been agreed. With each of these hands an opening bid of three notrump is the alternate description.

Example hand 101d) is a bit skimpy and should not be opened with three notrump if vulnerable vs. not vulnerable opponents. This hand has only six winners with clubs as trumps and cannot commit itself to the four level at that vulnerability. Even at equal vulnerability three notrump exceeds the guidelines, but an opening bid of three clubs will suffice.

When three notrump has been opened responder may pass if he holds a fine hand with stoppers in all suits. His fitting honor card for opener's minor suit should provide for a source of tricks and if all other suits are stopped three notrump will probably make.

If instead responder holds any nondescript hand he bids four clubs which allows opener to pass if his suit is clubs, or correct to diamonds when that is his suit.

Responder's other possible actions depend upon the level at which he is willing to play in either or both of the minor suits. If responder has poor or short clubs but good diamonds and a reasonable hand and is willing to play a game or slam in diamonds but only a part score in clubs, he bids four clubs knowing that opener will pass if his suit is clubs. If opener's suit is diamonds and he corrects, responder will then raise to the level at which he wishes to play.

If responder's holdings are reversed and he is willing to play a game or slam in clubs but only a part score in diamonds, he bids four diamonds. Opener will pass if his suit is diamonds but will correct to five clubs if that is his suit and responder will have reached the contract he wants or can bid on.

If responder is willing to play game in either minor he bids five clubs and opener will either pass or correct. If responder is willing to play a slam in either suit he similarly bids six clubs. With thoughts of a diamond game or a club slam responder bids five diamonds knowing that opener will either pass or correct to clubs at the slam level.

A major suit response to the opening bid of three notrump should be treated as an **Asking Bid**. Responder is willing to play at least at game in either minor suit and seeks information about the major suit in which he needs a control to play a slam.

A response of four notrump can be used to ask opener to name his suit and describe its quality. If opener bids either five clubs or five diamonds he names his suit and denies holding either the ace or king.

If opener bids five hearts he shows clubs headed by either the ace or king. Similarly a bid of five spades shows diamonds headed by either the ace or king.

If opener bids six clubs or six diamonds he names his suit and shows that it is headed by the ace-queen or king-queen. If opener bids five notrump he does not name his suit but promises that it is headed by the ace-king.

Responder may bid a grand slam if he holds a hand which will produce thirteen tricks facing an eight card suit with that heading. Responder's next call will be six or seven clubs which opener should correct if it is the wrong suit, or six or seven notrump which opener must pass.

Example 102:

a) Responder
♠A952
♥KQ3
♦Q102
♣K63

b) Responder
♠A943
♥K6542
♦95
♣83

c) Responder
♠6
♥AK10732
♦A95
♣A62

d) Responder
♠AQ742
♥AK92
♦6
♣KJ5

With Example hand 102a) you have heard partner open with a *Namyats* bid of three notrump showing a broken eight card minor suit. With honor cards in all suits you should expect to be able to take nine tricks or more at notrump, and should pass.

With Example hand 102b) if opener has bid three notrump you should bid four clubs. You want to get out cheaply in either minor suit.

With Example hand 102c) bid six clubs. Your are willing to play a slam in either minor suit.

With Example hand 102d) bid four diamonds. You are willing to play a game in clubs if that is opener's suit, but if his suit is diamonds you want to play only in a part score.

CHAPTER VII
COMPETITIVE BIDDING

It is clear that any style or philosophy of competitive bidding that is acceptable to the partnership may be used. This Chapter presents the competitive bidding style that is most consistent with the system itself, which suggests sound bidding and slow auctions when good hands are known, and frequent preemption with weak distributional hands.

PART I - COMPETITIVE BIDS

Overcalls in Suits

Overcalls in suits can be made with very little in values at the one level. It is often important to make a lead directing call while it is possible rather than leave partner a guess as to what to lead against an opposing contract. Your failure to overcall when you might have done so also conveys negative inferences. Partner might choose the suit of his opening lead simply on the basis that you did not overcall.

Of course, lead direction is not the only reason to overcall. When you have a hand which warrants an attempt to declare, an overcall will often be your entry into the auction.

At the one level you will sometimes find that the only way to enter the auction intelligently is by making an overcall in a four card suit. This is most likely to be true when you have length in the suit of the opening bidder. When both you and he have length in his suit your partner is likely to be short in that suit, and will usually either have support for your suit or be able to offer a suit of his own.

An overcall at the two level should enjoy the safety of a good suit. Those who make two level overcalls on bad suits just because they were dealt thirteen points often come a cropper. Responder often turns up with a trump stack, and the overcaller wonders why he got such a bad result when he had such good values. A ten point hand with a good suit makes a better two level overcall than a hand with thirteen points and a bad suit virtually all of the time.

System overcalls traditionally extend to include some very good hands, even at the one level. However, when partner is a passed hand the overcaller has license to do whatever appears to fit the situation and the hand he holds.

Example 103:

a) Overcaller	b) Overcaller	c) Overcaller
♠643	♠AQ1095	♠AQ1095
♡KQJ95	♡KJ3	♡963
◇K5	◇5	◇54
♣A54	♣Q954	♣Q83

d) Overcaller	e) Overcaller	f) Overcaller
♠A6	♠A6	♠104
♡95	♡K53	♡AQJ6
◇542	◇Q106	◇AQ1082
♣AQJ963	♣KJ852	♣93

Example hand 103a) is a good overcall by all standards. Even if the opening bid has been one spade and the overcaller must bid at the two level his good suit and good values are adequate.

Example hand 103b) is a good overcall of any opening one bid. If the opening bid has been one diamond this hand does have support for all unbid suits, but a takeout double will nearly always find partner bidding hearts on a four card holding when a five-three spade fit exists. It is better to overcall in spades, then double at your next turn if the opposition continues in diamonds or bids one notrump. The double at your second turn shows support for hearts and clubs as well as the spade suit shown by your overcall, and the desire to compete further rather than sell out cheaply.

Example hand 103c) is skimpy and would not meet the requirements for an overcall in the early Walsh system. Those system practitioners might well have made a jump overcall despite having only five cards in the spade suit. Today's tendency is to overcall one spade for lead directing purposes unless partner is a passed hand, in which case a jump overcall has greater appeal.

Example hand 103d) is a sound overcall of two clubs. The good suit augurs against the possibility that an opponent will be able to punish this two level action.

Example hand 103e) has opening bid values but an overcall of two clubs is fraught with danger. The bad club suit makes likely the possibility that after the overcall there will be two passes, a reopening double, and a penalty pass by responder.

Example hand 103f) illustrates the kind of hand that should overcall with a four card suit at the one level. If the opening bid has been one diamond this overcaller should bid one heart on his good four card suit. No other entry into the auction has any merit.

Responses to Overcalls in Suits

Responses to overcalls in suits are often made without thought or partnership agreement as to what various calls mean. The system presents a well coordinated set of responses to be used by the advancer (this is the accepted term to designate the partner of the overcaller). The advancer's considerations should be as follows:

1) A raise of the overcall shows the same type of hand with which one would raise an opening bid in a major suit. Advancer will have three or four card support and a hand in the range of a good five to a bad nine points.

One of the greatest sins of omission occurs when the advancer has a hand that warrants a raise and fails to do so. When the opponents bid further the overcaller never knows when to compete since he believes that there is no fit, or advancer has no values, (or both).

Example 104:

a) Advancer	b) Advancer
♠ J83	♠ 1092
♡ K74	♡ KJ
♢ Q9763	♢ A97
♣ 82	♣ 87654

With Example hand 104a) if partner has overcalled in either major suit or in diamonds advancer needs to raise. Failure on his part to make a single raise and describe his hand will leave the overcaller without the necessary knowledge of the fit and values for a raise if the opponents compete further.

With Example hand 104b) advancer should raise an overcall in any suit. Although his hand would not raise an opening bid of one heart, when the bid of one heart has been an overcall a raise on a very good doubleton may be the only descriptive call available to advancer. A bid of one notrump would be fine if partner's one heart bid were an opening bid, but since it is an overcall one notrump would be a poor description by advancer.

2) A change of suit is not forcing and should be considered to be corrective in nature. If advancer has removed his partner's overcall in a major suit to a minor suit, his support for the major suit will be poor. He will usually have a void or singleton, but might have a doubleton if his own suit is quite good.

If advancer removes his partner's overcall from a minor suit to a major suit it is possible that he does have a fit for the suit of the overcall. Advancer will offer a major suit in an attempt to improve the contract and possibly even reach game in the major suit if the overcaller has a fit and good values. If the overcaller has no fit and bids again after advancer's correction, advancer will be able to support the original minor suit of the overcall or will have a good enough suit of his own to be able to repeat it, not needing support from the overcaller.

Example 105:

a) Advancer
♠QJ1063
♡A9
◇643
♣K105

b) Advancer
♠Q96
♡KQJ984
◇643
♣3

c) Advancer
♠K10642
♡AQJ3
◇7
♣K63

d) Advancer
♠Q8642
♡K532
◇86
♣J4

With Example hand 105a) you have heard partner overcall an opening bid of one diamond by bidding two clubs. Your should bid two spades to attempt to improve the contract. If partner cannot stand spades you are more than willing to play three clubs.

With Example hand 105b) correct partner's two club overcall to two hearts. Even if partner removes to deny heart support your suit is so good that you can next bid three hearts.

With Example hand 105c) your hand is too good to make a simple raise and a correction to spades would be unilateral. Make a simple cue bid of two diamonds and the overcaller's next bid will give you a better idea of how to proceed.

With Example hand 105d) you should pass. Any attempt to improve the contract could meet with disaster. You do not have enough in values, fit, or independent suit quality to make a call.

3) A jump in a new suit is highly invitational but not forcing. Advancer shows a hand with a good suit and opening bid values. His hand will look like a typical intermediate jump overcall. Advancer may have a fit for the overcaller, but his forward going action promises just that he has a very good suit and about the values of an opening bid.

4) A jump raise of the overcall is strictly preemptive. Advancer will have a four or five card fit for the overcall, some distributional feature, and very little in values. The jump raise of the overcall often has devastating effects on the opposition, taking away their bidding space before they are able to determine where they might play.

5) A jump cue bid by the advancer is a "power" raise. The advancer promises a hand with four card or longer support for the overcall and about ten to fourteen high card points. His hand will also either have distributional merit or "hard" values. When he is a passed hand advancer will have a hand with the lower portion of the described range.

6) Advancer's cue bid is an all purpose force. His hand will have reasonable values and he will visualize the possibility of game. Often advancer will have good values and a three card fit for the overcall.

On other occasions advancer will need to create a forcing auction, and makes a cue bid prior to showing a suit of his own. If advancer first cue bids, then bids a new suit of his own, the auction is forcing.

When the overcaller hears a cue bid from his partner his obligation is to indicate whether his overcall is good or bad. When his overcall is minimum, after a cue bid from advancer the overcaller will repeat his suit. This is necessary even when the suit of the overcall is only four cards long. The rebid of the suit of the overcall says nothing about suit length, only that the overcall is minimum in nature.

When the advancer has cue bid and the overcall was made with a good hand, the overcaller continues by telling more about the nature of his hand. He may bid a second suit in which he has a concentration of values in lieu of length, he may bid notrump with values in the opener's suit, or he may jump rebid his own suit when it is a good suit of six cards or more.

The one thing that the overcaller may not do when he has a good over-call and the advancer has cue bid is repeat the suit of his overcall at the cheapest level. That bid identifies his overcall as minimum, and a good game contract might be missed if misinformation is conveyed in this manner.

Example 106:

a) Advancer
♠95432
♡QJ62
◊6
♣Q62

b) Advancer
♠9542
♡K106
◊63
♣AJ64

c) Advancer
♠A63
♡K1064
◊63
♣A954

d) Advancer
♠A1093
♡KJ9
◊64
♣AQ95

e) Advancer
♠AQJ963
♡K4
◊6
♣Q742

f) Advancer
♠AQJ963
♡K4
◊6
♣AQ42

With Example hand 106a) you have heard partner make a major suit overcall after an opening bid of one diamond. Regardless of responder's action you should make a jump raise of partner's suit to the three level. This preemptive action will make life quite difficult for the opponents.

With Example hand 106b) after an opening bid of one diamond and an overcall in any other suit by partner, you should make a single raise to show your fit and values.

With Example hand 106c) if partner's overcall after the one diamond opening bid is one spade, make a simple cue bid and then show your support for spades. If the overcall is either in hearts or clubs, jump to three diamonds to show your good raise with four card support for partner's suit.

With Example hand 106d) you will again make a power jump raise if partner's overcall is either in spades or clubs, but will make a simple cue bid followed by a heart raise if the overcall is in that suit.

With Example hand 106e) if partner has overcalled one heart after an opening bid in either minor suit, jump to two spades. This jump shows your good suit and opening bid values. It is not forcing but it is highly invitational.

With Example hand 106f) when partner has overcalled with one heart your first action should be a cue bid of the opening bidder's suit. At your following turn you will bid spades and your bid will be forcing. A cue bid followed by a change of suit by advancer is absolutely forcing in all auctions.

Example 107:

a) Overcaller
♠J865
♡KQ1097
♢52
♣94

b) Advancer
♠AKQ3
♡64
♢7
♣AKJ853

This pair of hands occurred in a Regional Championship event. With Example hand 107a) after an opening bid of one diamond a lead directing overcall of one heart was made. The overcall was necessary despite this hand's meager values since the auction might have continued directly to a three notrump contract by responder. Overcaller most certainly wanted a heart lead from his partner against any contract, particularly a contract in notrump.

With Example hand 107b) the advancer made a cue bid of two diamonds, and overcaller bid two hearts to show a minimum overcall. Advancer now was able to bid three clubs which was forcing. Having no real options overcaller bid three hearts. Advancer next bid three spades which was again a forcing call. Overcaller knew to raise to four spades and the best contract had been reached. This auction was possible only because each call had definition due to systemic agreements. Most pairs floundered at a part score in clubs, although some did manage to get to spades but not to game.

The Jump Overcall

Jump overcalls in suits are preemptive except when they have a conventional meaning. When partner has not passed the preemptive jump overcall should be much like a minimum weak two bid, showing a six card suit at the two level. When made at the three level the jump overcall shows a hand much like a typical opening three bid, with good offensive strength and very little defensive strength.

When the jump overcall has been made at the two level the advancer may try for game by bidding two notrump. By agreement the two notrump call should seek some specific information about the nature of the jump overcall. It should ask for an **Ogust** rebid, or it should ask for a side feature if the jump has been made with a maximum hand, or it should ask for side shortness. Whatever the information it seeks, that is something that should be predetermined. Two notrump should never be misinterpreted as an attempt to escape from the jump overcaller's suit.

Two special jump overcalls may be agreed which are descriptive rather than preemptive. These two special bids function best when the partnership has agreed to play **Top and Bottom Cue Bids** since they show hands of the same type.

The **Top and Bottom Cue Bid** shows the highest and lowest ranking unbid suits while emphasizing the lower suit. Typical shapes will be four-six or four-five, or five-five when the lower suit is of good quality and the upper suit poor. These hands are normally hard to bid since the upper suit which is a major and more to be sought than the longer or better minor suit will often get lost if the bidder has no choice but to overcall in the lower suit.

When the overcaller has the two lower ranking suits and the minor suit is longer or stronger than his heart suit, the overcaller has a similar problem. If he overcalls in his longer or stronger minor suit a fit in hearts could be lost. An overcall in the shorter heart suit would be a distortion and might easily lead to the wrong contract.

Conventional jump overcalls solve this problem. When the opening bid has been one club, the jump overcall of two diamonds shows diamonds and hearts with longer or stronger diamonds. If hearts were the longer or stronger suit the overcaller could begin by bidding hearts and show his diamond suit later.

When the opening bid has been one diamond a jump overcall of three clubs shows clubs and hearts with longer or stronger clubs. Again if hearts were longer or stronger the overcaller would bid hearts first.

Addition of these two special jump overcalls to the competitive bidding agreements of the partnership cares for these problem hands that are otherwise virtually impossible to describe.

Example 108:

a) Overcaller
♠AQ10963
♡95
◊J1093
♡7

b) Overcaller
♠64
♡Q109863
◊K54
♣J6

c) Overcaller
♠853
♡7
◊KQJ9742
♣74

d) Overcaller
♠104
♡AQJ6
◊AQ1095
♣83

e) Overcaller
♠104
♡AQJ6
◊3
♣KQ10862

Example hand 108a) is a maximum weak jump overcall of two spades over an opening bid in any lower suit. If advancer bids two notrump you should show a good hand with a good suit if your agreement is *Ogust*, a side feature in diamonds is that if what is sought by two notrump, or shortness in clubs if that is your agreement.

Example hand 108b) is a fine hand for a jump to two hearts after an opening bid in a minor suit. If the opening bid has been one spade this hand should not jump to three hearts unless not vulnerable and facing a passed partner.

Example hand 108c) has a fine suit and no defense and clearly is entitled to make a jump overcall of three diamonds after an opening major suit bid. If the opening bid has been one club this hand's jump overcall of three diamonds may effectively keep the opponents from finding their best game.

Example hand 108d) will jump to two diamonds after an opening bid of one club if the partnership agreement is that this bid shows diamonds and hearts with longer or stronger diamonds.

Example hand 108e) will similarly jump to three clubs after an opening bid of one diamond to show this otherwise difficult to describe hand. This hand is a typical *Top and Bottom Cue Bid* if the opening bid has been one spade.

Overcalls in Notrump

Overcalls of one notrump after an opening suit bid are much as they are in standard bidding. The major difference is in the response structure. System players use the same reponse complex after an overcall of one notrump that they use facing a one notrump opening bid.

When it is agreed that the response structure will be used facing an overcall of one notrump that is used facing a one notrump opening bid, one idle bid exists. The one idle bid is a transfer to the major suit of the opening bidder. Advancer could not possibly want to play in that suit when the opener will usually have five or more cards there.

The otherwise idle transfer to the opening bidder's suit can be used as a check on the quality of stoppers in the notrump overcaller's hand. The availability of this stopper quality check will allow overcalls in notrump with hands that otherwise fully qualify, but have a shaky stopper in opener's suit, or perhaps something like four small cards.

When the advancer transfers to the major suit of the opening bid he asks the notrump overcaller to tell him both how good his stoppers are and how good his hand is. When the overcaller has the suit well stopped he bids two notrump to show a minimum overcall and jumps to three notrump if his values are maximum.

If the overcaller's stopper in the opening bidder's major suit is tenuous he indicates that fact by accepting the transfer. When advancer hears acceptance of the transfer bid he knows that notrump will not be a good contract and can begin a search for an alternate place to play while the auction is still at a low level. If the advancer continues by introducing a new suit his call is forcing since his original probe showed values enough to seek a game.

Example 109:

	a) Overcaller	b) Overcaller
♠	AQ54	J63
♡	J63	AQ75
◇	KQ94	AQ94
♣	K4	A4

With either Example 109 hand if the opening bid has been one club you should not overcall one notrump. Your correct action is to make a takeout double. If the opening bid is in any other suit the system permits you to overcall one notrump.

With Example hand 109a) if the opening bid has been one spade and advancer transfers to that suit, bid two notrump to show that spades are well stopped and your overcall was made with minimum values. If the opening bid has been one heart and advancer transfers to that suit, bid two hearts to indicate that your heart stopper is poor.

With Example hand 109b) if the opening bid has been one heart and advancer transfers to that suit, jump to three notrump to show good stoppers and maximum values. If the opening bid has been one spade and advancer transfers to that suit, bid two spades and listen to advancer's next (forcing) call.

Unusual Notrump

A basic principle of bidding is that when it is illogical for a bid to mean what its definition says it means, its meaning is exactly the opposite. A classic example of this concept is the takeout double. In its most literal use, the call "double" states that the bidder who has doubled is well equipped to defeat the contract that he has doubled, and suggests that he has an unexpectedly good holding in the trump suit that has been bid by the opponents, particularly if the double is at a low level.

The takeout double uses that term to mean exactly the opposite of its literal meaning. Since it would be illogical to double an opening bid for penalties, instead of suggesting penalties and showing a trump stack in the suit of the opening bidder the double shows values and support for the other suits. Instead of asking his partner to pass and defend the takeout doubler asks his partner to bid and declare.

This concept is extended to bids in notrump that cannot possibly suggest a notrump contract. Instead of showing a strong balanced hand, a bid in notrump when it is illogical for the bidder to want to play in notrump shows a weak unbalanced hand.

For example in the auction: P-1♠-P-3♠, 3NT, the dealer who has passed could not possibly want to play a contract of three notrump. His initial pass has denied the values of an opening bid, and the strong spade holding shown by the bidding of the opponents indicates that they will be able to take several spade tricks against a notrump contract. Certainly this is a very "unusual" notrump call.

Likewise a jump overcall in notrump at the level of two, four or five should not be construed as indicating a desire to play a notrump contract. Balanced hands in the range of about twenty points are rare, and they are described by a takeout double followed by a voluntary bid in notrump from the takeout doubler. Jumps beyond the game level in notrump again make no sense if their intent is to convey the message of some excellent balanced hand.

Since these unusual calls in notrump do not describe strong balanced hands, their message is exactly the opposite. These calls are used to describe an unbalanced hand that has two long suits. The two suits shown will be the two lowest ranking suits that have not yet been bid.

The most common mistake made by users of the **unusual notrump** is an incorrect statement of values. The values shown cannot logically be indeterminate. The value range should be understood as either very weak defensively but offensively potent because of the two long suits, or it should be at the other end of the value scale, showing a very powerful two suited hand.

In short, the unusual notrump bid should show either a preemptive bid in two suits or a slam try in two suits. When the call is preemptive in nature the **unusual notrump** bidder should select the level at which he wishes to preempt and make his **unusual notrump** call, then never bid again. When the call is intended as a slam try, after forcing his partner to select between the two suits he has shown, the **unusual notrump** bidder bids once more, either raising the suit his partner has selected or making some other descriptive call such as a cue bid.

When a hand with the proper distribution has the wrong values, the **Unusual notrump** should not be used. With intermediate to good values, an overcall in the higher ranking of the two suits followed by a rebid in the other suit shows the distribution and the strength of the hand.

The bidder who mistakenly uses the **unusual notrump** with opening bid values can never tell what to do after his partner selects one of his suits. Should he pass? Should he raise? How can he tell?

But his partner may have an even more difficult time if he has no idea of the value range shown by the **unusual notrump** if the opponents bid further. Should he defend? Should he sacrifice? Who knows?

When the **unusual notrump** has been made with an appropriate hand the answers to all of these questions are easy. If the **unusual notrump** bidder has preempted he bids no more and his partner knows when it is right to defend and when it is right to bid on. If the **unusual notrump** bidder bids again he has a huge hand that can virtually make game in one of his suits with little more than a fit for one of his suits in his partner's hand, and could easily make a slam when his partner has more than that.

The second most common error made in the use of this conventional tool occurs when the bidder does not have the suit lengths promised by his bid. The **unusual notrump** shows at least five-five distribution in the two suits shown when he jumps to two notrump. When he jumps to four or five notrump his suits will be even longer, at least six-five or six-six for four, and six-six or seven-six for five notrump. Those who err by jumping to two notrump with only five-four clearly earn the bad results they will attain by either getting too high or to the wrong suit.

Example 110:

a) Overcaller	b) Overcaller	c) Overcaller
♠6	♠63	♠6
♡95	♡95	♡95
◇QJ1085	◇QJ1085	◇AQJ83
♣KQ1063	♣KQ106	♣KQ1063

d) Overcaller	e) Overcaller
♠6	♠6
♡AQJ106	♡--
◇A5	◇KJ10542
♣AKJ95	♣QJ10986

With Example hand 110a) bid two notrump over a major suit opening bid. Your hand has very little defense and will be good offensively if partner fits with either of your suits.

With Example hand 110b) do not use the *unusual notrump*. Your five-four distribution is not adequate for two suited pre-emption.

With Example hand 110c) when there has been a major suit opening bid you should overcall two diamonds and bid clubs later if you are able. Your hand has the wrong value range for the *unusual notrump*.

With Example hand 110d) bid two notrump over an opening bid of one diamond. When partner selects one of your suits you will raise, thereby showing a huge hand with interest in slam.

With Example hand 110e) do not bid two notrump after an opposing major suit opening bid. Your suit lengths make two notrump an insufficient preempt, and having preempted you must not bid again. Tell your whole story the first time. Bid four notrump.

The requirement of at least five cards in each of the two suits shown by the use of **unusual notrump** does not necessarily apply in balancing position. If the opponents have bid and raised a major suit and you are in balance position, if you have shortness in the unbid major suit you might balance by bidding an "unusual" two notrump with as little as four-four length in the minor suits. You do not wish to balance and hear partner bid in your short major suit unless he does so entirely on his own, not expecting any support from you.

A variation of the theme occurs when someone who has already bid later bids notrump when it is clear that he cannot wish to play in notrump. The belated notrump bidder will have a hand with a good suit that he has already bid, but will also have another suit to tell his partner about. The second suit will usually be two cards shorter than the bidder's first suit. If he were to bid his second suit he would suggest that his partner select between them as though they were about equal in length, but when the length disparity is of two cards the bidder wants to play in his first suit if no real fit for his second suit exists.

Example 111:

a) Opener	b) Overcaller	c) Balancer
♠A5	♠6	♠8653
♡7	♡95	♡7
◇AKJ1063	◇K1083	◇AQJ5
♣AQ94	♣AKJ1062	♣KQ106

With Example hand 111a) you have opened with one diamond and heard your left hand opponent bid four spades followed by two passes. You should now bid four notrump to show a hand with a good diamond suit and another four card suit. If partner has four clubs and short diamonds he will bid five clubs. He knows that if your second suit is hearts and not clubs that you will correct to five diamonds. If he has fewer than four clubs he will bid five diamonds.

With Example hand 111b) you have overcalled two clubs after an opening bid of one heart. Your left hand opponent raises to two hearts and two passes follow. You should balance with a call of two notrump to show a good long club suit and a four card diamond suit as well. Your second suit must be diamonds since if it were spades you could balance by bidding two spades instead, or might have first made a *Top and Bottom Cue Bid* if that is what you play.

With Example hand 111c) your right hand opponent has bid one spade and after your pass his partner has raised to two spades. After two passes it is your turn and you should balance by bidding two notrump. You know that your partner is short in spades and you want him to bid a minor suit.

Takeout Doubles

Takeout doubles are usually the same as in standard bidding. The takeout doubler will have support for the unbid suits, particularly unbid major suits, and values enough to produce a good dummy. The notion that a takeout double shows the values of an opening bid without regard for distribution is totally false and has no relation whatever to the real language of bidding in the system.

If the takeout doubler next makes a call in a new suit after the response to his takeout double, his message is not that his partner has bid a suit for which he was unprepared and he is taking corrective action. The message sent by the takeout doubler who has next bid a suit of his own is that he really wanted to overcall, but his hand was so good that he feared an overcall would understate his values to the extent that a game that should be bid might be missed.

If the takeout doubler corrects to notrump his hand is too good for an overcall in notrump. It will be a balanced hand with a good eighteen points or more. If the takeout doubler corrects to a suit of his own he has a good suit and a hand that is worth about eighteen or more points.

Example 112:

a) Doubler	b) Doubler	c) Doubler
♠AKJ1072	♠84	♠AQ4
♡83	♡AJ93	♡AJ93
◇AQ4	◇KQ6	◇KQ6
♣A93	♣K1092	♣K92

With Example hand 112a) you hear an opening bid in one of the three lower ranking suits on your right. You might overcall one spade, but the possibility of making a game is so great that a better description is to first make a takeout double, then bid spades. When partner hears the takeout double he will think you have a hand with support for all of the unbid suits, but when you next bid spades he will expect a hand such as this.

With Example hand 112b) if the opening bid has been one spade you have a reasonable takeout double with support for all of the unbid suits. Many make the error of doubling an opening bid in a minor suit just to show that they have opening bid values. When partner bids spades they feel that they can correct to notrump at the cheapest level and thereby describe the hand that they hold. This is a great fallacy, for the double followed by the correction does not describe a hand of these values. With this hand if you absolutely must enter the auction after a minor suit opening bid, overcall one heart on your reasonable four card suit. This is not an exceptionally good call, but it is far better than a takeout double.

Example hand 112c) is the hand that first makes a takeout double and then bids notrump. The message conveyed is that the hand is of notrump shape, but that the values were too great for an original overcall in notrump.

If the agreement has been made to use **Top and Bottom Cue Bids** the emphasis of the takeout double shifts to the two higher ranking unbid suits. Although the takeout doubler may have a classic hand with support for all unbid suits, he has only promised that he has the two that are highest in rank.

Responder to the takeout double should strain to respond in one of those suits, and should bid the lowest ranking of the three unbid suits only when it is the only possible action that will describe his hand. Holding five cards in the lowest ranking suit and four cards in a higher ranking (major) suit, responder to the takeout double should always bid the major suit. If he later also bids the lowest ranking suit the takeout doubler should expect that suit to be longer than the major suit of the original response to the takeout double.

If the responder to the takeout double does bid the lowest ranking suit and the takeout doubler corrects to the lower ranking of the two remaining suits, he does not show extra values. He indicates that his takeout double was intended to show the two higher ranking suits, and that he cannot afford to pass and allow his partner to play in the lowest ranking suit. If his correction is to diamonds his diamond suit will be longer than the unbid major suit. If he corrects to hearts he may have five-five in the majors with a hand that he could not adequately describe by overcalling in spades and later bidding hearts.

The takeout double of a minor suit opening bid should show at least four-three distribution in the major suits, although with a hand such as: ♠AKx ♡AJx ◇xx ♣Jxxxx a takeout double of an opening bid of one diamond is certainly the most descriptive action available.

The takeout doubler will more often have four-four in the majors, or five-four with a five card suit not good enough to overcall. With a five-five hand and marginal values a takeout double is better than a spade overcall, but with a sound hand a spade overcall and a later bid in hearts is superior.

With a holding of five-three in the major suits an overcall in the five card suit will be the best action unless the five card suit is very weak and the three card holding quite good. If a takeout double is made with this major suit pattern, partner of the takeout doubler is almost certain to respond in the major suit for which the takeout doubler has only three card support. This will result in reaching many four-three fits while five-three fits exist in the other major suit.

Example 113:

a) Doubler	b) Doubler	c) Doubler
♠KJ53	♠KJ53	♠KJ53
♡Q1094	♡AK4	♡A10654
◇6	◇63	◇63
♣AJ85	♣Q954	♣K5

d) Doubler	e) Doubler	f) Doubler
♠KJ954	♠84	♠KJ1063
♡AQ3	♡AQ103	♡AQ954
◇63	◇AQ10962	◇7
♣K85	♣5	♣65

With Example hand 113a) you have a fine takeout double of an opening bid of one diamond. Even though your values are slim when compared with opening bid requirements, your excellent shape and support for all suits make this takeout double a good dummy for partner no matter what suit he bids.

With Example hand 113b) your shape is not quite as good, but your values are better. You have no apologies for your takeout double of a one diamond opening bid.

With Example hand 113c) a takeout double of an opening one diamond bid has more appeal than an overcall of one heart. The overcall might cause your side to miss a spade fit. If partner bids clubs in response to your takeout double you should pass. Even though you have only a doubleton club, partner knew that you did not want to hear him bid that suit, and the quality of your doubleton should provide enough support for his club suit.

With Example 113d) do not make a takeout double, overcall one spade. Even though you do have support for all of the unbid suits, partner will often respond in hearts when he has four hearts and three spades, and you will play in a four-three fit rather than a five-three. It would be wrong to double and then bid spades as that would show a much better hand.

With Example hand 113e) if the opening bid is one club you can jump to two diamonds to show this hand with longer diamonds than hearts. If the opening bid has been one spade you can make a takeout double. If partner responds in clubs you can correct to diamonds. This correction does not show additional values and indicates a hand just like the one that you hold.

With Example hand 113f) you hope to be playing *Michaels Cue Bids* rather than *Top and Bottom* when the opening bid is in a minor suit. However, since you are playing *Top and Bottom Cue Bids* you would best describe this hand with a takeout double. Your values are not good enough to overcall in spades and then bid hearts at a higher level. If partner responds in the unbid minor suit you will correct to hearts at the cheapest level to require him to select one of the major suits.

Responsive Doubles

A **responsive double** is a tool to be used after an opponent has opened the bidding, partner has taken action by either overcalling or making a takeout double, and responder has either raised the opening bid or has bid one notrump. The function of the **responsive double** is to solve an otherwise difficult bidding problem.

When partner has overcalled and responder has either raised the opening bid or bid one notrump, two suits remain unbid. Often, advancer will have length in both of the unbid suits. If he elects to bid one of them a fit in the other may be missed. The responsive double by advancer shows some values and length in both unbid suits.

Ideally advancer will have five or more cards in each of the unbid suits, but on occasion he may have only four card length in one of the suits but still have no call that is more expressive. The overcaller is encouraged to bid one of the suits shown by the responsive double on a three card holding.

When partner has made a takeout double rather than an overcall the responsive double only applies when responder raises the suit of the opening bid, and cares for a different kind of bidding problem. The responsive double indicates that the takeout doubler's partner has some useful values but cannot reasonably express those values. If he were to bid freely rather than use a **responsive double** he would overstate his values and the auction could easily get out of hand.

Oklahoma City expert Mike Aliotta has suggested that an even finer gradation of values can be expressed when the takeout doubler's partner would have to go to the three level to show a long suit with extremely limited values. Rather than make a **responsive double** the takeout doubler's partner can bid two notrump, using that call as **Lebensohl** in this type of auction. The **responsive double** can be reserved for hands that are not sure what the trump suit should be when **Lebensohl** is also available in such an auction.

Example 114:

a) Advancer	b) Advancer	c) Advancer
♠K97	♠J97	♠KJ976
♡874	♡86	♡8
◇Q976	◇65	◇AJ1054
♣J108	♣Q108742	♣Q3

With Example hand 114a) you have heard you left hand opponent open with one heart. Partner has made a takeout double and right hand opponent has raised to two hearts. A bid of three diamonds would overstate your values, but a *responsive double* will convey to partner that you have some useful cards and allow him to bid his best suit, expecting that you will have some support.

With Example hand 114b) you have heard an opening bid of one spade and a raise to two spades after partner's takeout double. You do not have the values to bid three clubs, and a *responsive double* might cause partner to bypass clubs and bid a red suit. Your *Lebensohl* bid of two notrump requires partner to bid three clubs which you will pass.

With Example hand 114c) you have heard partner overcall one heart after an opening bid of one club, and responder has bid one notrump. A bid by you in either of your suits risks missing a fit in the other one. You can best describe this hand by making a responsive double to show both of your suits. Partner is expected to bid the one of your suits in which he has three cards, expecting you to have five card support.

Snapdragon

A somewhat similar situation occurs when three suits have been bid. If advancer has support for the suit of his partner's overcall but also would like to bid the fourth suit, he has a bidding dilemma. If he raises the overcall it is possible to miss a better contract in the fourth suit. If he bids the fourth suit he may play there when his partner has no fit rather than comfortably in the overcaller's suit.

The solution to this problem is called **Snapdragon**. Advancer uses an artificial double to show the hand that has at least five cards in the unbid suit, and support (or at least a tolerance) for the overcaller's suit.

Example 115:

	a) Advancer	b) Advancer
♠	42	542
♡	KQ1075	KQ
◇	KJ6	AJ9863
♣	875	76

With Example hand 115a) advancer hears his partner overcall an opening one club bid by bidding one diamond, and responder bids one spade. Advancer makes a *Snapdragon* double to show that he has a heart suit as well as support for diamonds.

With Example hand 115b) advancer's partner has overcalled one heart after an opening bid of one club, and responder again bids one spade. Advancer's *Snapdragon* double shows that he has diamonds and a tolerance for hearts.

Cue Bids

Once used to show a very powerful hand with first round control of the opponents' suit, the cue bid today is standardly used to show some two suited hand with moderate values. The use of this cue bid makes more sense than the older application since the very strong hand rarely occurs, while two suiters with moderate values are quite common.

1) Probably the most popular use of the cue bid today was promulgated by the late Mike Michaels, a Florida expert. The **Michaels Cue Bid** shows a hand with two suits, each of which is expected to be of five or more cards in length, and between six and eleven high card points.

If the opening bid has been in a minor suit, **Michaels** promises both major suits. If the opening bid has been in a major suit, **Michaels** shows the unbid major suit and one of the minor suits. At the time of the cue bid it is not known which minor suit the cue bidder holds. If his partner wishes to know which minor the cue bidder holds he artificially bids two notrump to ask the cue bidder to name his minor suit.

When the responder to the cue bid has a fit for one of the suits shown and wants to have that suit become the trump suit, he bids that suit at a level that shows the extent of his values facing the expected range of six to eleven in the cue bidder's hand. If his bid is made cheaply in one of the cue bidder's suits, he may not even have much of a fit, and is trying to keep the auction as low as possible. If he jumps to the three level in a major suit known to be held by the cue bidder, he is inviting the cue bidder to carry on to game if he has maximum values within the limited range that has already been described.

Responder to the **Michaels Cue Bid** can also jump directly to game, or can make a return cue bid to show a very good hand with interest in slam.

Example 116:

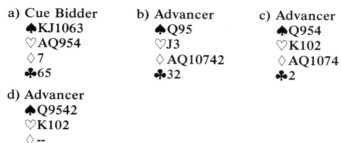

a) Cue Bidder
♠KJ1063
♡AQ954
◇7
♣65

b) Advancer
♠Q95
♡J3
◇AQ10742
♣32

c) Advancer
♠Q954
♡K102
◇AQ1074
♣2

d) Advancer
♠Q9542
♡K102
◇ --
♣A10742

Example hand 116a) is a very good hand for a *Michaels Cue Bid* after a minor suit opening bid. If advancer jumps to three in either major suit this cue bidder will continue to game.

Example hand 116b) finds advancer with only a moderate fit in spades and marginal secondary values in diamonds. This advancer bids as cheaply as possible in spades.

Example hand 116c) has good values and expects to make game facing a maximum *Michaels Cue Bid*. He invites game by jumping to three spades.

Example 116d) has a fifth spade and good holdings in all suits. This advancer expects to make a game facing even a minimum *Michaels Cue Bid* hand. He jumps to four spades.

2) Also in extensive use by system players is the **Top and Bottom Cue Bid**. This use of the cue bid shows the highest and lowest ranking unbid suits, but tends to emphasize the low suit. Generally the lower ranking suit will be either longer or stronger than the upper suit.

When the opening bid is in clubs the cue bid shows diamonds and spades. When the opening bid is either in diamonds or hearts, the cue bid shows clubs and spades. When the opening bid has been in spades the cue bid shows clubs and hearts. The strength of the hand is not severely limited and the cue bidder will judge his values based on the vulnerability and the situation.

Responder to the **Top and Bottom Cue Bid** will bid the top suit only when he holds four of them, or to escape with three cards when his holding in the bottom suit is a singleton or void. With hands that are ordinary and do not justify forward going action advancer will usually take refuge in the bottom suit at the cheapest level.

Responder to the **Top and Bottom Cue Bid** can also take forward going action by jumping in the suit indicated by his hand and the knowledge of what to expect from the cue bidder. With a hand that suggests slam he can also cue bid to find out more about the **Top and Bottom Cue Bidder's** hand.

The reason for emphasis on the bottom suit is that the major suit which is more important can be overcalled if it is substantial. The difficult hand to show is the one that suggests an overcall in the low ranking suit that also has a four card major. If one must overcall when this tool is not available, the major suit may be lost when the advancer has a fit for it, and the better scoring contract will never be reached.

If the **Top and Bottom Cue Bidder** at his next turn voluntarily introduces the top suit which was indicated by his cue bid and not chosen by the responder to the cue bid, he indicates that the top suit is a good suit at least five cards long, and that he has a very good hand. He is able to show a hand which was too good for a simple overcall due to the two suited nature of the hand and abundance of high cards, while also indicating exactly which two suits he holds.

The **Top and Bottom Cue Bid** is complimented by other bidding tools which have been presented earlier. These include takeout doubles which are oriented toward the two higher ranking suits, and jump overcalls in some auctions to show a good minor suit and a lesser heart suit. The basic hand type for these two jump overcalls is the same hand type that is typical for **Top and Bottom**.

Many partnerships choose to combine the use of both types of cue bids that have just been presented here. They use **Michaels** when the opening bid has been in a minor suit to show length in both majors, and they use **Top and Bottom** when the opening bid has been in a major suit to show the difficult hand that has club length and strength as well as a lesser holding in the unbid major suit.

Example 117:

a) Cue Bidder	b) Cue Bidder	c) Cue Bidder
♠8	♠QJ103	♠J9532
♡KJ105	♡86	♡6
◇63	◇AQJ106	◇42
♣KQ9543	♣95	♣KQJ94

d) Cue Bidder
♠ AKJ85
♡ 7
◇ K7
♣ KQJ98

With Example hand 117a) the cue bidder bids two spades after an opposing one spade opening bid. His call shows a hand with clubs and hearts, with clubs expected to be either longer or stronger.

With Example hand 117b) the cue bidder bids two clubs after an opposing opening bid of one club to show diamonds and spades with longer or stronger diamonds.

With Example hand 117c) after an opening bid in either red suit a cue bid shows clubs and spades with longer or stronger clubs.

With Example hand 117d) you should cue bid after an opening bid in either red suit. At your next turn you will voluntarily bid spades to show your good hand with two good suits.

3) When the opponents have bid two suits as opener and responder, a bid by your side in either of the two suits that have already been shown is natural. Your statement is that although they have bid the suit that you now bid, your holding is long and strong enough that you feel it should become the trump suit for your side.

When the auction has been, for example, one club by opener and one heart by responder, opener might have as few as three small clubs. Likewise responder might have four small hearts. When you have been dealt a very good long suit you do not care that there may be a trump stack in the hand of the opponent who has bid the suit. Your own holding is sufficient to overcome the mild stack and it is to your advantage to have your good suit as trumps.

There is no need to have this apparent cue bid be for takeout. When the opponents have bid two suits, a double is still for takeout and suggests that you want partner to bid one of the two remaining suits. In addition to showing the two remaining suits, a double in this auction also shows that you have reasonable defensive strength.

When you wish to compete because you have the two unbid suits but do not have defensive strength you can express your good offensive two suiter by using the **unusual notrump**. If you have not previously passed and bid one notrump partner will expect that you have a strong balanced hand, so you will need to jump in notrump to show that your call is for takeout.

Example 118:

a) Overcaller
♠A4
♡6
◇AKQ1042
♣J654

b) Overcaller
♠AJ10863
♡7
◇K
♣KQJ98

c) Doubler
♠103
♡AQJ75
◇AJ1064
♣7

d) Overcaller
♠103
♡KQJ75
◇KJ1064
♣7

With Example hand 118a) you hear an opening bid on your left of one diamond and a major suit response on your right. Your overcall of two diamonds is natural.

With Example hand 118b) the opening bid on your left has been one diamond and right hand opponent has responded one spade. Your best plan of action is to bid two spades (natural) at this turn and later bid clubs. If you eschew spades at this turn and bid clubs you will never be able to convince your partner that you really have spades no matter how vigorously you bid that suit later.

With Example hand 118c) you have heard left hand opponent bid one club and a one spade response on your right. You do not need to cue bid to show this hand. Since it has good support for both unbid suits and good defensive cards you can describe this hand quite well with a takeout double.

With Example hand 118d) you have again heard an opening bid on your left of one club and a response of one spade on your right. You want to show your two suits but deny good defensive values so you should use the *unusual notrump*. If you are a passed hand you can bid one notrump, but if you have not previously passed you need to jump to two notrump.

Defending Against Weak Two Bids

1) In defending against an opening weak two bid the general rule is that a bid in the immediate seat tends to show very sound values. When the values in the hand of the immediate bidder are less than very sound that fact can only be justified when he has extreme shortness in the suit of the weak two bid. Partner of the immediate seat defender should expect a solid hand from his partner, but should be warned when he has length in the suit of the weak two bid that his partner may be a little light since he is certain to be short in the suit of the weak two bid.

An overcall of the weak two bid shows a good hand with a good suit. A jump overcall, unless conventional, shows an even better hand. There is no such thing as a preemptive jump when the opposing opening bid has also been preemptive.

A takeout double of the weak two bid shows sound values, minimally about fourteen points in high cards. If the takeout doubler has a singleton or void in the suit of the weak two bid he can reasonably shade those values to about twelve high card points. In either case the takeout doubler should have the expected defensive strength of at least two plus tricks. The shorter his holding in the suit of the weak two bid, the greater likelihood that his partner may convert the double for penalties, and a hand with "slow" defensive values may not be sufficient.

An overcall of two notrump is NOT the **unusual notrump** showing a two suited hand. The two notrump overcall is a good balanced hand, but due to the fact that the auction has been crowded by the opening weak two bid, the high card requirement for the two notrump overcall must be somewhat elastic. The notrump overcaller will have from a good fourteen points to about nineteen.

Example 119:

a) Overcaller	b) Doubler	c) Overcaller
♠K4	♠KJ106	♠K4
♡7	♡7	♡AJ6
◇AKJ9832	◇AJ94	◇KQ94
♣A54	♣KQ73	♣K1087

With Example hand 119a) after a weak two heart opening bid an overcall of three diamonds is appropriate. With one fewer diamond and one less high honor card the overcall would be quite questionable.

Example hand 119b) is an excellent takeout double after an opening bid of two hearts. The fine shape would justify a takeout double even if a jack or queen were removed.

Example hand 119c) is a typical overcall of two notrump after an opening weak two bid in hearts. If the weak two bid had been in spades a takeout double would be in order instead.

It is possible to use a cue bid in the immediate seat after a weak two bid to show a two suited hand as with **Michaels** or **Top and Bottom**, but the values required would have to be substantially greater than after an opening one bid since the cue bid forces the auction to quite a high level. Because a very good hand is required, an alternate approach is recommended.

Holding a good two suited hand, after an opposing weak two bid a **Roman Jump Overcall** not only shows two suits, but it also identifies them. Since both suits become known immediately, further preemption cannot interfere with the auction as easily as it might if a cue bid were used to show a two suiter, one of which might never become known.

The **Roman Jump Overcall** shows the suit in which the bidder jumps and the next available suit. If the opening bid has been two hearts, a jump to three spades shows spades and clubs, a jump to four clubs shows clubs and diamonds, and a jump to four diamonds shows diamonds and spades. The **Roman Jump Overcaller** will have at least five-five distribution in his two suits, and his values will be such that he needs very little from advancer to make a contract at the level to which he has forced the auction.

When the agreement is to use **Roman Jump Overcalls** as a defense against weak two bids, the cue bid is released for other purposes. Since it is not needed to show two suited hands, the cue bid shows a solid single suited hand, usually with some side values but without a stopper in the suit of the weak two bid. With a running suit and a stopper it would be better to simply bid three notrump and expect to have a good chance to make that contract.

Responder to the cue bid knows that with a stopper in the suit of the weak two bid he can bid three notrump which will make more often than not. Lacking a stopper in the suit of the weak two bid he can make a waiting bid in the cheapest suit in order to find out which suit is held by the cue bidder. If he bids in any suit other than the cheapest suit at that point he shows a good suit of his own, and suggests that it be trumps rather than the solid suit known to be held by his partner.

Example 120:

a) Overcaller	b) Overcaller	c) Cue Bidder
♠AKJ105	♠AQJ1053	♠A4
♡6	♡--	♡2
◇ AKJ953	◇ 74	◇ AKQJ763
♣4	♣AK1095	♣Q103

After an opening bid of two hearts, Overcaller with Example hand 120a) will jump to four diamonds. This jump shows diamonds and spades and offers a choice of contracts.

With Example hand 120b) after an opening weak two bid of either two hearts or two diamonds you will jump to three spades to show spades and clubs.

With Example hand 120c) after an opening weak two bid in hearts you can make a cue bid of three hearts to show that you have a solid suit. Partner will bid three notrump if he has a heart stopper. If he instead bids three spades he is temporizing and denying a heart stopper. You will next bid four diamonds to show where your solid suit is located.

2) The partner of the bidder who takes immediate action after a weak two bid should know how to proceed. If his partner has overcalled, a change of suit by him should be forward going but not forcing. With a fit for the suit of his partner's overcall he can pass, raise, jump raise, or cue bid depending on the strength of his hand. Although a cue bid will imply a fit for the overcall, it may just show a hand too good to take any non-forcing action and the bidder will clarify the reason for his cue bid at his next turn. If he first cue bids and then bids a new suit, the auction is forcing.

If the immediate seat bidder after a weak two bid has made a takeout double, the **Lebensohl** convention should be used. If the responder to the takeout double bids at the two level in a higher ranking suit his call is not forward going in any sense. A jump to the three level in a higher ranking suit is a game invitation. The doubler should bid on if his values are slightly more than expected.

A response to the takeout double in a lower ranking suit at the three level promises values. The bidder will have a hand in the range of about seven to ten points. If his values are less, he bids two notrump, **Lebensohl**, to require the takeout doubler to bid three clubs and then pass after a correction to another suit. The takeout doubler will comply unless his values are so great that he wishes to push on toward a game even though he knows that his partner has fewer than seven points.

If the responder to the takeout double uses the **Lebensohl** bid of two notrump and then converts the required three club bid to a suit that ranks higher than the suit of the weak two bid, he shows that his values were not quite good enough to jump at his first turn and encourages the takeout doubler to bid more if he has extra values.

Example 121:

a) Advancer
♠ Q1074
♡ J3
◇ Q865
♣ 1092

b) Advancer
♠ KJ74
♡ 83
◇ K1094
♣ 1092

c) Advancer
♠ KJ742
♡ 83
◇ KQ94
♣ 102

d) Advancer
♠ KQ1074
♡ 8
◇ KQ94
♣ K102

e) Advancer
♠ Q104
♡ 83
◇ KQJ74
♣ J62

f) Advancer
♠ Q42
♡ 83
◇ QJ742
♣ 862

With all Example 121 hands you have heard an opening weak two heart bid on your left and your partner has made a takeout double.

With Example hand 121a) you make a simple bid of two spades. You are happy to be no higher than at the two level.

With Example hand 121b) you want to make a very mild game invitation. Your hand is not quite good enough to jump to three spades, so you bid two notrump. This requires the takeout doubler to bid three clubs. When you next correct to three spades you indicate that you have mild interest in a game if the takeout double is more than minimum.

With Example hand 121c) your values are good enough to make an immediate game invitation. Jump to three spades.

With Example hand 121d) your hand is too good to just invite a game. Jump to four spades.

With Example hand 121e) you can bid three diamonds. This voluntary bid at the three level shows the values of at least seven points.

With Example hand 121f) bid two notrump. This is *Lebensohl* and requires the takeout doubler to bid three clubs unless he has overwhelming values. You will correct his three club bid to three diamonds indicating that you always intended to be in diamonds but that your values are less than seven points.

When an overcall of two notrump has been made after the opening weak two bid, advancer has the tools to control the auction. All of his bids are transfer bids except a cue bid of the suit of the weak two bid which is **Stayman**. If the opening bid has been two hearts, for example, after the two notrump overcall advancer's bid of three clubs transfers to diamonds, three diamonds transfers to spades, three hearts is **Stayman**, and three spades is a transfer to clubs.

Without the availability of transfers·in this sort of auction the notrump overcaller would be hamstrung. If his partner bid in an unbid major suit at the three level the overcaller would not know whether that bid was based on a long suit with a weak hand, or whether it might show a five card suit with an eight or nine count. With advancer in control he can transfer and then pass when holding a long suit and a weak hand, but can transfer and then bid three notrump to show a five card suit and values that are probably enough to produce a game.

Example 122:

a) Advancer
♠J97532
♡6
♢Q854
♣95

b) Advancer
♠KQ1076
♡73
♢Q85
♣K109

c) Advancer
♠K1076
♡73
♢AQ8
♣Q1095

d) Advancer
♠J53
♡6
♢Q1098764
♣J5

In Example 122 there has been an opening weak two bid in hearts and the advancer's partner has overcalled with two notrump.

With Example hand 122a) advancer bids three diamonds to transfer to spades. When the overcaller bids three spades advancer passes, and the best contract has probably been reached.

With Example hand 122b) advancer again bids three diamonds to transfer to spades. After the overcaller bids three spades the advancer continues by bidding three notrump. This auction shows a five card spade suit and sufficient values for game. The overcaller can pass and play three notrump if he has only two spades, but can correct to four spades when he prefers to play there.

With Example hand 122c) advancer bids three hearts which is *Stayman*. If a four-four spade fit exists it will be found and game will be played in spades. If the overcaller cannot bid spades he will bid three notrump and that will become the contract.

With Example hand 122d) advancer bids three clubs which is a transfer to diamonds. Three diamonds will normally be a better contract than two notrump.

3) When a weak two bid is followed by two passes the bidder in fourth position has a different set of guidelines. His decision is whether to pass and defend or to compete. If his hand appears appropriate he should balance even with moderate values.

One of the keys to examine in making this decision is length in the suit of the weak two bid. When the balancer holds four or more cards in the suit of the weak two bid, with less than the strength of an opening notrump bid he should probably pass and defend. When his length in the suit of the weak two bid is a singleton or a void and the partner of the weak two bidder has not raised, it is likely that the balancing double will be left in by partner who holds four or five cards in the suit of the weak two bid. Balancer should take that probability into account if he decides to balance with a double.

The situation is less clear when the balancer holds two or three cards in the suit of the weak two bid. Since there has been no raise the balancer's partner may well also have two or three cards in the suit of the weak two bid. When two or three losers in the bid suit are possible, balancer should be reluctant unless other things about his hand are compelling.

A balancing bid should show a good five or a six card suit since it unilaterally suggests that balancer's suit will be the trump suit. A balancing bid in notrump should again show a good balanced hand with an elastic range of from a good fourteen to a bad nineteen points. A jump in a new suit in the balancing position will either show a good hand with a good suit, or it will be a **Roman Jump** if that is agreed in the partnership.

A balancing double can be made with good shape on values of about a good ten points or more. Since, as mentioned above, this double stands a good chance of being converted, the balancer should have reasonable defensive potential when he reopens with a double.

Example 123:

a) Balancer	b) Balancer	c) Balancer
♠K4	♠AJ87	♠A7
♡AJ6	♡5	♡53
◇KQ94	◇KQ10	◇KQ10
♣K1087	♣QJ863	♣AJ10974

Example 123 hands are in balancing position after an opening weak two bid in hearts.

With Example 123a) a balancing bid of two notrump is appropriate. This is the same hand that would bid two notrump in the direct seat after the weak two bid.

With Example hand 123b) balancer should double. He would be much happier to have doubled in immediate position since the auction at this point suggests that his partner may pass for penalties and his defensive values are slow. Still, a balancing double is mandatory.

With Example hand 123c) a balancing bid of three clubs is easy. Balancer has both good values and a reasonable suit.

PART II - DEFENDING AGAINST OPPOSING COMPETITIVE BIDS

Bidding After an Opposing Takeout Double

In all competitive situations it is important for responder to stretch to show a fit for opener's suit, particularly if it is a major suit. After a takeout double a simple raise by responder may be made with less in values than if the double had not occurred.

As in a non-competitive situation, three card support is sufficient to raise opener's major suit since he is known to have at least five card length. A raise in a minor suit promises very good support if only four cards, and five card support is expected if opener's suit is clubs. Three or four points in high cards is sufficient.

A jump raise in a major suit is primarily preemptive. Responder should either have four card support or should have values in the range of a normal single raise (5+ to 9-) with a distributional feature of some kind when his support is only three cards. In a minor suit the jump raise is identified by the term "flip-flop".

A jump to two notrump after the double of a major suit opening bid shows a good limit raise or better for the major suit. Until "flip-flop" was determined to be a superior approach the same was true if the opening bid had been in a minor suit. "Flip-flop" inverts the meaning of the jump raise and the jump to two notrump when the takeout double occurs after the opening bid of one of a minor suit. The jump raise becomes a limit raise for the minor suit, and the jump to two notrump becomes a preemptive raise.

The rationale for this inversion comes about because when opener knows that responder has a limit raise for his minor suit he often has the extra values that will allow his side to play three notrump. When this is so it will be more advantageous to have opener become declarer and force the takeout doubler to make the opening lead. When opener does not have the required extra values to bid three notrump he can pass and play at the three level in the agreed minor suit. If the response has been a preemptive jump to two notrump opener will nearly always correct and play the agreed minor suit at the three level.

Example 124:

a) Responder	b) Responder	c) Responder
♠K53	♠K953	♠KJ95
♡94	♡4	♡A4
◇J9762	◇J642	◇QJ64
♣1087	♣Q653	♣1087

d) Responder	e) Responder	f) Responder
♠85	♠8	♠85
♡J72	♡J72	♡A72
◇KJ93	◇KJ953	◇KJ953
♣9876	♣J976	♣K76

With Example hand 124a) you have heard partner open with one spade and your opponent has made a takeout double. Although you would most likely have passed if your opponent had passed, his action should cause you to raise to two spades. It is important to stretch to show a fit for partner in competitive situations.

With Example hand 124b) after partner's one spade bid and a takeout double you should jump to three spades. This action is primarily preemptive (but see *mini-splinters* later in this section).

With Example hand 124c) after the takeout double you should jump to two notrump to show a limit raise.

With Example hand 124d) your partner has opened with one diamond and there has been a takeout double. Your raise to two diamonds is no longer an *Inverted Minor Raise*, but shows limited values and a fit for diamonds.

With Example hand 124e) after the takeout double of partner's one diamond opening bid you should jump to two notrump. This "flip-flop" jump is a preemptive diamond raise.

With Example hand 124f) after the takeout double of partner's one diamond opening bid you should jump to three diamonds. This shows a limit raise for partner, and when he has extra values he will be able to play three notrump from his side.

After the takeout double if responder redoubles he will have a hand with good values (9+ or more) and no convenient call, or a hand with which he expects that his side will be able to penalize the opponents severely enough to outscore a contract that his side could declare.

If responder bids a new suit at the one level his bid ignores the double and says that he would have made this response in any case. If responder bids one notrump after the takeout double he shows a hand with the values of a response that is balanced and has scattered high cards. He will have less than the values required for a redouble, and if the opening bid was in a major suit this is not considered to be a **Forcing Notrump** response.

There was a time when the standard language of bidding stipulated that the only strong bid that could follow a takeout double was a redouble. Eventually, expert practice added the jump to two notrump which allowed responder to show a good hand with a fit. The rationale was that it is correct to get the opponents into the auction when responder holds no fit for opener, but that it is better to keep the opponents out of the auction and not allow exchange of information between them when responder does have a fit for opener.

One modern expert has rebutted the idea that only these two bids should show strong hands, and that any other bid by responder should indicate less than ten points. In his book **Judgment at Bridge**, many time World Champion Mike Lawrence shows why it is correct for responder to bid normally after a takeout double, even with a good hand, unless he feels that overwhelming penalties are in order or has no other expressive call.

Particularly when responder has a two suited hand, if he does not bid naturally at the one level, preemption by the responder to the takeout double may render him completely unable to express the nature of his hand. Unless he visualizes penalties as the ultimate objective with the hand that he holds, responder gives up far too much by not giving information about possible contracts his side might play if he randomly redoubles to show strength rather than make a descriptive forcing bid at the one level following the takeout double.

Aside: The book just recommended, **Judgment at Bridge**, is a must to further the education of aspiring intermediate players. Even advanced players will find much to learn here. A strong advocate of this book is Alfred Sheinwold (surely all readers here are acquainted with this Elder Statesman among all bridge columnists) who wrote the introduction to it.

A new suit bid at the two level after a takeout double is not forcing. It will usually be the bid of a minor suit after opener has bid a major suit. Responder's change of suit in this auction is corrective. He wants to indicate that a contract in opener's major suit is not attractive and that his own suit is a suggested alternative.

Responder will have shortness, a singleton or a void, in opener's major suit. He knows that the takeout doubler is also short in opener's suit and that the takeout doubler's partner may have the hand with which to make a penalty pass.

When responder removes from opener's major suit he both warns opener of this possibility and sets the defense if the opponents play the hand. Opener knows that responder will be able to ruff the first or second round of the major suit he has bid and responder has run from.

A jump shift by responder after a takeout double is preemptive. Again, if opener's suit was a major, responder suggests shortness in that suit as well as length in his own suit.

An alternate use of the jump shift if opener's suit is a major is the agreement that responder has a four card or longer fit for opener, less than the values to jump to two notrump to show a limit raise, and shortness in the suit of his jump. This **mini-splinter** may convey enough information about responder's hand to allow a very thin game to be bid, or for a good sacrifice to be taken against an opposing contract.

Example 125:

a) Responder
♠K83
♡Q105
◇974
♣K1098

b) Responder
♠KJ9865
♡54
◇J62
♣83

c) Responder
♠76
♡AKJ7
◇53
♣QJ854

d) Responder
♠6
♡KQ9753
◇AQ1098
♣Q

e) Responder
♠853
♡6
◇1084
♣AJ9874

f) Responder
♠KJ8
♡AQ10
◇763
♣J1095

g) Responder
♠K953
♡J642
◇4
♣Q653

246

With Example hand 125a) you have heard a takeout double of partner's opening bid of one diamond. Make the natural call of one notrump.

With Example hand 125b) in the same auction make a preemptive jump response of two spades.

With Example hand 125c) in the same auction bid one heart. Do not redouble. If you were to redouble and hear preemption in spades you would be poorly placed to continue.

With Example hand 125d) your partner's opening bid of one club has been doubled for takeout. Again, do not redouble. Make your natural call of one heart. If the opponents preempt in spades you will still be able to bid both of your suits.

With Example hand 125e) if partner has opened with one heart and there has been a takeout double you should bid two clubs. A preemptive bid of three clubs is also acceptable if the vulnerability is favorable. The important thing is not to pass since partner will not know what to do if your pass is followed by a penalty pass of the takeout double. If you pass he has the right to expect at least two hearts in your hand.

With Example hand 125f) if partner's one diamond opening bid has been doubled for takeout you can redouble. You announce that you have reasonable strength but no clear cut call to make. Partner will expect that you do not have a four card or longer major suit that you might have bid at the one level. If you later double a major suit bid by the opponents he will not expect you to have more than three cards in their suit.

With Example hand 125g) if partner's opening bid has been in a major suit and there has been a takeout double, if you have agreed to use a jump shift as a *mini-splinter* you can jump to three diamonds. This information may be all partner needs to bid a game that otherwise might not be reached.

Bidding After an Opponent Has Overcalled

When there has been an overcall of the opening bid, responder should stretch to raise when it is possible to raise. Particularly if the opening bid has been in a major suit, responder should not allow the opportunity to show a fit for opener's suit to slip away.

In other auctions responder should make the natural response at the one level that he would have made if the overcall had not occurred. If this response is in a higher ranking suit it is forcing unless responder has previously passed.

If the response after the overcall is a bid of one notrump it will show the values of about six to ten points, promise a stopper in the overcaller's suit, indicate that responder's hand is balanced, and usually deny that responder holds a four card or longer major suit. Since this one notrump call limits responder's hand both in shape and values it is not forcing.

None of the responses above is considered to be a **free bid**. At one time any call by responder after an overcall was considered to be a **free bid** and promised extra values, but when responder's call is either a raise of opener's suit or bid in a higher ranking denomination at the one level, it is no longer considered to be a **free bid**.

If the opponents overcall after a strong and artificial opening bid of two clubs, responder does well to affirm or deny values immediately. If responder passes, he promises that he has the positive values of at least an ace, a king, or two queens. If responder does not have such positive values, he doubles the overcall. Opener is then able to convert the double for penalties unless his hand has good enough offensive potential to seek a game contract despite responder's lack of values.

Free Bids

A **free bid** is a call made by responder after there has been an overcall, and occurs at the two level or higher in a new suit. The requirements for a **free bid** are twofold:

1) Responder promises that his suit is at least five cards long. If responder has the values to take action at this level but does not have a suit of five cards or more, he must take alternate action. Such alternate action may be a pass, a **negative double**, or a **cue bid** as his hand indicates. He must not make the error of making a **free bid** on a four card suit since partner will raise with three card support.

2) Responder promises certain minimum values when he makes a **free bid**. In standard bidding a **free bid** at the two level promises a minimum of ten points, and many system players retain that requirement. Other system players prefer that the **free bid** show the same values that would be necessary for a two over one response when there had been no overcall. Those who prefer this agreement know that a **free bid** promises values enough to produce game in the hands of the partnership, a minimum of about twelve points. Free bids at the three level are game forcing in either agreement.

Example 126:

a) Responder
♠A5
♡KJ1053
◊K42
♣K83

b) Responder
♠A5
♡KJ103
◊K965
♣K82

c) Responder
♠64
♡KQ853
◊K105
♣842

d) Responder
♠Q87
♡65
◊AKJ98
♣J109

e) Responder
♠AJ10975
♡K6
◊K
♣8643

With Example hand 126a) you have heard partner's opening bid of one club overcalled with a bid of one spade. You have an easy *free bid* regardless of the partnership agreement. You have both the values and the suit length to bid two hearts.

With Example hand 126b) in the same auction you have the values for a *free bid* but you do not have a five card or longer suit. You may not make a *free bid* but should make a *negative double* (detailed in the next section of this Chapter).

With Example hand 126c) in the same auction you do have adequate suit length for a *free bid*, but your values are not sufficient to take that action regardless of your partnership agreement. This hand again qualifies as a *negative double*.

With Example hand 125d) if your agreement is that a *free bid* is the same as in standard bidding, when your partner's opening bid of one club has been overcalled with a bid in either major suit you can make a *free bid* of two diamonds. Both your suit length and values are adequate. If your agreement is that opening bid values are required, your action will be determined by which major suit has been bid. This matter is discussed in detail in the next section on *negative doubles*.

With Example hand 125e) if partner's opening bid of one diamond has been overcalled with a bid of two clubs you can make a *free bid* of two spades regardless of your agreement. Your king of diamonds is known to be a working card and partner is known to be short in clubs. Your extra spade adds values to your hand, and even if your *free bid* of two spades is forcing to game your hand is good enough.

Negative Doubles

On many occasions, after an overcall responder will wish to enter the auction, but to do so he would have to make a **free bid** and he lacks one of the requisites. He may have values enough for a **free bid**, but lack a five card or longer suit. On the other hand he may have a suit of sufficient length (five or more cards), but lack the strength to make a **free bid**. In many of these cases responder will be able to make a **negative double**.

A **negative double**, as its name suggests, is a double that is not for penalties. It is for takeout and guarantees that responder has support for unbid suits, particularly for unbid major suits. With a few exceptions that will be explained, responder promises at least four cards in any unbid major suit when he makes his **negative double**. The exceptions are these:

1) If the overcall has been one heart, responder is still able to bid spades at the one level. When the partnership agreement is that a **free bid** promises ten points or more, a negative double shows that responder has exactly four spades. With five or more spades responder will instead bid one spade.

When the partnership agreement is that a **free bid** promises full opening bid values, the picture changes. Responder will frequently have five cards in the unbid minor suit and about ten points. He will be unable to make a **free bid** on this occasion since the partnership agreement is that he needs game forcing values to do so, but he should not be shut out of the auction.

In this circumstance, since responder is able to bid one spade whenever he holds four or more spades and that bid at the one level is not a **free bid**, the use of the **negative double** is disassociated from the spade suit. A bid of one spade by responder in this auction shows four or more spades, and a **negative double** denies that responder has as many as four spades.

The **negative double** in this auction expresses that responder would like to be able to make a **free bid** but cannot do so due to lack either of sufficient suit length or sufficient high card strength. Although responder does not promise five or more cards in the unbid minor suit, he shows values and denies that he holds four spades with a **negative double** in this auction.

2) When responder has a long spade suit without the values to make a **free bid** and the overcall has been in a minor suit at the two level after an opening bid in the other minor, he can make a **negative double**

even though he does not have support for hearts. Responder is prepared to correct from hearts to spades whenever opener bids hearts, prompted by the **negative double** into believing that responder has hearts, no matter how high the level.

With the exceptions having been noted, other situations in which responder makes a **negative double** assure his partner that he has four card or longer support for unbid major suits. Responder may have a major suit longer than four cards which he is unable to bid for lack of values. It is possible for him to make a **negative double** showing at least four cards in that major suit, and wait until the next round in the auction. If at his next turn he bids the major suit indicated by his **negative double** he indicates that his suit is at least five cards long, but that he lacked the values to bid it at his previous turn.

Conversely responder does not deny good values when he makes a **negative double**. His values are not limited by this action which simply indicates that for some reason he is unable to make a **free bid**. If he has made a negative double with excellent values because he has no five card or longer suit to bid freely, his next action will give some indication of the strength of his hand. He may well make a **cue bid** at that turn if no other descriptive bid is available.

There will be some rare situations in which responder is unable to either make a **free bid** or a **negative double** although he has a hand with values. He will have neither the suit length for a **free bid**, nor the required holding in an unbid major suit to make a **negative double**. In this instance responder may have no choice but to pass and await developments. It will be rare that the auction ends without giving him a chance to show the nature of his hand, for the opening bidder is well aware of the problem under discussion and will keep the auction open whenever it appears to him that a problem of this nature is to be anticipated.

Example 127:

a) Responder
♠A5
♡KJ103
◇K965
♣K82

With Example hand 127a) after partner's one club opening bid and an overcall of one spade you will make a *negative double*. Although your strength is great enough to insist upon reaching a game, you do not have a long enough suit in which to make a *free bid*.

b) Responder
♠64
♡KQ85
♢K1095
♣842

c) Responder
♠64
♡AQJ854
♢104
♣J95

d) Responder
♠875
♡65
♢AKJ98
♣J109

e) Responder
♠KQ10984
♡K6
♢73
♣864

With Example hand 127b) in the same auction you have a classic minimum hand for a *negative double*. The four card diamond holding is not necessary since your only promise is that you have four hearts.

With Example hand 127c) your heart suit is long enough for a *free bid*, but you do not have sufficient values for that action. Make a *negative double* and plan to bid hearts freely at your next turn since your values will have been limited by your failure to make a *free bid* at this turn.

With Example hand 127d) if the overcall has been one heart you can make a *negative double* to show this hand if your *free bid* would be game forcing. If the overcall has been one spade and your *free bid* would be game forcing, you have no choice but to pass at this turn since a *negative double* would show hearts which you do not have.

With Example hand 127e) if partner's bid of one diamond has been overcalled with two clubs, or if partner's one club bid has been overcalled with two diamonds, you can make a *negative double* despite not having length in hearts. If partner bids hearts, as is to be expected, your spades are long and good enough to correct to that suit no matter what the level.

When responder has a hand that would ordinarily punish the overcaller by making a penalty double, he must pass. Since double would be **negative**, responder needs help from the opening bidder if a penalty is to be extracted. When the overcall is passed back to the opener, he should consider why there was no response.

Opener can judge that responder might have the awkward hand that could not be expressed by either a **free bid** or a **negative double**. Or opener might deduce that responder wished to make a penalty double but was unable to do so since double would not have been for penalties. If either of these possibilities seems likely opener must care for the situation. Instead of passing to end the auction, he doubles, keeping the auction alive.

On those occasions where responder has the awkward hand, the reopening double allows him to bid what he would like to have bid at his previous turn but could not due to systemic restrictions. On those other occasions where responder wanted to double for penalties but could not, he is now able to pass and convert the reopening double into a penalty double.

Opener should not double to reopen the auction unless he is satisfied to defend against the overcall. If his hand is offensive in nature and he feels that his side should play rather than defend, his action after an overcall and two passes should be a bid that expresses the offensive nature of his hand.

Opener should rarely pass in this situation. When his holding in the suit of the overcall is so good that he knows responder cannot wish to penalize the overcall, he still must consider the fact that responder might have the awkward hand that could not bid after the overcall. If opener considers all of these factors and still feels that it is right to pass, only then should he do so.

When responder has made a **negative double**, opener has the obligation to bid the extent of his values at the time of his rebid. When he has four cards in a suit indicated by the **negative double** and minimum values, he will bid that suit as cheaply as possible.

When opener has a fit for a suit indicated by the **negative double** and greater values he has the obligation to show those values by jumping in the suit that is the indicated trump suit. Opener may even be able to jump to game when he has a good hand and feels that the values and suit fit of a minimum **negative double** will be enough to give game a good play.

When there has been an overcall and a **negative double** and the advancer raises the overcall, opener may have a problem. If he bids freely he may prod responder to bid more, and the result may be that the contract reached is a level too high. Opener needs to be able to indicate in such auctions that he has sufficient length in a suit shown by the **negative double** that he would have bid if the level had not been increased by the raise of the overcall. If he does bid at this point, opener needs to have sound values rather than a bare minimum for his opening bid.

To show a fit for the major suit indicated by the **negative double** and limit his values, opener makes a **responsive double** in such an auction. It would be rare that opener truly wished to make a penalty double when the overcall has been raised, so his double at this point should not be mistaken. Opener's **responsive double** after a **negative double** and a raise of the overcall shows a desire to bid a suit shown by the **negative double** but denies the values to make that bid freely.

When more than one suit exists that might be the suit that opener wants to bid, responder must be careful to bid in the lower ranking of those suits unless his values are sufficient to let the auction reach a higher level. If responder bids in the lower of the two indicated major suits and opener corrects to the higher ranking one, the auction has limited his values. If opener's desire was to play in the lower ranking of the two suits, he will pass when responder bids that suit.

Example 128:

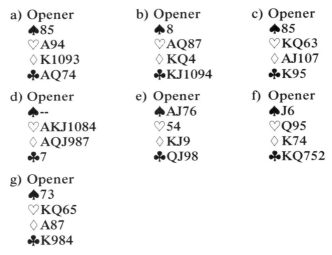

a) Opener
♠85
♡A94
◇K1093
♣AQ74

b) Opener
♠8
♡AQ87
◇KQ4
♣KJ1094

c) Opener
♠85
♡KQ63
◇AJ107
♣K95

d) Opener
♠--
♡AKJ1084
◇AQJ987
♣7

e) Opener
♠AJ76
♡54
◇KJ9
♣QJ98

f) Opener
♠J6
♡Q95
◇K74
♣KQ752

g) Opener
♠73
♡KQ65
◇A87
♣K984

With Example hand 128a) if you have opened with one club and partner has made a *negative double* after a one spade overcall you have an uncomfortable auction. You can bid two diamonds, or you might reach out for a three-four heart fit since you will be able to ruff spades in your hand rather than the hand with longer hearts. This particular auction is the one that causes many partnerships to prefer to open with one diamond rather than one club when balanced with four-four in the minor suits. If your opening bid has been one diamond, a rebid of two clubs after the *negative double* by partner is far more comfortable.

With Example hand 128b) you have again heard partner make a *negative double* after your one club opening bid and a one spade overcall. Bid the full value of your hand by jumping to four hearts.

With Example hand 128c) you have opened with one diamond and after a one spade overcall there have been two passes. It is likely that partner wants to penalize the overcall, and is waiting for you to reopen with a double. You have no reason to take any other action.

With Example hand 128d) you have opened with one heart and after an overcall of one spade there have been two passes. Even though partner may wish to penalize the overcall your hand is so powerful offensively that you need little more than a fit for one of your suits to make a slam. You should reopen with a jump shift of three diamonds to convey this message to partner.

With Example hand 128e) you have opened with one club and there has been a one spade overcall. After two passes you must decide whether it is right to reopen. You know that partner cannot have a penalty pass because of the quality of your own spade holding. Since he did not make a *negative double* he might have some values with diamond length and fewer than four hearts, but that possibility is slim. Partner's failure to make a negative double indicates that the opponents might have a better home in hearts, so your best decision is probably to pass and defend one spade.

With Example 128f) if you have opened with one club and there has been an overcall of one spade followed by two passes you must not develop cold feet. If you are ashamed of your opening bid you have good reason, but having elected to open you must now reopen with a double. If you pass because you do not like your hand your partner will lose confidence in you altogether. That is too high a price to pay for this indiscretion that you chose to call an opening bid.

With Example hand 128g) after your opening bid of one club and an overcall of one spade, partner has made a *negative double* and the overcall has been raised. You know that your side has a heart fit but if you bid hearts at this turn you will probably get too high. Make a *responsive double* and if partner bids either three clubs or three diamonds, correct to three hearts.

h) Opener	i) Opener
♠73	♠--
♡KQ65	♡AQJ6
◇ A87	◇ KQ1094
♣KQ98	♣AKJ7

With Example hand 128h) you face the same auction. After partner's *negative double* of the one spade overcall and the raise to two spades your values are good enough for a bid of three hearts. If partner raises to four hearts you will probably make it.

With Example hand 128i) you have opened with one diamond and after an overcall of one spade there have been two passes. You dare not double since partner will probably pass for penalties, and there is too good a chance for slam in any of three suits. A *cue bid* of two spades appears to be your best balancing action.

Responder's Cue Bid After an Overcall

Many pairs have agreed that when there is competition after an opening bid, particularly in a major suit, jump raises that would have been invitational without competition (limit raises showing 9+ to 12-) become preemptive. It is very likely that after an opposing overcall this agreement is superior to the continued use of a jump raise as invitational.

If after an overcall a jump raise is preemptive rather than invitational, the responder must have a way to show the hand of a limit raise when that is what he holds. In this situation responder uses a **cue bid** of the overcall to show that he has a fit for opener and invitational values.

On rare occasions the **cue bid** might be made with some other sort of hand with good values and no clear cut descriptive call to make, but when that is the case responder's continuation will clarify the situation. Opener should always continue expecting that the **cue bid** shows a limit raise for his suit.

Support Doubles

When the interference by the opponents does not occur until after the response, this different situation requires a different answer. When opener has bid a major suit and the response is a **forcing notrump**, opener has no special obligation after the overcall, and will pass with any minimum hand that does not have great distribution. When opener has a five-five hand he may well continue, particularly if he is able to bid his second suit at the two level, but hands of lesser distribution give him no impetus to bid again after an overcall on his right.

When responder has bid a new suit, opener has a different situation to face. Particularly when responder's suit is a major suit, it is very important for opener to show a fit for that suit after the interference bid. If opener fails to show a fit for responder's suit at this turn he may never be able to do so, and responder will not know when it is right to compete.

If opener has four card support for responder's major suit he has no problem. His raise after the overcall is comfortable since it is what he would have done if the overcall had not occurred. When opener has three card support for responder's major suit the situation is more difficult. Opener would not have raised responder in an uncontested auction but would have bid one notrump or would have continued in a second suit in nearly all instances.

Since the competition has made necessary that opener show his three card support for responder's major suit, the auction will be easier for both bidders if opener is able to distinguish between those raises that show four card support and those that show only three cards in responder's suit.

The systemic tool that enables opener to differentiate between four and three card support in this auction is the **support double**. When opener doubles after a response in a major suit and an overcall at his right, the double shows that he has three card support for responder's major suit. Of course this double requires an alert, but if opener fails to double at that turn responder should also alert, for the opponents are entitled to know that this failure to double tends to indicate that opener has fewer than three cards in responder's major suit.

Although most useful in auctions where responder has bid a major suit, **support doubles** can be used after any response and any overcall through the two level. This means that you can use the **support double** if it is possible to bid responder's suit and still be at the two level, but it does not apply if the overcall has been at the two level and a return to responder's suit must be at the three level. In such instances a double of the overcall should be for penalties. The exception to this limitation should occur if the responder's bid was game forcing. In that instance a support double can be made without regard for the fact that the auction is forced to the three level.

Example 129:

a) Opener
   ♠K65
   ♡93
   ◊ AQJ94
   ♣K73

b) Opener
   ♠J87
   ♡K75
   ◊ AJ8
   ♣KQ54

c) Opener
   ♠A3
   ♡KJ82
   ◊ Q97
   ♣A1087

d) Opener
   ♠7
   ♡AJ8
   ◊ K10985
   ♣AJ94

With Example hand 129a) you have opened with one diamond. If partner responds by bidding one spade and there is an overcall of two clubs or two hearts, double to show three card spade support. If partner's response was one heart and there has been an overcall your pass will deny holding as many as three hearts.

With Example hand 129b) you will make an opening bid of one club. After partner's response in any suit and any non-jump overcall you will double to show three card support.

With Example hand 129c) you have opened with one club. If partner responds by bidding one heart and there is an overcall in either spades or diamonds you will raise to two hearts to show four card support. If partner has responded one diamond and the overcall is one spade you should double to show your three card support for diamonds. However, if partner's response is one diamond and the overcall is one heart, a rebid of one notrump by you will be more expressive. A contract in notrump is always more desirable than one in a minor suit.

With Example hand 129d) you have opened with one diamond and partner has responded one heart. If there is an overcall in either spades or clubs you will double to show three card support for hearts. If the overcall is in clubs you would like to have the double be for penalties instead, but any conventional call must be understood to have the meaning assigned to it in the partnership.

When the Overcall Has Been One Notrump

When an opponent has overcalled naturally in notrump he shows a hand that has the values of an opening one notrump bid. Responder will very often have a nondescript hand and will pass.

If the opening bid has been in a major suit responder should be sure to raise the opening bid just as he would have without the one notrump overcall. The information that one opponent has a good balanced hand should not deter responder from describing his hand, and showing a fit in competition is of great importance.

Any time responder has sufficient values that he feels the hand belongs to his side but there is no bid for him to make that is clear cut, he should double the overcall for penalties. If there is some descriptive alternate action, it is usually better for responder to take that indicated course since the result at one notrump doubled may not be as good as the result that might be attained in a part score contract by the opener's side. Sometimes the notrump overcaller has an unexpected source of tricks that lets him win seven before the opposing side with more high cards can beat him.

When responder has a reasonable suit of his own and normal response values, after the overcall of one notrump he can introduce his suit. This suit will be at least five cards long, and responder will feel that opener's values combined with his own will be sufficient to produce eight tricks with his suit as the trump suit.

When opener has bid a minor suit responder knows that he may have length in one or both of the majors. When responder has length in the major suits he will often want to seek a major suit fit in opener's hand after the one notrump overcall. A special bid is available for this purpose.

When responder wants opener to bid a major suit he artificially uses a raise of opener's minor suit to the two level as a takeout for majors. Responder will be expected to have five-five in the majors when he takes this action, but in any case will have at least four cards in each major. When opener does not have a four card major suit to bid he should expect to be able to safely bid a three card major. This conventional application is called **Same Suit Stayman** since it asks opener to bid a major suit.

If responder truly wishes to raise opener's minor suit, a raise to the two level would serve no purpose. After the minor suit raise to the two level the advancer would have no problem bidding a major suit at the two level. In such an auction the advancer is favored to have major suit length and not much in high card values.

A raise in opener's minor suit to the three level by responder after the one notrump overcall has much greater effect. It will usually deny the advancer a chance to get into the auction with his five card major suit since his values will not be sufficient to bid at the three level.

Example 130:

a) Responder
♠8753
♡K98
◇5
♣QJ742

b) Responder
♠8
♡K5
◇Q9643
♣J10954

c) Responder
♠KJ109752
♡6
◇QJ4
♣K6

d) Responder
♠64
♡KQJ107
◇853
♣A52

e) Responder
♠KJ86
♡Q10963
◇75
♣43

f) Responder
♠7
♡QJ9853
◇Q76
♣J84

With Example hand 130a) you have heard partner open with one of a major suit. After an overcall of one notrump you should raise partner's major suit to two.

With Example hand 130b) you have heard partner open with one of a minor suit and there has been an overcall of one notrump. Make a jump raise to three of partner's minor suit. If you raise only to the two level you will give the advancer an easy two level bid in a five card major suit that he is favored to have. Besides, a raise to the two level is *Same Suit Stayman* and asks opener to bid a major suit.

With Example hand 130c) jump to three spades after a one no-trump overcall of partner's minor suit opening bid to invite a game. You need little more than two spades (or a singleton honor) and two aces to make four spades playable.

With Example hand 130d) after partner has opened with one spade and there has been a one notrump overcall your best action is to double. You have a good source of tricks and a good lead, and expect to collect a sizeable penalty.

With Example hand 130e) after a minor suit opening bid by partner and an overcall of one notrump bid two of partner's minor suit. This is *Same Suit Stayman* and asks partner to bid a major suit.

With Example hand 130f) after partner's minor suit or one spade opening bid and an overcall of one notrump, bid two hearts. This bid is non-forcing and asks partner to pass. You should have a reasonable play for this contract.

Unusual vs Unusual

When the opponents use the **unusual notrump** against us by jumping to two notrump after our opening suit bid, the defense we use against that interference call is called **unusual vs unusual**. It uses bids in the suits shown by the **unusual notrump** call to show various good hands, and bids in other suits to show limited hands.

If our opening bid has been in a major suit, the two notrump overcall shows minor suits. This will be the most common situation to be considered. After the overcall of two notrump, a bid by responder in either major suit at the three level will be natural and very limited.

A raise of the major suit in which opener has first bid will show the strength of a single raise (5+ to 9-) and will not be forward going. It will be strictly competitive. We have noted several times that it is important to stretch to show a fit for partner in competitive situations.

A bid in the other major at that point in the auction shows a good suit and little else. It will be like a maximum weak two bid in the other major.

A bid of three clubs will show a hand with hearts and game invitational values or better. A bid of three diamonds will show a hand with spades and game invitational values or better. These definitions will apply regardless of the major suit in which the opening bid was made. If this "cue bid" shows the opener's major suit, it shows a limit raise or better for that major. If this "cue bid" shows the unbid major suit, it promises a good suit that is five cards or longer and values in the game invitational range (9+ to 12-) or better.

When opener hears responder's "cue bid" in one of the suits shown by the **unusual notrump** call, he can sign off in his own major suit or in the other major suit which has been shown by responder at the three level when his values are minimum. If his values are good enough to accept a game invitation, he can bid game in the major suit indicated by responder's auction and his own opening hand. If opener attempts to sign off and responder's values are adequate for game, he bids on to the most likely game contract.

Example 131:

a) Responder	b) Responder	c) Responder
♠K95	♠95	♠QJ5
♡J7643	♡AQJ963	♡AJ76
◇A62	◇10832	◇K842
♣54	♣5	♣54

d) Responder
♠K5
♡AQJ963
◇A832
♣5

With Example 131 hands responder has heard an opening bid of one spade from his partner and an *unusual* two notrump overcall. Using the defense known as *unusual vs unusual* responder continues as indicated.

With Example hand 131a) responder bids three spades. Opener will know that this raise is not forward going, and that responder would have only raised to two spades if the interference had not occurred.

With Example hand 131b) responder will bid three hearts. Opener knows that this is a non-forcing bid that simply shows a good heart suit.

With Example hand 131c) responder bids three diamonds. This promises a limit raise or better in spades. Opener will decline the game invitation and bid three spades when his values are minimum (12 or 13) but will bid four spades when his values are better.

With Example hand 131d) responder bids three clubs. This shows a hand with a good heart suit and at least game invitational values. If opener rejects the game invitation by bidding only three hearts or three spades, responder will show his extra values by bidding four hearts.

If the opening bid has been in a minor suit and the **unusual notrump** call shows the other minor suit and hearts, responder's defense is the same. The difference will be that a "cue bid" in the lower ranking suit shown by the overcall will show the lower ranking unbid suit, and a "cue bid" in the higher ranking of the two suits shown by the **unusual notrump** overcall will show spades.

When the Opponents Double Our One Notrump Opening Bid

When the opponents have doubled either an opening bid or an overcall of one notrump, all systemic responses are still possible and will apply. The double does allow for another response, since redouble becomes available. Redouble is used to allow us to escape in a minor suit at the two level rather than requiring us to get to the three level with a weak hand and a long minor suit as we would have to do without competition.

When responder (or advancer) has redoubled, the notrump bidder is asked to bid two clubs. Responder (advancer) will then pass if his suit is clubs, or correct to two diamonds if that is his suit. If responder (advancer) instead corrects to two hearts he shows a major two suiter. If he had held a one suiter in hearts he would have made a **Jacoby Transfer** bid instead, so the auction of redouble followed by a correction to two hearts is used to ask the notrump bidder to select a major suit. Responder (advancer) will have five-five in the major suits.

If after an overcall of one notrump responder bids, either raising the opener's suit or introducing a suit of his own, advancer uses **Lebensohl**. The only exception will be the circumstance in which the opponents are using **Hamilton** or **Cappelletti** as a defense against the one notrump overcall, and artificially bid two clubs to show a one suited hand. In that specific auction advancer's double is **Stayman** and normal notrump responses apply.

Balancing

For those who are interested in detailed information regarding the topic of balancing, a bible is available. **The Complete Book on Balancing in Contract Bridge**, by Mike Lawrence, will tell you everything you could possibly want to know about balancing. If you are a serious bridge player, your library is incomplete without this title.

The basic rule for balancing is that when the opponents have found a fit and have stopped at the two level, it is rarely right to let them play there. Each side has about half of the high card values, and when they have a fit, it will inevitably be true that we also have a fit in which to play.

A balancing bid might get us to a contract that we can make, even at the three level. If we cannot make that contract and go down one, our score is better than the 110 or more that we were going to lose, even when we are vulnerable.

Often the opponents will not be content to defend after we have balanced. Since they know that they have a fit and reasonable values, they may decide to "take the push" and bid in their established denomination one level higher. If they can make that contract our balancing bid has cost us nothing, but if they are one trick too high and go down, the fact that we have balanced has turned a minus for our side into a plus.

1) Balancing When the Opening Bid Has Been Passed by Responder

When there have been two passes after the opening bid, the bidder in the balancing position knows these things: a) He knows that the opener's partner has little in values, usually less than a good five points. b) He also knows that his partner had no action to take over the opening bid. His partner will not have a hand with which to overcall, or make a takeout double, or to **cue bid**. Before he decides whether or not to balance he must try to determine whether the balancing bid will help his side or the opposing side.

Sometimes the opening bidder has a good hand and has opened in a minor suit preparing to jump to two notrump at his rebid. A balancing bid in this situation will allow him to correct from his minor suit to one notrump, or even from a three card minor to a good four card major. When the potential balancer has length in opener's minor suit, the best for his side is often to pass and defend. Even if opener makes his contract, his score will often not be as good as those scores achieved by others holding his hand who managed to find their way to one notrump or a major suit contract which is superior to the one level minor suit contract that he might have been allowed to play.

When it appears right to balance, if the balancer bids a higher ranking suit at the one level it will be assumed that his suit is five cards or longer. On occasion he might have an awkward hand that would require him to balance by bidding a good four card major suit, but his partner should assume that the suit in which he balanced is five cards or longer.

A takeout double in balancing position may be light in values if it has support for all unbid suits. Often a balancing double will be made with some very good hand that could not be otherwise described. One such hand is the hand which would have opened with one notrump, since a balancing bid in notrump shows less than the values of a one notrump opening bid.

A balancing bid of one notrump shows a hand in the range of about ten to thirteen points, and suggests stoppers in the opener's suit. Sometimes the balancer will have a balanced hand without a stopper but have no other descriptive bid to make. It would be better for the balancer's partner to have those stoppers which would then be better placed, and that will often be the case.

If the opening bid has been in a minor suit, balancer will have reasonable latitude, and the stated range will almost always apply. If the opening bid has been in a major suit, particularly in spades, when balancer has a square hand he has fewer options, and his range may expand to as much as fifteen points. When balancer has a hand that would be opened with one notrump, in the balancing position he must double, then bid notrump at his next turn unless a more descriptive bid becomes available.

A jump in the balancing position is never a weak bid. If the balancer jumps in a suit he shows a good opening bid with a good suit. His hand will fulfill the requirements for a typical intermediate jump overcall. His suit will rarely be five cards unless it is a very good suit. Most six card suits will be appropriate and the high card values for this jump are about twelve to sixteen points.

A jump in notrump by the balancer is not the **unusual notrump**. This jump shows a very good balanced hand, about a good eighteen to twenty points. It would be otherwise difficult to show a hand of this range since the balancer must double and then bid notrump when his hand is in the range of a normal opening notrump.

Example 132:

a) Balancer	b) Balancer	c) Balancer
♠K106	♠J106	♠Q4
♡Q104	♡Q4	♡KQ94
◇KJ9	◇KJ963	◇863
♣A974	♣A95	♣A1072

With Example hand 132a) after any opening bid and two passes you might balance by bidding one notrump.

With Example hand 132b) if you are balancing against one heart, double is probably the best of your bad choices. Against one of either black suit the choice is between one notrump or a balance in diamonds. One notrump is probably most flexible.

With Example hand 131c) if there have been two passes after an opening bid of one diamond your best choice is probably one heart on your good four card suit. Double is not to be considered since your spade holding is so poor.

d) Balancer	e) Balancer
♠KQ9	♠K1063
♡AQJ975	♡AQ5
◇63	◇63
♣A2	♣Q1098

With Example hand 132d) after a minor suit opening bid and two passes your hand is classic for a jump to two hearts. This jump should not be confused with a jump overcall which is preemptive. Balancer is not making a weak jump overcall.

With Example hand 132e) you have a classic balancing double after one diamond and two passes, but if the opening bid has been in any other suit you should bid one notrump.

2) Balancing When the Opponents Have Stopped at One Notrump

When the opponents arrive at one notrump your decision to balance is not easy. They will have shown that they have some values in each of the four suits, and whatever suit you select to be trumps may be one in which one of the opponents is well heeled. You will rarely have a good suit in this circumstance for you might have overcalled at the one level if you did have such a suit. Only rarely will you be able to balance by bidding such a suit.

There will be times when you wish to balance by making a takeout bid. In those situations the system provides a special set of bids which is superior to standard. A balancing double is not for takeout, but says that the opponent in front of you has bid a suit in which you have values, thereby keeping you out of the auction. When you double, partner is encouraged to pass if he has values, and lead the suit that has been bid on his left. In this situation a good penalty is likely since the cards are well placed for your side.

If you wish to make a takeout call as you balance, you must artificially bid two clubs. It does not matter whether or not clubs have been bid on the way to one notrump. Your balancing bid of two clubs tells your partner that you feel that defending against one notrump will give your side a bad result, and you want to find a place for your side to play at the two level. If partner has more than one suit to suggest he should begin by bidding the lower ranking one so that your side can correct to a higher ranking denomination without increasing the level when you do not fit the suit that he first expresses.

Example 133:

a) Balancer
♠K4
♡AQ1097
◇QJ9
♣873

b) Balancer
♠K1083
♡54
◇AQ96
♣Q104

c) Balancer
♠KQ109
♡A98
◇53
♣K1098

d) Balancer
♠62
♡KJ98
◇A873
♣Q105

With Example hand 133a) you have heard a one club opening bid at your left, pass by partner, one heart on your right, pass by you, one notrump by opener and two passes to you. Double by you at this point shows good heart values and asks partner, if he has reasonable values, to pass and lead a heart.

With Example hand 133b) in the same auction you might have made a takeout double after the one heart response, but that would have been risky. Now that the opponents have limited their values, rather than sell out to one notrump you can bid two clubs for takeout.

With Example hand 133c) the auction has begun with one spade on your right and a one notrump response after your pass. Two more passes follow and you can balance with a double to show good spade values and suggest that partner pass and lead a spade if his values are sufficient to defend.

With Example 133d) the auction has been the same. You can balance by bidding two clubs to ask partner to select a suit.

3) Balancing After Preempts

After a preemptive opening bid the opponent in immediate seat needs good values or good shape or both to enter the auction. Because of this when there have been two passes after a preemptive opening bid, the need to balance will often occur.

The principles presented in the section dealing with defending against weak two bids will also apply against preemptive bids at higher levels. The immediate seat bidder needs good values and the balancer needs much less. If you are short in the preemptor's suit, be sure that you can cope when partner converts the double for penalties. When you have length in the preemptor's suit, it will usually be right to pass and defend.

Action Doubles

Sometimes the responder will find himself in the balancing position because after his response there has been an overcall, and opener has passed as has the overcaller's partner. When responder in this situation has bid the extent of his values his only reason to bid again is due to a good and long suit of his own, or because he has an undisclosed fit for opener's suit. Without one of these reasons to bid, responder will pass and defend against the overcall.

When responder does have extra values and knows that game should be reached, he can propel the auction forward with a forcing bid in a new suit, or with a **cue bid**. Although opener has limited his values and denies a fit for responder's suit with his pass after the overcall, if prompted he will be able to tell more about his hand so that the most appropriate contract can be reached.

When responder's values are in the invitational range (9+ to 12-) and he finds himself in the balancing position, he will not be able to make a bid that forces his side to game. With a good suit he can make a jump rebid which is descriptive and invitational but not forcing. With a fit for opener's first suit he will be able to make a jump preference to that suit.

When responder has invitational values and no clear cut call, he can express his hand with a double at that point in the auction. The double is not for penalties, but simply expresses the fact that he feels that his values warrant another call, and no call suggests itself. This double is called an **action double**.

Example 134:

a) Responder	b) Responder	c) Responder
♠KJ973	♠A965	♠AQ86
♡A4	♡J105	♡54
◇1076	◇43	◇AJ3
♣Q97	♣AJ87	♣9543

In Example 134 the auction has proceeded one diamond by opener and one spade by responder after which there has been an overcall of two hearts followed by two passes. With each of the Example 134 hands responder might make an *action double*. This is not a penalty double but simply shows values and suggests that responder's side should not sell out to the overcall, and at the very least should defend the contract doubled if opener does not choose to bid on.

Maximal Overcall Doubles

The subject of game tries has been covered in some detail in previous Chapters. It becomes more difficult to make a game try when the opponents have entered the auction. Also, it is necessary to distinguish in competitive situations those calls which are tries for game from those that are simply competitive.

The first rule is that in any competitive auction, a reraise of an agreed major suit is competitive and not a try for game. If opener has been raised and wishes to try for game he must do so by bidding in a denomination other than the agreed suit. Similarly, if responder has been raised and the auction is contested, a rebid of the agreed suit is competitive and not a try for game.

In most competitive situations, although the opponents are bidding, a suit or suits will be available in which a game try can be made. When either opener or responder wishes to make a game try, he will bid in one of the available suits. When two suits are available, the game try is expressive as game tries are when there is no competition. The bidder who tries for game bids the suit in which he wants his partner to evaluate his cards.

If only one suit is available in which a game try might be made, the game try is less expressive. The bidder who makes a try for game cannot ask for help in a specific suit, but can only let it be known that he thinks game is possible. The try will be accepted or rejected on a general basis by the partner of the bidder who has made the try for game.

In one specific type of auction, competition by the opponents takes away all of the suits that might be used by either opener or responder as a game try. This occurs when the opponents are competing in the suit that ranks directly below the suit agreed by opener and responder as their potential trump suit.

If both opener and responder bid spades and both opponents bid hearts, there is no suit available in which to make a game try. The same is true when both opener and responder bid hearts and both opponents bid diamonds.

In such situations, when both opponents have bid or shown the same suit it will be rare that the opener's side can extract a significant penalty. Since a penalty double would almost never be a profitable action, double becomes an artificial game try.

These are some of the auctions in which a **maximal overcall double** might occur:

1) 1♠-2♡-2♠-3♡, Dbl.
2) 1♠-Dbl-2♠-3♡, Dbl.
3) 1♡-2◊-2♡-3◊, Dbl.
4) 1♣-P-1♠-2♡, 2♠-3♡-Dbl.
5) 1♣-P-1♡-2◊, 2♡-3◊-Dbl.

In each of these examples the bidder who might have wanted to make a game try might also have wanted to bid one more time competitively. In each of the auctions shown if the doubler had bid the agreed suit instead of doubling, his call would have been competitive instead of an artificial try for game.

Honor Redoubles

A common auction is one in which after an opening bid and an overcall there is a negative double. The advancer will often have a hand with which he then raises the overcall. When the advancer is silent, it will be assumed that he either has no fit for the overcall or that he has no values.

Sometimes the advancer does have a fit for the overcall but knows it is likely that his side will defend. When that likelihood looms large, advancer may wish to send a message about the quality of his support for the overcall which will eventually aid the defense. The honor redouble serves this purpose.

A redouble after the **negative double** carries the message that the advancer has a top honor card in the overcaller's suit. He promises that he holds the ace or the king, and that he has at least two card support for the suit of the overcall. If the overcalling side does eventually defend, the overcaller can lead his suit knowing that his partner has a key card which makes that lead right, even when the overcaller's holding would normally make it appear wrong.

Holding AQxxx or AJxxx it would normally be wrong to lead your suit. If the auction tells you that your partner has the king and may have only a doubleton, an underlead of your honor holding can be quite profitable.

The negative inference that is available is also quite valuable. If advancer has raised the overcall he tends to deny holding either of the top two honor cards. Holding AQxxx or AJxxx you will know that it is wrong to either lead or underlead your honor combination.

CHAPTER VIII
SLAM BIDDING

The foundation for good slam bidding is a good early auction. The nature of the systemic aproach is such that when slam is a prospect, the early auction will have been slow and revealing. Bidding space is conserved particularly when responder has a good hand, for instead of having to jump and use precious bidding space, responder will often establish a game force with a simple two over one response, or by the use of **New Minor Forcing** or **Fourth Suit Forcing** auctions.

The conduct of a low level dialogue should exchange enough information that when a step toward slam is made it will usually seek information about controls, either by number or in specific suits. Certain modern bidding tools make a pursuit of this type much easier, and are recommended to system users.

Roman Key Card Auctions

Introduction of the **Roman Key Card** variation to **Blackwood** and other ace asking conventions has met with universal acceptance in the tournament world. This variation has the advantage of locating not only the aces and kings that are sought by the bidder who investigates the possibility of slam, but also conveys information about the quality of the trump suit. Since information about both of these vital things, controls and trump quality, is exchanged quite readily, **Roman Key Card** has proved to be a very valuable tool.

For **Roman Key Card** to function there must be an agreed trump suit. Each partnership will establish its own criteria for determining the suit in which quality information is to be conveyed when the trump suit has not been clearly established.

It is possible to agree that when there is no clearly agreed trump suit **Roman Key Card** does not apply. It is also possible to agree that when there is not a clearly agreed trump suit the last suit bid prior to the **RKC** ask is the suit in which quality will be shown, although this will often lead to using useful bidding steps to convey useless information.

One matter that should be clearly agreed is that when responder's first bid is a leap to four notrump, **RKC** does not apply in opener's suit. It does not apply at all. Responder may simply need to know about the aces in opener's hand, and the king of opener's suit will not be a vital card. Opener should respond to **Blackwood** in traditional fashion rather than think and respond in terms of **RKC**.

When **RKC** is used, the mechanism is as follows. The king of the agreed trump suit is considered to be as vital as an ace. Responder to the ace asking bid considers that there are five aces as he replies to the question he has been asked. Assuming that the asking bid is a bid of four notrump, responder bids five clubs to show zero or three key cards, five diamonds to show one or four key cards, five hearts to show two or five key cards but deny that he holds the queen of the agreed trump suit, or five spades to again show two or five key cards but affirm that he does have the queen of the agreed trump suit.

When responder has bid either five clubs or five diamonds and it is not clear from the previous auction whether he holds the greater or lesser number of key cards shown by his response, if the four notrump bidder signs off in the agreed trump suit responder will carry forward and bid a slam when he holds the greater number. If the earlier auction leaves no doubt as to the number of key cards responder has shown and the four notrump bidder signs off in the agreed trump suit, responder will honor that signoff and pass.

When the response has been either five clubs or five diamonds, neither of which speaks of the trump queen, and the four notrump bidder wants to ask for the queen of the agreed trump suit, he continues by making the cheapest bid which is not a signoff in the agreed trump suit. Responder can affirm or deny holding the trump queen in more than one way, and the method in use in the partnership should be determined in advance.

1) Responder can affirm or deny possession of the trump queen by using a step progression. The first step after the question is asked denies that responder holds the trump queen and the second step affirms that he does have that card.

2) A more sophisticated approach is to have responder deny the trump queen by returning to the agreed trump suit as cheaply as possible. When he does have the trump queen he affirms that fact by bidding in the nearest suit in which he holds a king. If he has no side kings he can show the trump queen either by bidding five notrump or by jumping to six of the agreed trump suit.

Whether or not he asks for the queen of the agreed trump suit, if the **Blackwood** bidder continues by bidding in a new suit that is not a queen ask, he is asking for the king of the suit in which he is bidding. His message is that that particular king is what he needs to make a grand slam. Responder can deny that king in one of several agreed ways. He can bid in steps, denying that king with the first step and showing it with the second step, or he can deny that king by returning to the agreed suit and show it by either bidding notrump or jumping to a slam in the agreed suit. Partnerships that use this tool should be sure to agree on the choice of method to show or deny a king in such an **RKC** auction.

When the **Blackwood** bidder continues by bidding five notrump, he announces that all five key cards are accounted for and seeks a grand slam. If responder has a hand with a previously undisclosed source of tricks and feels that thirteen tricks can be taken, he has license to jump directly to a grand slam. If his hand does not warrant a direct grand slam bid, he will tell the **Blackwood** bidder about kings in his hand. Of course, the king of the trump suit has already been spoken of, and will not be included when kings are shown at this point in the auction.

There are two modern approaches to the showing of kings in response to five notrump. The traditional way is to show them by number. When that is the partnership agreement, six clubs will show zero or three kings (excluding the trump king), six diamonds will show one king, and six hearts will show two kings.

The alternate method of responding to five notrump is for responder to bid the suit of the lowest ranking king that he holds. If that king is all the **Blackwood** bidder needs to know about to bid a grand slam, he does so. If that information is not what he needs, he then bids the suit in which he needs to find the king in order to make a grand slam. If responder has that king he bids the grand, but if not he signs off at the six level in the agreed suit.

The showing of voids in conjunction with the use of **RKC** is again a subject for partnership discussion and agreement. It is fairly standard to use bids of five notrump and higher in response to four notrump to show voids and some number of aces or key cards. Most commonly five notrump shows two key cards (or two aces if you prefer) and a working void, and six clubs shows one key card (or one ace) and a working void.

It is most important that the void be shown only when the earlier auction indicates that its presence will be an asset rather than a potential liability. Indiscriminate showing of voids just because they are there will lead to bad results.

RKC Gerber

When the responder to an opening bid of one or two notrump uses **Stayman** and finds a fit, his bid of four clubs becomes **RKC Gerber** in the suit of the **Stayman** response. The response steps to **RKC Gerber** are the same as shown above. The first step, four diamonds, shows zero or three key cards, four hearts shows one or four key cards, four spades shows two or five key cards but denies the trump queen, and four notrump shows two or five key cards and promises the trump queen.

When **Gerber** is a direct jump from notrump to four clubs and no trump suit has been established, the **RKC** application is as follows. Four diamonds shows zero or three aces, four hearts shows one or four aces, four spades shows two aces but denies interest in slam, four notrump again shows two aces, but shows an interest in slam due to an undisclosed source of tricks in the notrump bidder's hand.

Minor Suit Raises as RKC

In many auctions where minor suits are established as trumps and a slam probe follows, the use of **Blackwood** consumes too much space, and alternate means of asking for key cards are more practical. There are two particular auctions where a raise of the agreed minor suit to the four level should trigger a response that shows key cards.

1) When a strong **Inverted Minor Raise** has been made, if opener continues by jumping to four of the agreed minor suit, that call should ask responder to show key cards beginning with the first available step from opener's bid.

2) When **Minor Suit Stayman** has elicited a four card or longer minor suit from the opening notrump bidder, if responder continues by bidding four of that minor suit, this raise should again ask opener to show key cards in the agreed minor suit.

Generally, when any auction finds a minor suit fit and one partner has bid four of that suit, it is possible to play that when the auction to that point is forcing and the other partner will bid again, the bid that he chooses as he continues shows key cards in the agreed minor suit. Thereafter, a bid by the other partner of either four notrump or five of the agreed minor suit is a signoff.

Kickback

One of the problems brought about by the use of **RKC** is that the responses will sometimes put the bidding side in a position of being too high and having no way to recover. For example, if hearts is the agreed trump suit and the **Blackwood** bidder has one key card, when the responder bids five spades to show two key cards and the heart queen, the bidding side is forced to the six level in hearts despite the fact that two key cards are missing.

The **RKC** response complex appears to need a full bidding level in order that this problem not occur. When spades are trumps, four no-trump creates no problem since a full bidding level is available.

Marty Bergen's solution to this problem is called **Kickback**. The use of **Kickback** provides a full bidding level by modifying the choice of call that asks for key cards. When spades is the trump suit, four no-trump is still used to ask for key cards. When any other suit is the trump suit, in order to provide the full bidding level needed, the bid that asks for controls is the denomination that ranks immediately above the agreed suit.

When hearts is the agreed trump suit, four spades becomes **RKC Blackwood**. When diamonds is the agreed trump suit, four hearts becomes **RKC Blackwood**. When clubs is the agreed trump suit, four diamonds becomes **RKC Blackwood**. This agreement is **Kickback**.

Auctions With Six Key Cards

In some auctions the bidding side is known to have fits in two suits. When slam is sought and this is known to be true, the kings and queens of both suits are equally important, and **RKC** should seek information about all of those cards.

The most common of these situations are the ones in which two suits have been shown facing a balanced hand as in **Minor Suit Stayman** auctions, **Puppet Stayman** auctions, and possibly others such as **Michaels** or **Top and Bottom Cue Bid** auctions.

The responses remain the same as when only five key cards exist. There will almost never be a case in which the responder to a key card ask will have so many key cards that the usual responses will not suffice.

When six key card auctions occur and queens in the agreed suits are asked for, step responses are necessary. The first step will deny both queens, the second step shows the queen of the lower ranking suit, the third step shows the queen of the higher ranking suit, and the fourth step shows both queens.

Example 135:

	a) Opener	b) Responder
♠	AK876	QJ4
♡	K3	AQJ107
◇	975	AK4
♣	A54	83

The Bidding

Opener	Responder
1♠	2♡*
2♠	3♠*
4♣	4NT
5♣	5♡*
5NT*	7NT

or

	4NT
5♣	5NT
6♡*	7NT

(Bids with asterisks are alertable)

With Example hand 135 after an opening one spade bid and the natural and game forcing response of two hearts, opener marks time by rebidding two spades. Responder's rebid of three spades is stronger than a jump to four would have been and sets the trump suit so that *RKC* can be used. Holding extra values opener uses available space to show his club ace. Responder then uses *RKC* and finds three key cards. Five hearts now asks for the heart king (five diamonds would have asked for the spade queen but responder doesn't need that information) and five notrump shows that opener has it. Responder can now count thirteen tricks and bids the grand slam.

The alternate auction shows responder continuing with *Blackwood* to seek a specific king. When opener shows the heart king responder bids the grand slam.

Example 136:

	a) Opener		b) Responder
	♠743		♠ —
	♡AKJ93		♡Q10872
	♢KQJ6		♢A954
	♣4		♣A1063

The Bidding

Opener	Responder
1♡	3♢ *
3♡*	3♠*
3NT*	4♡*
4NT	5♠
7♡	

or

4♠*	5♡*
7♡	

In Example hand 136 the three diamond response to the one heart opening bid is an "under jump shift" showing the values of a limit raise with four or more trumps and some side shortness. Opener's rebid of three hearts asks about the shortness and responder's call of three spades identifies that shortness as being a void. Opener then asks where the void is by bidding three notrump and responder shows that it is in spades with his bid of four hearts. Opener then uses either *RKC Blackwood* or *Kickback* to ask about key cards and when responder shows two aces and the heart queen he is known to have all of the right cards to produce a grand slam on 24 high card points.

Example 137:

	a) Opener	b) Responder
	♠AJ2	♠KQ54
	♡AQ1073	♡KJ4
	◊AQ9	◊5
	♣K9	♣Q7643

The Bidding

Opener	Responder
2NT	3♣*
3♡*	4NT
5♣	5◊*
5♠*	6♡

or

	4♠*
4NT*	5♣*
6♣*	6♡

In Example 137 responder uses *Puppet Stayman* and discovers the five-three heart fit. When *RKC Blackwood* indicates that a control is missing responder decides to take a shot at slam if opener has the trump queen but knows that he can stop at the five level if opener lacks that card. Five diamonds asks for the trump queen and five spades shows it.

In the alternate auction responder uses *kickback* to find the three key cards and continues to ask for the heart queen. Opener shows the heart queen and the club king, a card responder is glad to hear about.

Example 138:

	a) Opener		b) Responder
	♠7		♠A83
	♡A5		♡J6
	◇KQJ94		◇A10852
	♣AQJ63		♣K94

The Bidding

Opener	Responder
1◇	2◇*
4◇*	4NT*
6♣*	6♡*
7◇	

or

5♡*	6♣*
7◇	

In Example 138 the *Inverted Minor Raise* suggests slam to opener, so he jumps to four diamonds which is *RKC*. When responder's bid of four notrump shows the two missing key cards, opener jumps to six clubs to ask for the king of that suit (five clubs would ask for the diamond queen which opener has). When responder shows the club king opener bids the grand slam.

In the alternate auction opener continues his *RKC* quest by bidding five hearts. Since five diamonds would be a signoff, the *RKC* continuation must be a *kickback* call. Showing specific kings by agreement, responder bids six clubs, and opener bids the grand slam.

Example 139:

a) Opener	b) Responder
♠K83	♠A8
♡A8	♡72
◇A52	◇KQJ843
♣KQJ109	♣A82

The Bidding

Opener	Responder
1NT	4♣
4NT*	5♣
5NT*	7NT

In Example 139 responder to the opening bid of one notrump checks for aces by using *Gerber*. Opener's *RKC* response shows two aces and interest in a slam. Responder continues by asking for kings and opener again shows two as he reaffirms interest in slam. This double expression of slam interest causes responder to bid the good grand slam.

Example 140:

a) Opener	b) Responder
♠A1092	♠K852
♡A5	♡J1073
◇AQ93	◇K3
♣K96	♣AQ5

The Bidding

Opener	Responder
1NT	2♣*
2♠	4♣*
4◇*	4♡*
4♠*	Pass

In Example 140 responder first uses *Stayman* and finds a fit in spades, then uses *RKC Gerber*. When opener shows three key cards responder next asks for the spade queen. When opener denies that card responder gives up on slam. The combined point count is only between 29 and 31 and responder expects another probable loser in addition to a loser in the trump suit. Responder might instead have bid four diamonds after discovering the trump fit, but in a slam search it would be hard for him to show all of his secondary values, so he decided to ask instead. In case you have forgotten, *Stayman* is alertable since it might be a relay for the purpose of raising to two notrump.

Example 141:

a) Opener	b) Responder
♠A1092	♠7
♡A5	♡K4
◇AQ93	◇KJ1062
♣K96	♣AQ874

The Bidding

Opener	Responder
1NT	2♠*
3◇*	4◇*
4♡*	4♠*
5♣*	6♣*
6♡*	7◇

or

5♣*	7◇

In Example 141 responder uses *Minor Suit Stayman* in response to one notrump and finds opener with a four card fit in diamonds. Responder's continuation to four diamonds is *RKC* and opener shows three key cards. Responder's four spade bid asks about the diamond queen and five clubs shows that card. Responder then asks for the club king and when opener shows that card responder bids the grand slam.

In the alternate auction opener's bid of five clubs shows both the diamond queen and the club king, so responder gets the necessary information to bid the grand in one less round of bidding.

Asking Bids

As the search for controls is the gateway to slam, often the problem will not revolve around the number of controls, but will hinge on the discovery of specific controls. For this purpose, **Asking Bids** are available.

The following situations are among those in which **Asking Bids** are used:

1) A jump shift response to a weak two bid or an opening three bid is an **Asking Bid**.

2) A new suit response to the opening bid of four in a major suit is an **Asking Bid**.

3) After an opening **Namyats** transfer bid of four clubs or four diamonds, a response in a suit beyond the anchor suit shown by the opening bid is an **Asking Bid**.

4) A major suit response to an opening **Namyats** three notrump bid is an **Asking Bid**.

5) Any unusual jump not otherwise assigned systemic meaning is an **Asking Bid**. Most unusual jumps are **Splinters**. When the unusual jump is one level higher than the jump that would be a **splinter**, that jump is an **Asking Bid**. The single exception to this general rule is the double jump reverse which is a **void splinter** rather than an **Asking Bid**.

6) After the opening bid of two clubs and the waiting response of two diamonds, if opener jumps to three of a major suit he announces that his completely solid suit will be trumps regardless of responder's holding in that suit, and requires responder to show controls. Responder must next bid a suit in which he has an ace. With more than one ace he shows the nearest one.

When responder has no first round controls but does have some second round controls, he bids three notrump to convey that message. With no first or second round controls, responder bids game in opener's major suit.

If responder has shown some second round controls by bidding three notrump, opener can continue by asking for controls where he needs to find them. All of opener's further bids that are not in his established trump suit are **Asking Bids**. If responder has denied holding any first or second round controls and opener continues to seek a control in a particular suit, responder is asked to show a third round control in that suit.

Responses to Asking Bids

With one exception, when an **Asking Bid** has been made, responder to that bid replies in steps to show his exact holding in the suit he has been asked about.

When responder to the **Asking Bid** makes the cheapest bid available in notrump he shows that he holds the king of the suit he has been asked about, and that it is not a singleton. Since responder to the **Asking Bid** shows his king in this fashion, if notrump has not previously been bid in the auction, he will be declarer if a notrump contract is established. When a control in this trouble suit is the only problem and tricks are plentiful, the **Asking Bidder** who is in charge of the auction can elect to play a slam in notrump with the king of the trouble suit protected on the opening lead.

With notrump deleted from the list of available calls, all other responses to an **Asking Bid** are made in steps as follows:

1) The first step shows no control. This means no ace, king, void, or singleton.

2) The second step shows second round control. This means a singleton with some length in the known trump suit, or the king and queen, since the king without the queen is not clearly a second round control and is shown by a bid in notrump.

3) The third step shows first round control. This means the ace, or a void with poor trump length.

4) The fourth step shows absolute control. This means a void or singleton ace with adequate trump length, or the ace and king.

A third round control can be sought in situations where either an **Asking Bid** has already denied a first or second round control, or when responder's bidding has systemically denied a first or second round control. This use of the **Asking Bid** or repeated **Asking Bid** is answered as follows:

1) The first step denies a third round control.

2) The second step shows third round control in the form of a doubleton.

3) The third step shows third round control in the form of the queen.

Example 142:

a) Opener
♠5
♥KJ10975
♦ Q73
♣984

b) Responder
♠86
♥AQ8
♦ A4
♣AKQ762

The Bidding

Opener	Responder
2♥	3♠*
4♦*	6♥

In Example 142 after the opening bid of two hearts responder makes an *Asking Bid* by jumping to three spades. When opener shows second round control of spades by bidding four diamonds, responder jumps to six hearts. Surely the weak two bidder will have one top honor in his suit.

Example 143:

a) Opener
♠Q75
♥8
♦ 82
♣KQ109876

b) Responder
♠ —
♥Q54
♦ AKQ753
♣A542

The Bidding

Opener	Responder
3♣	4♥*
5♣*	6♣

In Example 143 responder to the opening preemptive bid of three clubs jumps to four hearts to ask about controls in that suit. When he hears about second round control he goes directly to slam in clubs. If the responder had held a heart suit he would first have bid three hearts (forcing), then four hearts to play there.

Example 144:

a) Opener
♠ AQJ10953
♡ 7
♢ K63
♣ 93

b) Responder
♠ K62
♡ 85
♢ A2
♣ AKQ852

The Bidding

Opener	Responder
4♠	5♡*
6♣*	6♠

After the opening bid of four spades, responder asks by bidding five hearts. If opener had no heart control his response to the *Asking Bid* would be five spades and responder would pass. When opener is able to show second round heart control slam is a good proposition.

Example 145:

a) Opener
♠ AKJ653
♡ 4
♢ 965
♣ 842

b) Responder
♠ Q107
♡ 976
♢ AKQJ3
♣ A7

The Bidding

Opener	Responder
2♠	2NT
3♢*	4♡*
5♣*	6♠

In Example 145 responder uses *Ogust* after the opening weak two bid to determine opener's suit quality. When opener shows a good suit, responder jumps in hearts to ask about controls in that suit. The four heart bid should not be confusing, since if responder held hearts he would have no reason to use *Ogust* prior to bidding his heart game, and once responder has started seeking information from opener there is no reason for him to change course and start giving information by making a *splinter bid*. Thus, the jump to four hearts is clearly an *Asking Bid*, and when opener shows a heart control responder bids the slam.

Example 146:

	a) Opener	b) Responder
	♠A5	♠9
	♡AKQJ943	♡65
	◇AQ8	◇K654
	♣A	♣987542

The Bidding

Opener	Responder
2♣	2◇*
3♡*	3NT*
4◇*	4NT*
5♠*	6◇*
7♡	

In Example 146 opener hears a two diamond response to his two club opening bid and jumps to three hearts to set the trump suit and start a control showing auction. Responder's bid of three no-trump denies an ace but shows some second round controls. Opener asks in diamonds and responder shows the king. Opener then asks in spades and when he finds second round control of that suit can bid the grand slam.

Example 147:

	a) Opener	b) Responder
	♠AKQJ874	♠96
	♡A	♡8754
	◇AK952	◇Q63
	♣ —	♣9852

The Bidding

Opener	Responder
2♣	2◇*
3♠*	4♠*
5◇*	5NT*
7♠	

In Example 147 opener hears a waiting two diamond response to his two club opening bid, then jumps to three spades to set the trump suit and start a control showing sequence. Responder's next bid of four spades denies any first or second round control. Opener's five diamond bid asks for third round control of that suit. When responder shows the queen of diamonds by bidding five notrump (third step) opener bids the grand slam since he has found the only card he needs to make that contract.

Exclusion Blackwood

When a strong hand wishes to find out about controls in his partner's hand but his own holding includes a void, information about aces by number is irrelevant since partner might hold the ace of the suit in which the bidder is void. The solution to this problem is to use an unusual jump in certain auctions as **Exclusion Blackwood.**

Auctions in which **Exclusion Blackwood** is used will for the most part be auctions in which a fit has been found or a trump suit has been otherwise determined. When after being raised, an unlimited hand makes a jump to a new suit at the five level, that jump should be to the suit in which the good hand has a void. As he bids his void, the bidder asks his partner to show key cards, but not to show the ace of the excluded suit.

Specific situations in which **Exclusion Blackwood** will apply are:

1) Immediately following a suit raise.

2) As the next call by the user of a **Texas Transfer.**

3) After a **Namyats** opening transfer bid followed by a relay to the anchor suit shown by the opening bid, responder's next bid in a new suit is **Exclusion Blackwood.**

Example 148:

a) Opener	b) Opener	c) Responder
♠KJ1073	♠KJ1073	♠A9852
♡A98	♡J85	♡KQ742
◇5	◇5	◇AKJ
♣KQ43	♣AQJ4	♣ —

With Example 148a) and 148b) opener first bids one spade and when responder makes a *Jacoby Two Notrump* response bids three diamonds to show his shortness there.

Responder with Example hand 148c) then bids five clubs, *Exclusion Blackwood* in clubs.

Opener 148a) shows two key cards outside of clubs. Since they must be the spade king and heart ace responder can bid seven spades.

Opener 148b) shows one key card outside of clubs. Since either the heart ace or spade king is missing, responder settles for the small slam in spades.

Example 149:

a) Opener	b) Opener	c) Responder
♠ AJ43	♠ AJ43	♠ KQ2
♡ A93	♡ A93	♡ KQ108742
◇ AQ8	◇ QJ5	◇ —
♣ J105	♣ A108	♣ KQ3

With Example hands 149a) and 149b) opener bids one notrump. Responder with Example 149c) bids four diamonds, a *Texas Transfer* and opener dutifully bids four hearts. Responder then bids five diamonds, *Exclusion Blackwood* and opener shows his key cards excluding the ace of diamonds.

With Example hand 149a) opener five notrump to show two key cards without the heart queen. Responder settles in six hearts.

With Example hand 149b) opener bids five hearts to show three key cards. Responder knows they are the right ones and can bid seven hearts.

The Grand Slam Force

A traditional tool, the **Grand Slam Force** is activated in any of three ways.

1) A direct leap to five notrump is the simplest version of the **Grand Slam Force**.

2) Introduction of a new suit at the six level after **Blackwood** has been used is a second form of the **Grand Slam Force**. The new suit will be lower ranking than the agreed trump suit.

3) A third form of the **Grand Slam Force** occurs when in a **Blackwood** auction a signoff at five notrump is required, and then removed to six of the agreed suit. The suit will usually be a low ranking suit since the second method of introducing a new suit below the level of the agreed suit will not be available.

When the **Grand Slam Force** is used, responder to that call is asked to bid a grand slam in the agreed suit if he holds two of the top three honor cards in the trump suit, but to sign off at the six level when his trump quality is not that good. Most expert partnerships use some form of coded answers at the six level so that responder can show what his trump holding is as he denies holding two of the top three honor cards.

A most effective method of identifying lesser trump holdings is to have the bidder sign off at the agreed trump suit when he has the queen or no top honor, but to artificially bid six clubs to announce that he has either the ace or the king. When the ace or the king is shown, if the user of the **Grand Slam Force** has the other of those two cards it may still be possible to get to a good grand slam missing the queen of trumps if the bidding side has ten or more cards in the suit between the two hands.

When the user of the **Grand Slam Force** knows that ten or more cards are present, when he hears that both the ace and king are accounted for he can bid the grand slam knowing that the queen is missing. If he needs to know about trump length in his partner's hand, he artificially bids six diamonds to ask for extra length.

Responder's earlier auction will have promised a trump fit of minimum length, based upon the auction. A single raise in a major suit promises three card support. A jump limit raise may have three card or longer support depending upon other facets of responder's hand. A raise of responder's major suit shows four card support. A raise of opener's minor suit usually shows a good four cards, or five or more cards. Other situations exist in which a minimum length has been established for the trump fit which will have been shown in the earlier auction.

When the user of the **Grand Slam Force** asks for extra length and his responder has greater length than has been promised by the earlier auction, it is to be assumed that the length of the suit in the partnership is ten or more cards, and responder bids the grand slam.

Super Gerber

Confusion often exists as to when the **Gerber** convention applies in an auction. Although the partnership may agree to use **Gerber** in auctions where it would not normally apply, there is a general rule as to when a bid of four clubs is, in fact, **Gerber**.

A jump from a natural notrump call to four clubs is **Gerber**. These auctions are auctions in which the **Gerber** convention clearly applies: 1NT-P-4♣; 2NT-P-4♣; 1♣-P-1♡-P, 1NT-P-4♣; 1♡-P-2NT-P, 4♣. The common denominator in all of these auctions is that the last bid before a jump to four clubs was a natural bid in notrump.

Unless the partnership has a specific agreement to the contrary, when a contract of three notrump has been reached and removed to four clubs, that four club bid is not **Gerber**. The bid of four clubs in this auction will be either a restatement of a club suit that has been previously bid and is now being suggested as the trump suit at a slam, or it will be a cue bid of the ace of clubs in support of a slam in a suit that has previously been shown.

When a bid of four clubs will not be **Gerber** and the bidder wants to ask about controls, he will often be able to use **Super Gerber**. **Super Gerber** utilizes a jump to five clubs as asking for aces when four clubs would have another meaning.

When a contract of three notrump has been reached and the next bidder wants to ask about controls, rather than bid four clubs which does not have that meaning, he jumps to five clubs, using **Super Gerber** to find out about controls. In an auction such as: 2♣-P-2◇-P, 3NT-P-?, a bid of four clubs would be **Stayman** rather than **Gerber**, and if the bidder wished to ask for controls he would jump to five clubs, employing **Super Gerber**.

In an auction such as: 1♣-P-3NT-P, ?, again a bid of four clubs would show a good club suit and try for slam, while a bid of five clubs would be **Super Gerber**, asking for controls.

General

In addition to the specific inclusions in this Chapter, all standard slam seeking tools are also available. Quantitative jumps in notrump, leaps to five in an agreed major suit, and simple cue bids are all as they would be in any standard bidding approach.

CHAPTER IX
DUPLICATE PROCEDURES

If you have read this book and are attempting to use its contents you are most probably playing duplicate bridge. It is necessary for you to have filled out your convention card properly, to know when you must alert, and be able to explain concisely and accurately the meaning of your systemic agreements when asked. The purpose of this Chapter is to furnish you with information you will need in order to fulfill those obligations.

The Convention Card

ACBL regulations require that at tournaments each member of the partnership have a convention card, that they be legible and identical, and that they bear the first and last names of the members of the pair. In club games one such card is ample unless the director stipulates otherwise, but a second card is a courtesy you should extend if you have an abundance of conventional agreements.

Under the specification of general approach, the most easily understood is the title of this book. It is sufficient to write 2/1 = Game Force.

In the section of the card which covers notrump opening bids and responses, the box for non-forcing **Stayman** should be checked, and next to it a reference made that hearts are bid first when both majors are held. A reference to **Puppet Stayman** next to the opening two notrump range is appropriate. The box on the line for transfers marked "other" should be checked and **Smolen** written on the line that follows. To indicate which variety of **Smolen** you have agreed to use write "2 & 3 levels" if you use **Invitational Smolen**, and write "3 level" if you use **Forcing Smolen**. Other items to include are **Lebensohl**, two spades is **Minor Suit Stayman**, two notrump relays to three clubs, **Walsh Relays**, redouble requires three clubs, and **negative doubles** at the three level if you use them. Of course the boxes for **Jacoby** and **Texas Transfers** and the box for invitational jump responses in minor suits should all be checked. Indicate also that 3NT shows a broken minor suit, and fill in the blanks to show your opening bid ranges in such fashion as to truly reflect what your agreement is.

In the box on major suit opening bids indicate never for first and second seats and often for third and fourth seat (or seldom if that is your agreement). Check the box for limit raises, but indicate that they must show either side shortness or four cards. For conventional raises show three spades, three notrump, **Inverted Trump Swiss**, **Jacoby Two Notrump**, 1♠-3♡, and 1♡-3♢. Check the box for 1NT Forcing, but indicate that it applies by an unpassed hand. Check the **Drury** box, but write in above it the words "reverse" or "two way" or both if you use them. Under the **Drury** box write "SSGT" to indicate that game tries are made in short suits after **Drury**. On the line for other agreements indicate that you use **Mathe Asking Bids** by writing the known abbreviation **MAB**.

In the section for minor suit openings and responses, check the box that shows three card length is promised in clubs. In diamonds, check both boxes (3+ and 4+) but next to the 3+ box indicate "only when 4-4-3-2". Check the boxes for double raise preemptive and single raise forcing, but between them write your agreement such as "off in all competition", or "off after double". Fill the blanks for one notrump over one club with 8 to 10 but below indicate 6 to 10 if passed. After one diamond response write in "usually no four card major". On the "other" line indicate that responses of three clubs and two notrump to an opening one diamond bid show 10-12.

In the section on two bids check the black box for two clubs strong, indicate that two diamonds is a waiting bid, and either show that the cheapest bid at the three level is a "second negative" or show that an immediate response of two hearts is negative. Check the appropriate box for other two bids, using the black box if they are natural and the red box if they are conventional. Describe conventional two bids, and include relevant response and rebid information.

In the area marked "Other Conventional Calls" show all of your agreements that do not have a place of their own on the card. Included here should be **New Minor Forcing**, **Fourth Suit Forcing**, **Wolff Signoff**, two clubs takeout versus one notrump in balance seat, **Splinters**, preemptive jump shifts, **Unusual vs Unusual** and anything else that needs to be shown.

In the section on special doubles, indicate the level through which you have agreed to use **negative doubles**. On the next line, if you have agreed to play **free bids** forcing to game, enter the fact that a negative double of one heart denies four spades. The level through which you have agreed to play **responsive doubles** must be indicated, and on the last two lines you will list **Snapdragon, maximal overcall, support,** and other doubles you may have agreed to use, as well as **honor redoubles**.

292

In the section on direct notrump overcalls, fill in the range agreed and check the appropriate box to express your agreement on the use of **unusual notrump**. Indicate on the line marked "other" that you have agreed to use the same responses to a notrump overcall that you use after opening notrump bids.

In the box for simple overcalls, fill in the range you have agreed. Check that a **cue bid** is a one round force. Write in the words "jump cue" and check the box for limit raise. Use the last line to show that a jump raise is weak. To be absolutely complete, you should write in that an overcall at the one level could be four cards.

Circle the appropriate suit symbols to indicate your agreed defense against an opposing opening bid of one notrump. If your conventional approach has a name that would be widely recognized, it helps to include that name on the bottom line of the section.

Check the box for preemptive jump overcalls and indicate the nature of two notrump as a game try. Also write in here that 2♢ over 1♣ shows ♢ & ♡, and that 3♣ over 1♢ shows ♣ & ♡.

Over the opponents' takeout doubles, check the boxes that show new suits forcing at the one level, jump shift weak, and redouble implies no fit. On the bottom line indicate that two notrump is a good major raise or a preemptive minor raise. A standard way of indicating this is the simple designation "Flip-flop".

Check the box that expresses your style of preemptive bidding. On the line write in that four clubs and four diamonds are transfers, then write in the word **Namyats**.

Versus opponents' preempts double is for takeout and that box should be checked. If your agreement is that double shows a notrump type hand and some other call is for takeout, check the box marked optional and also indicate what your takeout call is. Many players incorrectly check optional when they have no agreed conventional call for takeout, and their doubles are, in fact, takeout doubles. If you use **Lebensohl** after the double of a weak two bid, that should be indicated in this box. You should also write in **Stayman** and **Jacoby** if they apply after notrump overcalls, and **Roman Jump Overcalls** should be shown here if you use them after an opposing weak two bid.

Under Psychics, enter expectancy. Once every four to six months is "seldom" for frequent players, and if the frequency is greater, you should correctly indicate "often". Psychic controls are no longer permitted in ACBL events.

In the Direct Cuebid area, check the box that indicates two suits, and write in **Top and Bottom** or **Michaels** or both, or another preference that is agreed in your partnership.

In the section relating to slam conventions, include reference to **RKC, Exclusion Blackwood, Kickback, Asking Bids,** and **RKC** and **Super Gerber.**

Be thorough in showing your card play agreements in the section provided, and affix a red dot if so required by your carding agreements.

Alerts and Explanations

Whenever your partner makes a conventional call, with a few exceptions that call is likely to require an alert. The exceptions that should not be alerted are these:

1) **Stayman.** (but in the system since it could be a relay instead of just **Stayman** an alert is required).

2) **Blackwood** and any variations including **RKC.** Do not alert 4NT or the response to 4NT, but do alert continuation sequences within the **RKC** complex.

3) Takeout doubles.

4) A two notrump response to a **weak two bid** that asks for information about the nature of the **weak two bid.**

Other conventional calls do require alerts. There is an additional guideline that must be observed.

Whenever partner's call conveys information to you that your opponents are not also expected to receive, you must alert. This means that any departure from what would be standard is alertable.

Many simple things may seem to need no alert, but an alert is necessary because of departure from standard or special partnership agreements. Here are some examples of situations where alerts are often not given although they are necessary:

1) In the system when the auction begins with one club and responder bids one of a major suit, opener must alert. If asked, opener should reply that although the call is natural, responder might have bypassed a longer diamond suit.

2) A major suit limit raise should be alerted for the reason that opener knows that responder shows either three trumps with side shortness or four trumps without side shortness. Opener knows this, but the opponents do not, so they are entitled to an alert.

ACBL CONVENTION CARD

All conventions marked in red and all non-standard partnership agreements must be alerted.

SPECIAL DOUBLES (Describe)	DIRECT NT OVERCALLS	Names MARY & MAX HARDY
Negative →3S	1NT __15__ to __18__ HCP	General Approach 2/1 = GAME FORCE Pair # ____
OF 1H DENIES 4S	Jump to 2NT: ___ to ___ HCP	
Responsive →3S	Unusual for Minors ☐	Strong Forcing Opening: 2♣ ■ 2 bids ☐ 1♦ ☐ Other 4C-4D
Other MAX OKALL SUPPORT	2 Lower Unbid ■	
HONOR XX SNAPDRAGON ACTION	Other SYSTEM ON	PUPPET 3S→3NT

		NOTRUMP OPENING BIDS	
SIMPLE OVERCALL	Vs. Wk. ■ Strong ■ NT Opening	1NT __15+__ to __18-__	2NT __20__ to __22__ HCP
7 to 17 HCP/occ. light ■	Direct ■ Balance ■	1NT ___ to ___♥/1ST	3NT ___ to ___ HCP
MAY BE 4 CARDS AT ONE LEVEL	2♣ shows ♠—♦ ♥ ♦	2♣ Forc.☐ Non-Forc.■ Stayman	BROKEN MINOR Solid Suit ■
Responses: New Suit Forcing ■ AT ONE LEVEL	2♦ shows ♠—♦ ♥ ♦	2♦ Forc.☐ Non-Forc.☐ Stayman	LEBENSOHL (SLOW SHOWS)
Cuebid is: One-Round Force ■ JUMP Q	2♥ shows ♠ ♦ ♥ ♦	Transfers. Jacoby ■ Texas ■ Other ■	SMOLEN (2+3 LEVELS)
Game Force Limit Raise	2♠ shows ♠ ♦ ♥ ♠	1NT - 3♠/3♦	IsInvitational ☐ Preemptive ☐ Forcing ☐
Other JUMP RAISE WEAK	Other ASTRO	Other 2S = MSS 2NT→3C WALSH RELAYS XX→2C
		NEG X AT 3 LEVEL X AT 2 LEVEL = RAISE

JUMP OVERCALL	OVER OPP'S TAKEOUT DOUBLE		
	New Suit Force 1-level ☐ 2-level ☐	MAJOR OPENINGS	MINOR OPENINGS
Strong ☐ Interm ☐ Preempt ■	Jp. Shift Force☐ Good☐ Weak■	1 ♥-1 ♠ Opening on 4 Cards	Length Promised
Special Responses 2NT→OGUST	Redouble Implies No Fit ■	Often Seldom Never	4 + 3 + Shorter
2D/1C = D&H 3C/1D = C&H	Other FLIP - FLOP	1st-2nd ☐ ■←→☐ ☐	1♣ ☐ ■ ☐
		3rd-4th ■←→☐ ☐ ☐	1♦ ☐ ■ ■ 4-4-3-2 ONLY
OPENING PREEMPTS	Vs. Opp's Preempts Dbl. Is	RESPONSES W/STIFF ♣♦	1-2-4 ■ RESPONSES
Sound Light Solid Minor	LEBENSOHL Takeout Opt. Penalty	Double Raise Forcing ☐ Limit ■	RKC Double Raise
3-bids ■	Wk. 2's ■ ☐ ☐	Preemptive ■ in Comp. ☐	Forcing ☐ Limit ☐ Preempt ■
Other 4C-4D TRANSFERS (NAMYATS)	3 Bids ☐ ☐ ☐	Conv. Raise: 2NT ■ 3NT ■	OFF AFTER DBL & 1D-2C
4C = RKC GERBER	Conv. takeout STAYMAN COMM JUMPS - TRANSFERS	INV Swiss ■ Splinter ☐	Single Raise Forcing ■
		TRUMP Conv. Responses: 1NT Forcing ■	1NT/1♦ __8__ to __10__ HCP UPH
PSYCHICS Systemic ☐	Strong Takeout: Minor ☐ Major ☐	REV 2 WAY DRURY ■ Single Raise Constr. ☐	1. Resp. Conv. usually AID P4
Never Rare Occ. Frequent	Natural: ♠ ☐ ♥ ☐ ♦ ☐ Artif. Bids ☐	Other 1S-3H 1H-3D MAB	4 CARD MAJOR SPLINTERS
☐ ☐ ☐ ☐	Two Suits ■ TOP & BOTTOM	3C = GUARD RAISE	Other 3C 1D=10-12
Describe: Q			2NT 1D=10-12
Controls			

SUPER & RKC SLAM CONVENTIONS ASKING BIDS		2♣	WK ☐ ☐ 23 to BAL HCP. Describe 2D WAITING = POSITIVE		INT ■ ☐ ☐ X OR XX = NEG 2H = NEGATIVE 2♠ Neg.		STR ■ ■ Conv. Resp. 2S = H 2NT = S 2NT Neg.☐
Gerber ■ NT & PREEMPTS 4NT Var ■ RKC - KICKBACK	2♦	WK ■ ☐ ☐ _5_ to _11_ HCP. Describe OGUST / 2NT
Interference over 4♣ or 4NT: D = PEN P = Do x 3 (RKC)		INT ☐ ☐ ☐ 2NT BPH 2NT Neg.☐
EXCLUSION RAISES - TEXAS - NAMYATS		STR ☐ ☐ Conv. Resp.
	2♥	WK ■ ☐ ☐ _5_ to _11_ HCP. Describe ASKS STIFF
DEFENSIVE CARD PLAY	K♣10		INT ☐ ☐ NEW MAJOR FORCING
Opening lead vs. SUITS: 3rd best ■ 4th best ■ 5th best ■ Other 7TH		STR ☐ ☐ Conv. Resp. J.S. ASKING 2NT Neg.☐
Mark card led: x x⑧ Ⓐ K x Ⓚ Q x Ⓠ J x ⓙ 10 x ⑩ 9 x	2♠	WK ■ ☐ ☐ _5_ to _11_ HCP. Describe MCCABE / DOUBLE
K J⑩ x K 10⑨ x x x x x⑧		INT ☐ ☐ 2NT Neg.☐
Opening lead vs. NT: 3rd best ■ 4th best ■ Other 5TH 7TH		STR ☐ ☐ Conv. Resp.

Mark card led Q⑨ x x Ⓐ K J x A Q⑩ x A J⑩ x
A 10⑨ 8 Ⓚ Q J x K⑩ 10 9 K J⑩ 9 K 10⑨ 8
⑩ J 10 x Q 10⑨ 8 ⑩ J 10 9 x ⑩ 9 8 x x x x x⑥

Special Carding _____ Frequent Count Signals ■

OTHER CONVENTIONAL CALLS
NMF - HARDY ADJ ___ PJS EXCEPT WHEN CONVENTIONAL
4TH SUIT SPLINTERS CRASH VS 1C & 2C ARTIFICIAL
UNUS VS UNUS SAME SUIT STAYMAN WOLFF SIGNOFF
2C T.O. VS DEAD NT LEBENSOHL / REVERSES DALLAS

If in doubt as to the meaning of a conventional call — ASK AT YOUR TURN!

The convention card above is the actual card used by Mary and Max Hardy in tournament competition. It is filled out as completely as the form itself will allow. You should endeavor to be as complete as possible in indicating the agreements in your partnership as you fill out your own card.

3) People who play forcing club systems miss this one with great frequency. Facing an opening bid of one club, responder bids one heart or one spade. In most forcing club systems, this promises a five card suit. In standard bidding responder does not promise more than a four card suit. Since this is a deviation from standard, opener is required to alert.

Whether or not an alert is required, you must be sure not to volunteer explanations of partner's bids. Only if the opponents ask are you permitted to explain, and then your explanation should be both thorough and concise.

When an explanation is in order, giving the name of a convention is appropriate only when that convention is so common that the opponents are expected to know it. Facing an overcall of one notrump, for example, if partner bids two clubs and the opening bid by the opposition was not in clubs, partner's bid requires an alert. The reason for this is that in standard bidding facing a one notrump overcall a cue bid is used for **Stayman**, and a bid of two clubs is natural and non-forcing. Since in the system we use the same responses facing an overcall of one notrump as facing an opening bid in notrump we know that the bid of two clubs is **Stayman**, but the opponents may not. After you alert them, if they ask it is sufficient to tell them that partner's bid of two clubs is **Stayman**, for they understand what **Stayman** is.

In an auction where you have overcalled an opponent's opening bid and the responder bids a third suit, if partner doubles you will alert. If you are asked what the alert is for, do not say, "Snapdragon". The opponents probably have never heard of "Snapdragon" and telling them the name of the convention does nothing toward explaining what the bid means. Your correct description of the meaning of partner's double is, "That shows that he has at least five cards in the unbid suit and tolerance for the suit of my overcall."

It is not enough to remember to alert. You must also know not to explain unless asked, and when asked to give a description of the meaning of partner's call rather than a conventional name that may have no meaning at all to your opponents.

In the following section we have attempted to give capsule explanations to be used if the opponents ask about any bid made in any system auction. The list cannot possibly be complete, but will cover most circumstances.

Opening Bids

One Club. Three or more clubs and normal opening bid values.

One Diamond. Four or more diamonds unless exactly 4-4-3-2 with normal opening bid values.

One Heart or One Spade. If in first or second seat, at least a five card suit and normal opening bid values. In third or fourth seat could be a four card suit, and if four cards must be light in values.

One Notrump. Balanced or semibalanced with honors in short suits, with a good fifteen to a bad eighteen points. May contain a five card major if there are three cards in the other major and no bad doubleton.

Two Clubs. Strong, artificial and forcing. At least 23 points if balanced. For suit play at least eight tricks with a solid major suit, or nine tricks otherwise.

Two Diamonds. Weak two bid. Five to eleven points. Six cards in first or second seat (rarely a good five), but often five cards in third or four seat (or describe the conventional two diamond bid your partnership has agreed to use).

Two Hearts or Two Spades. A weak two bid with five to eleven points. Six cards (or a good five) in first or second seat but frequently five in third or fourth.

Two Notrump. Balanced, or semibalanced with 20+ to 22 in high cards. May contain a five card major.

Three of Any Suit. Normal preempt. I expect a seven card suit and little defense.

Three Notrump*. Artificial, showing a broken eight card minor suit.

Four Clubs*. Artificial, showing a good but not solid heart suit and eight or eight and one half playing tricks.

Four Diamonds*. Artificial, showing a good but not solid spade suit and eight or eight and one half playing tricks.

Four Hearts* or Four Spades*. A normal preempt, but alertable since we also play **Namyats**.

Responses

To One Club:

One Diamond*. Denies a four card major unless he has a hand of opening bid strength and five or more diamonds as well. Could be artificial with two or three diamonds, no four card major, and not enough to respond with one notrump.

One Heart* or One Spade*. Natural with at least four cards and five or more points, but he may have bypassed a longer diamond suit.

One Notrump. A balanced and tenaced eight to ten points and no four card major. If passed, six to ten points.

Two Clubs*. An **Inverted** strong raise with a good nine points or more and no four card major. By an unpassed hand it is unlimited and forcing. Applies after an overcall but not after a takeout double (or — does not apply in competition).

Two Diamonds*, *Two Hearts** or *Two Spades**. A preemptive jump shift.

Two Notrump. Standard. A balanced and tenaced hand with a good twelve to a bad fifteen points. Denies a four card major.

Three Clubs*. An **Inverted** raise. A weak hand of less than nine points with no four card major, at least five clubs, and some distributional merit.

Three Diamonds*, *Three Hearts** or *Three Spades**. A **splinter** bid showing shortness in the suit bid and opening bid values with good support for clubs. All higher level responses are standard.

To One Diamond:

One Heart or One Spade. Natural with five or more points and four or more cards in the suit.

One Notrump. Natural and non-forcing. A good five to a bad nine points and no four card major.

Two Clubs*. Natural and forcing to game.

Two Diamonds*. An **Inverted** strong raise with a good nine points or more and no four card major. By an unpassed hand it is unlimited and forcing. Applies after an overcall but not after a takeout double (or does not apply in competition).

Two Hearts* or Two Spades* A preemptive jump shift.

Two Notrump*. A limited balanced hand in the range of a good nine to a bad twelve with no four card major. Not forcing.

Three Clubs*. An invitational hand in the range of a good nine to a bad twelve points with a good club suit, probably six cards.

Three Diamonds*. An **Inverted** raise. A weak hand of less than nine points with at least four diamonds and no four card major, and some distributional merit.

Three Hearts* or Three Spades*. **Splinter** bids showing shortness in the bid suit, opening bid values and good support for diamonds. All higher level responses are standard.

To One Heart:

One Spade. Natural and forcing if by an unpassed hand. With a minimum response and heart shortness can be a good three card suit.

Two Spades*. A preemptive jump shift.

Three Diamonds*. Artificial, showing a good nine to a bad twelve in high cards, four or five card heart support, and some singleton or void.

298

Three Spades*. Artificial, showing a good twelve to a bad fifteen in high cards, four or five card heart support, and some singleton or void.

Three Notrump* Natural and non-forcing showing a tenaced hand with exactly 3-2-4-4-distribution and a good fifteen to seventeen points.

Four Hearts. Standard and preemptive. Shows little in high cards with lots of hearts and some distributional merit.

To One Spade:

Two Hearts*. Natural and game forcing. At least five hearts and a good twelve points or more.

Three Diamonds*. A preemptive jump shift. By a passed hand if **Two Way Drury** is agreed shows a six card diamond suit with spade shortness and invitational (9+ to 12-) values.

Three Hearts*. Artificial, showing a good nine to a bad twelve in high cards, at least four card support for spades, and some side singleton or void.

Three Notrump*. Artificial, showing a good twelve to a bad fifteen in high cards, at least four card support for spades, and some side singleton or void.

Four Hearts. Natural and preemptive.

Four Spades. Natural and preemptive. Lots of spades and little in high cards with some distributional merit.

To One Heart or One Spade:

One Notrump*. By an unpassed hand is forcing for one round. Shows a hand in the range of a good five to a bad twelve. Can have a three card fit for opener if balanced and in the range of nine plus to twelve minus. By a passed hand is natural and non-forcing.

Two Clubs* ***or Two Diamonds****. Natural and forcing to game if by an unpassed hand. By a passed hand two clubs is **Drury**, promising a limit raise for opener's major suit. If two diamonds is also agreed as **Drury** by a passed hand, the two club bid shows exactly three card support for opener's major suit, and the two diamond bid shows four card or longer support with nine plus to twelve minus points.

Single Raise. Natural and non-forcing. Shows a good five to a bad nine points and three or four card support.

Two Notrump*. A **Jacoby Two Notrump** bid that promises at least a good fifteen points and four card or greater support for opener's major suit. Opener must observe a systemic set of rebids.

Three Clubs*. A preemptive jump shift. By a passed hand shows a club suit usually six cards long, invitational values (9+ to 12-) and shortness in the opener's major suit.

Jump Raise*. A limit raise of a good nine to a bad twelve points. It shows exactly three card support with some side shortness, or four card support without side shortness.

Four Clubs*. **Inverted Trump Swiss.** A balanced hand with a good twelve to a bad fifteen in high cards and four or five card trump support. If only four trumps must contain two of the top three honor cards. If five trumps must be headed by at least ace or king.

Four Diamonds*. **Inverted Trump Swiss.** A balanced hand with a good twelve to a bad fifteen points and four card or longer support for opener's major suit. Trumps will not be as good as for a bid of four clubs.

To One Notrump:

Most responses to one notrump are alertable. Explanations are to be made in keeping with the systemic calls explained in Chapter Five. A complete representation here would be redundant.

To Two Clubs:

Two Diamonds*. An artificial waiting bid. It does not deny values and leaves room for opener to describe his strong two bid. If two hearts is agreed as an immediate double negative, promises values of at least an ace, a king, or two queens.

Two Hearts*, Two Spades*, Three Clubs*, or Three Diamonds*. Natural promising at least five cards headed by two of the top three honor cards. The possible exception is in clubs which could just show a positive response with a reasonable club suit.

Two Hearts*. Alternately an artificial immediate double negative, denying as much as an ace, a king, or two queens.

Opener's Rebid of Three Hearts* or Three Spades* Promises a long and solid suit with nine or more winners. Sets in motion **Asking Bids** by opener and control showing calls by responder.

Opener's Rebid of Four Hearts* or Four Spades*. Promises a long and solid suit with exactly eight or eight and one half winners.

To a Weak Two Bid:

Responses are according to the preference of the users and should be listed on the convention card. If two notrump is forcing and seeks information it does not require an alert. If opener's rebids are artificial they must be alerted. If jump shifts are **Asking Bids** they require alerts.

To Two Notrump:

If three clubs is **Stayman** it requires no alert. If three clubs is **Puppet Stayman** it does require an alert. Systemic responses are the same as to an opening bid of one notrump except that a raise to three notrump is played by most as natural and not as a relay.

To Three of a Suit: If a jump shift is an **Asking Bid***, alert. In standard bidding a new suit is forcing. If your agreement is that a new suit is not forcing*, alert.

To Three Notrump: All responses are conventional and require alerts. The explanations are in keeping with your understanding of the convention.

To Four Clubs:

Four Diamonds*. A relay requiring opener to bid four hearts.
Four Hearts*. A natural signoff.
Four Spades*, Five Clubs* or Five Diamonds* Asking Bids.
Four Spades*, Five Clubs* or Five Diamonds* after a relay to Four Hearts. **Exclusion Blackwood**.

To Four Diamonds:

Four Hearts*. A relay requiring opener to bid four spades.
Four Spades*. A natural signoff.
Five Clubs*, Five Diamonds* or Five Hearts* Asking Bids.
Five Clubs*, Five Diamonds* or Five Hearts* after a relay to Four Spades. **Exclusion Blackwood**.

Rebids By Opener

Very few of opener's rebids require alerts. These are the notable exceptions:

1) After a one diamond* response to the opening bid of one club, if opener rebids either one heart* or one spade* he shows an unbalanced hand not suited to a rebid of one notrump. If opener instead bids one notrump* he shows any balanced minimum and may conceal one or two four card majors.

2) If opener makes a jump raise to game* in responder's major suit an alert is required since responder knows that opener's hand is balanced.

3) Opener's other jump rebids include **splinters*** and calls to show a six four pattern. These require alerts.

Rebids by Responder

Most of responder's rebids are natural and require no alerts. There are two notable exceptions:

1) **New Minor Forcing***. When responder uses the new minor after a rebid of one notrump by opener, that call is artificial and forcing and requires an alert. Subsequent calls will also be alertable since they carry specific meaning to the bidding partnership that may not be understood by the opponents.

2) **Fourth Suit Forcing***. From a purely theoretical standpoint, use of this bidding technique is standard, since there is documentation to prove that more than 95% of expert bidders consider it to be so. However, from a practical viewpoint, the artificial use of the fourth suit to establish a forcing auction is not understood by the masses of those who play bridge. It is therefore to be assumed that whenever partner uses the fourth suit, the message that you receive may not be understood by your opponents, and an alert is due. This practice is necessary even against expert opponents.

Correct Procedures

There will be times when you may fail to alert as has been required of you, or you may have given an incorrect explanation when an opponent has asked you about one of your partnership agreements. When you become aware that you have given misinformation in either of these ways, you must immediately make a correction. The sooner the correction is made, the less likely that the misinformation is to effect the bidding or play of your opponents, and the less likely that an adjudication of the result will be necessary.

If your partner fails to alert or gives an incorrect explanation, you must do nothing to correct him until the appropriate time has been reached. Further, you must ignore his failure to alert or his incorrect explanation and continue the auction with your actions based upon what you know your partnership agreements to be. Any inference you draw from partner's misinformation and act upon is improper.

The correct time to call attention to partner's misinformation is at the conclusion of the auction, but then only if your side is the declaring side. If your side will defend, you must continue to maintain silence until the play has been completed. The opponents are entitled to profit from any misdefense your partner may generate through his own misunderstanding of your partnership agreements. When play has been completed, you must then call attention to partner's misinformation so that if your opponents have been injured, they may properly seek redress at that time.

The final word is to know your system so that you will also know when to alert and how to explain when an opponent seeks information about your partnership agreements. Remember that any time a call made by your partner carries specific information which the opponents are not reasonably expected to also receive, you must alert. When in doubt, an unnecessary alert is a better idea than the omission of an alert which should have been made.

INDEX

304

INDEX OF EXAMPLES

THE TWO OVER ONE SEMINAR

An intensive presentation of the Two Over One System is available. A seminar in four sessions of between two and three hours each was developed by Max Hardy in response to the request of a bridge club and first presented in 1981. Since that time there has been a total of ten presentations of this seminar in various locations throughout the North American continent.

Sponsors of the presentation have sometimes been bridge organizations or clubs, but at other times individuals who are interested in the system have undertaken to organize and present the seminar in their home areas. Anyone with the initiative and desire to organize such a presentation need only make arrangements with Max Hardy and then promote the undertaking. With sufficient interest and promotion, it is possible that the seminar can become a money making proposition for the sponsor.

Contents of the Seminar

Participants are urged to bring tape recorders as well as take notes. Questions may be asked during the presentation, and topics that are related to the subject material may also be introduced. The schedule of topics is elastic and may extend beyond the material scheduled to be covered in each session. (At the Vancouver presentation of the seminar the sponsor video-taped the first three sessions. This is also permissible as long as use of the tapes is restricted to the local area of the presentation and no charge is made for viewing the tapes without permission of Max Hardy.)

Session One - After Natural Notrump. Discussion of responses and rebids after the opening bid of one or two notrump, or a rebid in notrump to show a hand of some specific size. Included are Stayman auctions, Minor Suit Stayman, Jacoby Transfers, Texas Transfers, Smolen Transfers, Walsh Relays, Lebensohl, Puppet Stayman, New Minor Forcing, Hardy Adjunct, Wolff Signoff, Roman Key Card Gerber.

Session Two - Forcing and Non-Forcing Auctions. Discussion of one over one auctions, two over one auctions, forcing notrump, preemptive jump shifts, fourth suit forcing, simple preferences, jump preferences, the principle of fast arrival, finding eight card fits, and competitive bidding not covered in other segments of the seminar.

Session Three - Suit Raises and Slam Bidding. Major suit raises including limit jumps, mini-splinters, maxi-splinters, Inverted Trump Swiss, Mathe Asking Bids, Jacoby Two Notrump, Inverted Minor Raises, raises after takeout doubles, Roman Key Card Blackwood, Kickback, Walsh Asking Bids.

Session Four - Testing What You Have Learned. This session includes the play of eight prepared hands, each of which presents some system component that has been discussed in the previous three sessions. Following play, group discussion is held on each of the hands, and each seminar participant receives a record of all eight hands and a commentary sheet.

History of the Seminar

The seminar has been enthusiastically received after each of these ten presentations, all prior to the presentation you are reading in the update of **Two Over One Game Force** issued in June of 1989.

Date	Location	Sponsor
Aug 81	San Diego, Ca.	The Pacific Club
Jul 83	Casper, Wy.	Casper Unit, ACBL
Mar 84	San Diego, Ca.	Gail Erickson's Bridge Club
Oct 84	Torrance, Ca.	Kings' Bridge Club
Oct 84	Colorado Spgs, Co.	Privately sponsored
Nov 84	Denver, Co.	Lakewood & Arvada Bridge Clubs
Feb. 85	Albuquerque, NM.	Privately sponsored
Jun 85	Vancouver, B.C.	Vancouver Unit, ACBL
May 87	Southfield, Mi.	SOMBA Regional Tournament
Oct 88	St. Louis, Mo.	Privately sponsored
Aug 91	Bellevue, Wa.	East Side Bridge Club
Sept 91	Denver, Co.	Denver Metropolitan Bridge Club

Some of the sponsors were sufficiently impressed to send letters indicating their pleasure with the presentation. Copies of those letters are available as recommendations.

Cost and Arrangements for the Seminar

The cost of the seminar (as of July 1989) is $1,000 plus all expenses. Most sponsors have arranged for presentation in conjunction with Max Hardy's normal travel, thereby reducing the travel expense to the sponsor. The Casper seminar was given immediately before a Sectional in Denver, and the travel expense to the sponsor was between Denver and Casper. The St. Louis seminar was given between a Denver Sectional and the Nashville NABC, requiring very little travel expense for the sponsor.

Housing arrangements can be in a hotel or in a private home. All meals during the duration of the seminar are included as part of the expense to be borne by the sponsor.

A suggested individual cost is $50 per person for the four sessions. At this price, an attendance of 30 participants will bring in $1,500 which will usually more than cover all expenses for the sponsor.

Two or three sessions in a day are possible. Many sponsors have scheduled one session in the late afternoon (about 3:30pm to 6:00pm) so that those who work could leave work early and not miss a full day, and followed with another session at about 7:30pm, ending shortly after 10:00pm.

If you or an organization that you represent would like to present this seminar, contact Max Hardy at the Post Office Box shown on the title pages of this book, or call (702) 368-0379. A machine will take your message if we are not there to answer your call.

The following presentation is a synopsis of each of the several bridge books that are available through this publisher. Ordering information is found at the end of the list.

BOOKS BY MAX HARDY

Two Over One Game Force Revised, Expanded, Updated for the 1990's. Paperback, 303pp, **$14.95.**

The third in a series of system books, replacing **Five Card Majors — Western Style** which was followed by the original **Two Over One Game Force.** The first book was published in 1974, and the replacement in 1982. This newest version is far more comprehensive than the earlier system books, includes greater amounts of explanation, and is graphically better in its layouts and larger type size.

The system discussed is the Western Five Card Major approach as developed by Richard Walsh, John Swanson and Paul Soloway in the late 60's. Each book that followed the original attempted to present the new ideas that have become part of the system as time has passed. The version most popular today includes many newer ideas that have emerged and been found to have merit in recent years.

New Minor FORCING, Fourth Suit FORCING, FORCING Notrump Responses. Paperback, 80pp, $7.95. Each topic available under separate cover, $2.95.

This book looks in depth at each of three important bidding tools. Each is a component of the **Two Over One** system, but can be used separately as part of anyone's bidding approach. No other source devotes as much space or attention to any of the three topics.

Splinters And Other Shortness Bids. Paperback, 88pp, $7.95.

Bidding to show shortness is mentioned in several bridge texts, but no other book undertakes to catalogue all of the methods in use that employ shortness showing bids and explains how hand evaluation can be achieved accurately through their use.

BOOKS BY MIKE LAWRENCE

Judgment at Bridge. Paperback, 151pp, **$9.95.**

Alfred Sheinwold did the introduction for this prime textbook for the advancing player. The theme is that of avoiding the common errors. Great attention is given to auctions which include takeout doubles and their responses. There are two valuable chapters on defense. Even very experienced players will find much here to help improve their understanding of the game.

The Complete Book on Overcalls in Contract Bridge. Hardcover, $14.95, Paperback, 202pp, $9.95.

The only complete coverage of this important aspect of bidding is found in this Lawrence classic. Sheinwold again wrote the introduction, awarded it his prize as "bridge book of the year" for 1980, and stated, "If you read only one bridge book per year, this should be it." The high regard in which this book is held throughout the world of bridge is shown by the fact that Victor Mollo sought and obtained the rights, and did a special edition for his British constituency.

The Complete Book on Balancing in Contract Bridge. Hardcover, $14.95, Paperback, 209pp, **$11.95.**

Again Mike Lawrence took a specialized topic that had largely been ignored in the bridge literature and produced a classic. And once again Alfred Sheinwold produced an Introduction that urges the serious player not to be without this book. Understanding this topic can upgrade your bidding tremendously, and Lawrence presents it in easily readable style.

The Complete Book on Hand Evaluation in Contract Bridge. Paperback, 194pp, **$11.95.**

Once more Mike Lawrence has written exhaustively about a topic dear to the hearts of all bridge players who would be successful. "Reading this book is a special experience", says Sheinwold in his Introduction of it. "A must for the library of the player with any depth. A tremendous value for the money." said the ACBL Bulletin.

50 HIGHLY-RECOMMENDED TITLES

FOR BEGINNERS
#0300 Future Champions' Bridge Series 9.95
#2130 Kantar-Introduction to Declarer's Play 10.00
#2135 Kantar-Introduction to Defender's Play 10.00
#0101 Stewart-Baron-The Bridge Book 1 .... 9.95
#1121 Silverman-Elementary Bridge
      Five Card Major Student Text 4.95
#0660 Penick-Beginning Bridge Complete 9.95
#0661 Penick-Beginning Bridge Quizzes 6.95
#3230 Lampert-Fun Way to Serious Bridge 10.00

FOR ADVANCED PLAYERS
#2250 Reese-Master Play 5.95
#1420 Klinger-Modern Losing Trick Count 14.95
#2240 Love-Bridge Squeezes Complete 7.95
#0103 Stewart-Baron-The Bridge Book 3 .... 9.95
#0740 Woolsey-Matchpoints 14.95
#0741 Woolsey-Partnership Defense 12.95
#1702 Bergen-Competitive Auctions 9.95
#0636 Lawrence-Falsecards 9.95

BIDDING — 2 OVER 1 GAME FORCE
#4750 Bruno & Hardy-Two-Over-One Game Force:
      An Introduction 9.95
#1750 Hardy-Two-Over-One Game Force 14.95
#1790 Lawrence-Workbook on the Two Over One System 11.95
#4525 Lawrence-Bidding Quizzes Book 1 .... 13.95

DEFENSE
#0520 Blackwood-Complete Book of Opening Leads 17.95
#3030 Ewen-Opening Leads 15.95
#0104 Stewart-Baron-The Bridge Book 4 .... 7.95
#0631 Lawrence-Dynamic Defense 11.95
#1200 Woolsey-Modern Defensive Signalling 4.95

FOR INTERMEDIATE PLAYERS
#2120 Kantar-Complete Defensive Bridge 20.00
#3015 Root-Commonsense Bidding 15.00
#0630 Lawrence-Card Combinations 12.95
#0102 Stewart-Baron-The Bridge Book 2 .... 9.95
#1122 Silverman-Intermediate Bridge Five
      Card Major Student Text 4.95
#0575 Lampert-The Fun Way to Advanced Bridge 11.95
#0633 Lawrence-How to Read Your Opponents' Cards 11.95
#3672 Truscott-Bid Better, Play Better 12.95
#1765 Lawrence-Judgment at Bridge 9.95

PLAY OF THE HAND
#2150 Kantar-Test your Bridge Play, Vol. 1 .... 10.00
#3675 Watson-Watson's Classic Book on
      the Play of the Hand 15.00
#1932 Mollo-Gardener-Card Play Technique 12.95
#3009 Root-How to Play a Bridge Hand 15.00
#1124 Silverman-Play of the Hand as
      Declarer and Defender 4.95
#2175 Truscott-Winning Declarer Play 10.00
#3803 Sydnor-Bridge Made Easy Book 3 .... 8.00

CONVENTIONS
#2115 Kantar-Bridge Conventions.......................... 10.00
#0610 Kearse-Bridge Conventions Complete 29.95
#3011 Root-Pavlicek-Modern Bridge Conventions 15.00
#0240 Championship Bridge Series (All 36) 25.95

DUPLICATE STRATEGY
#1600 Klinger-50 Winning Duplicate Tips 12.95
#2260 Sheinwold-Duplicate Bridge............................. 4.95

FOR ALL PLAYERS
#3889 Darvas & de V. Hart-Right Through The Pack 14.95
#0790 Simon: Why You Lose at Bridge 11.95
#4850 Encyclopedia of Bridge, Official (ACBL) 39.95